# Step by Step

## Microsoft
# FrontPage
### Version 2002
Microsoft® Office XP Application

Online Training Solutions, Inc.

Creating a
Web Site

Lists and
Tables

Enhancing
Your
Web Site

Creating a
Site From
Scratch

Changing
Page
Layout

Enhancing
Capabilities

Communicating
with
Visitors

Team
Project
Web Sites

Connecting
to a
Database

Publishing
Your
Web Site

Managing
Your
Web Site

PUBLISHED BY
Microsoft Press
A Division of Microsoft Corporation
One Microsoft Way
Redmond, Washington 98052-6399

Library of Congress Cataloging-in-Publication Data
Microsoft FrontPage Version 2002 Step by Step / Online Training Solutions, Inc.
     p. cm.
   Includes index.
   ISBN 0-7356-1300-1
   1. Microsoft FrontPage.  2. Web sites--Design--Computer programs.  I. Online Training
Solutions (Firm).

TK5105.888 .M535   2001
005.7'2--dc21                          2001030585

Printed and bound in the United States of America.

5 6 7 8 9   QWT   7 6 5 4 3 2

Distributed in Canada by H.B. Fenn and Company Ltd.

A CIP catalogue record for this book is available from the British Library.

Microsoft Press books are available through booksellers and distributors worldwide. For further information about international editions, contact your local Microsoft Corporation office or contact Microsoft Press International directly at fax (425) 936-7329. Visit our Web site at www.microsoft.com/mspress. Send comments to mspinput@microsoft.com.

Information and photographs from the Carnivorous Plant Database at www2.labs.agilent.com/bot/cp_home/ are used by permission of Agilent Labs. ActiveX, bCentral, FrontPage, IntelliMouse, Links, Microsoft, Microsoft Press, MSDN, MSN, Outlook, PivotTable, PowerPoint, Revenue Avenue, SharePoint, SourceSafe, Verdana, VGA, Visual InterDev, Visual SourceSafe, Webdings, Windows, and Windows NT are either registered trademarks or trademarks of Microsoft Corporation in the United States and/or other countries. Other product and company names mentioned herein may be the trademarks of their respective owners.

The example companies, organizations, products, domain names, e-mail addresses, logos, people, places, and events depicted herein are fictitious. No association with any real company, organization, product, domain name, e-mail address, logo, person, place, or event is intended or should be inferred.

**Acquisitions Editor:** Kong Cheung
**Project Editors:** Jean Cockburn and Wendy Zucker

Body Part No. X08-06236

# Contents

## 1 Understanding How FrontPage Works    1

## 2 Creating a Web Site to Promote Yourself or Your Company    24

Contents

# 7 Enhancing the Capabilities of Your Web Site 158

# 8 Communicating with Your Visitors 190

# 9 Creating a Web Site to Support Team Projects 208

# 10 Connecting Your Web Site to a Database 230

# What's New in Microsoft FrontPage 2002

You'll notice some changes as soon as you start Microsoft FrontPage 2002. The toolbars and menu bar have a new look, and there's a new task pane on the right side of your screen. But the features that are new or greatly improved in this version of FrontPage go beyond just changes in appearance. Some changes won't be apparent to you until you start using the program.

The following table lists the new features that you might be interested in, as well as the chapters in which those features are discussed.

| To learn how to | Using this new feature | See |
| --- | --- | --- |
| Open a new page or Web | The **New Page or Web** task pane | Chapter 1, page 3 |
| View your Web site in a variety of ways | Page view, Folders view, Reports view, Navigation view, Hyperlinks view, and Tasks view | Chapter 1, page 13 |
| Get help | The FrontPage 2002 Help file | Chapter 1, page 18 |
| Copy and paste content from other Microsoft Office programs into an existing Web page | Office Clipboard task pane | Chapter 2, page 38 |
| Choose to apply the destination styles, keep the source formatting, or keep only the text for your pasted selection | Paste the way you want | Chapter 2, page 39 |
| Format a table | More table formatting options | Chapter 3, page 67 |
| Access and organize media files | Updated Clip Organizer | Chapter 4, page 76 |
| Incorporate specially formatted lines, a wide variety of preformed shapes, WordArt objects, text boxes, and shadowing | Cross browser enhanced drawing tools | Chapter 4, page 87 |
| Create an attractive display of personal or business photos or images | Photo Gallery | Chapter 4, page 95 |

*(continued)*

*(continued)*

| To learn how to | Using this new feature | See |
| --- | --- | --- |
| Generate an automatically refreshed list of the top 10 pages on your site in order of **page hits**, **unique users**, referral source, search strings, or many other factors | Top 10 Lists | Chapter 7, page 178 |
| Add links to maps, driving directions, search capabilities, up-to-the-minute stock market information, news, business, technology, and sports headlines to your Web pages | Automatically updated Web content | Chapter 7, page 179 |
| Create a full-scale team **collaboration site** | SharePoint team Web site | Chapter 9, page 221 |
| Edit SharePoint team Web site content, upload documents, and participate in threaded discussions directly from your Internet browser | Browser-based editing of Web sites based on SharePoint Team Services | Chapter 9, page 222 |
| Customize SharePoint team Web sites; create and apply custom themes; insert graphics, link bars, and automatic live content; and insert lists such as Announcements, Events, Contacts, Surveys, and Links on the Web site for the entire team to view | Customization and integration with FrontPage 2002 | Chapter 9, page 222 |
| Add a document library to your team Web site so that documents can be stored centrally for general or restricted access | Document libraries | Chapter 9, page 222 |
| Publish only the files that you want to rather than the entire Web site | Single-page publishing | Chapter 11, page 271 |
| Know something about the people who come to take a look at your Web site | Usage analysis reports | Chapter 12, page 289 |

For more information about the FrontPage product, see *www.microsoft.com/frontpage/*

# Getting Help

Every effort has been made to ensure the accuracy of this book and the contents of its CD-ROM. If you do run into problems, please contact the appropriate source for help and assistance.

## Getting Help with This Book and Its CD-ROM

If your question or issue concerns the content of this book or its companion CD-ROM, please first search the online Microsoft Knowledge Base, which provides support information for known errors in or corrections to this book, at the following Web site:

*mspress.microsoft.com/support/search.htm*

If you do not find your answer at the online Knowledge Base, send your comments or questions to Microsoft Press Technical Support at:

*mspinput@microsoft.com*

## Getting Help with Microsoft FrontPage 2002

If your question is about a Microsoft software product, including FrontPage 2002, and not about the content of this Microsoft Press book, please search the Microsoft Knowledge Base at:

*support.microsoft.com/directory/*

In the United States, Microsoft software product support issues not covered by the Microsoft Knowledge Base are addressed by Microsoft Product Support Services. The Microsoft software support options available from Microsoft Product Support Services are listed at:

*support.microsoft.com/directory/*

Outside the United States, for support information specific to your location, please refer to the Worldwide Support menu on the Microsoft Product Support Services Web site for the site specific to your country:

*support.microsoft.com/directory/*

# Using the Book's CD-ROM

The CD-ROM inside the back cover of this book contains all the practice files you'll use as you work through the exercises in this book. By using practice files, you won't waste time creating sample content with which to experiment—instead, you can jump right in and concentrate on learning how to use Microsoft FrontPage 2002.

## Important

The CD-ROM for this book does not contain the FrontPage 2002 software. You should purchase and install the program before using this book.

## Minimum System Requirements

To use this book, your computer should meet the following requirements:

**Computer/Processor**

Computer with a Pentium 133-megahertz (MHz) or higher processor

**Memory**

RAM requirements depend on the operating system used.

■ Microsoft Windows 98, or Windows 98 Second Edition

24 MB of RAM plus an additional 8 MB of RAM for each Microsoft Office program (such as Microsoft Word) running simultaneously

■ Microsoft Windows Millennium Edition (Windows Me), or Microsoft Windows NT

32 MB of RAM plus an additional 8 MB of RAM for each Office program (such as Microsoft Word) running simultaneously

■ Microsoft Windows 2000 Professional

64 MB of RAM plus an additional 8 MB of RAM for each Office program (such as Microsoft Word) running simultaneously

**Hard Disk**

Hard disk space requirements will vary depending on configuration; custom installation choices may require more or less hard disk space.

■ 245 MB of available hard disk space with 115 MB on the hard disk where the operating system is installed. (Users without Windows 2000, Windows Me, or Office 2000 Service Release 1 require an extra 50 MB of hard disk space for System Files Update.)

■ An additional 25 MB of hard disk space is required for installing the practice files.

### Operating System

Windows 98, Windows 98 Second Edition, Windows Me, Windows NT 4.0 with Service Pack 6 or later, or Windows 2000 or later. (On systems running Windows NT 4.0 with Service Pack 6, the version of Microsoft Internet Explorer must be upgraded to at least version 4.01 with Service Pack 1.)

**Important**

The exercises in the book were created on a computer running Windows 98. Other operating systems might display different results than those shown in this book.

### Drive

CD-ROM drive

### Display

Super VGA (800 × 600) or higher-resolution monitor with 256 colors

### Peripherals

Microsoft Mouse, Microsoft IntelliMouse, or compatible pointing device

### Applications

Microsoft FrontPage 2002

## Installing the Practice Files

You need to install the practice files on your hard disk before you use them in the chapters' exercises. Follow these steps to prepare the CD-ROM's files for your use:

1   Insert the CD-ROM into the CD-ROM drive of your computer.

A menu screen appears.

**Important**

If the menu screen does not appear, start Windows Explorer. In the left pane, locate the icon for your CD-ROM drive, and click this icon. In the right pane, double-click the file named *StartCd*.

2   Click **Install Practice Files**.
3   Click **OK** in the initial message box.
4   If you want to install the practice files to a location other than the default folder (*C:\SBS\FrontPage*), click the **Change Folder** button, select the new drive and path, and then click **OK**.

## Important

If you install the practice files to a location other than the default folder, the file location listed in some of the book's exercises will be incorrect.

5   Click the **Continue** button to install the selected practice files.

6   After the practice files have been installed, click **OK**.

Within the installation folder are subfolders for each chapter in the book.

7   Remove the CD-ROM from the CD-ROM drive, and return it to its envelope.

# Using the Practice Files

Each chapter's introduction lists the folders where you will find the files that are needed for that chapter. Each topic in the chapter explains how and when to use any practice files. The majority of the topics use the GardenCo Web site, a sample site created for a fictitious garden and plant store called The Garden Company. However, the Web site varies from topic to topic, so be sure to use the one in the folder specified for the particular topic you are working on. The file or files that you'll need are indicated in the margin at the beginning of the procedure above the CD icon, like this:

GardenCo

The following table lists each chapter's practice files.

| Chapter | Folder Name | Subfolder Name |
|---------|-------------|----------------|
| Chapter 1: Understanding How FrontPage Works | Understanding | |
| Chapter 2: Creating a Web Site to Promote Yourself or Your Company | CreateWeb | TasksList InsertText InsertExist FormatText InsertHype PreviewPages |
| Chapter 3: Presenting Information in Lists and Tables | ListsTables | CreateList CreateTable TableText TableStruct FormatTable TableInTable |
| Chapter 4: Enhancing Your Web Site with Graphics | Pictures | AddPicture Thumbnail PhotoGallery |

*(continued)*

*(continued)*

| Chapter | Folder Name | Subfolder Name |
|---|---|---|
| Chapter 5: Creating a Web Site from Scratch | FromScratch | NewPage<br>PageTitle<br>Backgrounds<br>Borders<br>Banners<br>Themes |
| Chapter 6: Changing Web Page Layout | PageLayout | Tables<br>Elements<br>ApplyTemp<br>Frames<br>LayOutFrame |
| Chapter 7: Enhancing the Capabilities of Your Web Site | Capabilities | Organize<br>Subweb<br>Permissions<br>LinkPages<br>LinkSites<br>Components<br>Elements |
| Chapter 8: Communicating with Your Visitors | Communicate | AutoUpdate<br>VisitorInput<br>FindInfo |
| Chapter 9: Creating a Web Site to Support Team Projects | TeamWeb | Productivity<br>Source |
| Chapter 10: Connecting Your Web Site to a Database | Database | ConnectDB<br>Publish |
| Chapter 11: Publishing Your Web Site | PublishWeb | |
| Chapter 12: Managing Your Web Site | ManageSite | |

## Uninstalling the Practice Files

After you finish working through this book, you should uninstall the practice files.

1.  On the Windows task bar, click the **Start** button, point to **Settings**, and then click **Control Panel**.
2.  Double-click the **Add/Remove Programs** icon.
3.  Click **Microsoft FrontPage 2002 SBS Files**, and click **Add/Remove**. (If you're using Windows 2000 Professional, click the **Remove** or **Change/Remove** button.)
4.  Click **Yes** when the confirmation dialog box appears.

### Important

If you need additional help installing or uninstalling the practice files, please see the "Getting Help" section earlier in this book.

# Conventions and Features

You can save time when you use this book by understanding how the *Step by Step* series shows special instructions, keys to press, buttons to click, and so on.

| Convention | Meaning |
| --- | --- |
| **1**<br>**2** | Numbered steps guide you through hands-on exercises in each topic. |
| (CD icon) | This icon at the beginning of a chapter indicates the list of folders that contain the files that the lesson will use. |
| FileName<br>(CD icon) | At the beginning of an exercise, this icon often appears (preceded by a list of the practice files or the practice Web site required to complete the exercise. |
| FP2002-3-5<br>(MOUS icon) | This icon indicates a section that covers a Microsoft Office User Specialist (MOUS) exam objective. The specific MOUS objective number is listed above the icon. Multiple objectives may be covered in each exercise. |
| new for<br>**Office**XP | This icon indicates a new or greatly improved feature in this version of Microsoft FrontPage. |
| **Tip** | This section provides useful background information or a helpful hint or shortcut that makes working through a task easier. |
| Important | This section points out information that you need to know to complete the procedure. |
| **Troubleshooting** | This section shows you how to fix a common problem. |
| Save<br>(Save button icon) | When a button is referenced in a topic, a picture of the button appears in the margin area, preceded by the name of the button. |
| Alt + Tab | A plus sign (+) between two key names means that you must press those keys at the same time. For example, "Press Alt+Tab" means that you hold down the Alt key while you press Tab. |
| **Black boldface type** | Program features that you click are shown in black boldface type. |
| **Blue boldface type** | Terms explained in the glossary are shown in blue boldface type. |
| **Red boldface type** | Text that you are supposed to type appears in red boldface type in the procedures. |
| *Italic type* | Folder paths, URLs, and emphasized words appear in italic type. |

# MOUS Objectives

Each Microsoft Office User Specialist (MOUS) certification level (Core and Expert) has a set of objectives. To prepare for the MOUS certification exam, you should confirm that you can meet its respective objectives.

This book will prepare you fully for the MOUS exam at either the core or the expert level because it addresses all the objectives for both exams. Throughout this book, topics that pertain to MOUS objectives are identified with the MOUS logo and objective number in the margin, like this:

FP2002-3-5

Multiple MOUS objectives may be covered within one topic.

## Core Microsoft FrontPage 2002 MOUS Objectives

| Objective | Skill | On Page |
|---|---|---|
| **FP2002-1** | **Creating and Modifying Web Sites** | |
| FP2002-1-1 | Create and manage a FrontPage Web site | 26, 31, 103, 210, 214, 221 |
| FP2002-1-2 | Create and preview Web pages | 2, 7, 48, 106, 165, 172, 177, 186, 192, 197, 201, 210, 243 |
| FP2002-1-3 | Open, view, and rename Web pages | 2, 7, 13 |
| FP2002-1-4 | Rename a Web page | 38, 108 |
| FP2002-1-5 | Change the title for a Web page on banners and buttons | 38, 108 |
| **FP2002-2** | **Importing Web Content** | |
| FP2002-2-1 | Insert text and images | 35, 38, 54, 76, 79, 86 |
| FP2002-2-2 | Insert Office drawings, AutoShapes, and Word Art | 87, 98 |
| **FP2002-3** | **Formatting Web Pages** | |
| FP2002-3-1 | Apply text and paragraph formats | 43, 54, 58, 263 |

*(continued)*

| Objective | Skill | On Page |
|---|---|---|
| FP2002-3-2 | Insert hyperlinks | 47, 140, 165, 172, 236, 249 |
| FP2002-3-3 | Insert a date using shared borders | 119 |
| FP2002-3-4 | Create and edit tables | 58, 64, 135 |
| FP2002-3-5 | Apply Web site themes | 123, 236, 249 |
| **FP2002-4** | **Formatting Web Pages** | |
| FP2002-4-1 | Edit graphic elements | 81, 87 |
| FP2002-4-2 | Create image maps | 165 |
| FP2002-4-3 | Add FrontPage components to Web pages | 165, 177, 186, 192 |
| FP2002-4-4 | Add a photo gallery | 95 |
| **FP2002-5** | **Organizing and Viewing FrontPage Web Sites** | |
| FP2002-5-1 | Use FrontPage views | 13, 34, 35, 38, 108, 123, 160, 236, 249, 282, 289 |
| FP2002-5-2 | Manage Web site structure | 160 |
| FP2002-5-3 | Organize Web site files | 160 |
| FP2002-5-4 | Manage tasks | 34 |
| **FP2002-6** | **Managing Web Sites** | |
| FP2002-6-1 | Publish a Web page | 214, 232, 234, 267, 270, 277, 282, 289 |
| FP2002-6-2 | Create custom reports | 282, 289 |

# Expert Microsoft FrontPage 2002 MOUS Objectives

| Objective | Skill Set | On Page |
|---|---|---|
| **FP2002e-1** | **Creating and Customizing Web Sites** | |
| FP2002e-1-1 | Modify Web page layout | 135, 151 |
| FP2002e-1-2 | Create subwebs | 163, 278 |
| FP2002e-1-3 | Manage permissions for subwebs | 278 |
| FP2002e-1-4 | Create and apply custom themes | 127 |
| FP2002e-1-5 | Customize shared borders | 119 |
| FP2002e-1-6 | Add and modify background images | 110, 116 |
| **FP2002e-2** | **Using Navigational Features** | |
| FP2002e-2-1 | Manage the structure of a Web site | 165 |
| FP2002e-2-2 | Add navigation bars to page banners | 165 |

# Taking a MOUS Exam

As desktop computing technology advances, more employers rely on the objectivity and consistency of technology certification when screening, hiring, and training employees to ensure the competence of these professionals. As an employee, you can use technology certification to prove that you meet the standards set by your current or potential employer. The Microsoft Office User Specialist (MOUS) program is the only Microsoft-approved certification program designed to assist employees in validating their competence using Microsoft Office applications.

## About the MOUS Program

A Microsoft Office User Specialist is an individual who has certified his or her skills in one or more of the Microsoft Office desktop applications of Microsoft Word, Microsoft Excel, Microsoft PowerPoint, Microsoft Outlook, Microsoft Access, Microsoft FrontPage, or Microsoft Project. The Microsoft Office User Specialist Program typically offers certification exams at the "core" and "expert" skill levels. (The availability of Microsoft Office User Specialist certification exams varies by application, application version, and language. Visit *www.mous.net* for exam availability.) The Microsoft Office User Specialist Program is the only Microsoft-approved program in the world for certifying proficiency in Microsoft Office desktop applications and Microsoft Project. This certification can be a valuable asset in any job search or career advancement.

### What Does This Logo Mean?

APPROVED COURSEWARE

It means this courseware has been approved by the Microsoft Office User Specialist Program to be among the finest available for learning FrontPage 2002. It also means that upon completion of this courseware, you may be prepared to become a Microsoft Office User Specialist.

## Selecting a MOUS Certification Level

In selecting the MOUS certification(s) level that you would like to pursue, you should assess the following:

- The Office application and version(s) of the application with which you are familiar
- The length of time you have used the application
- Whether you have had formal or informal training

Candidates for the core-level MOUS certification exams are expected to successfully complete a wide range of standard business tasks, such as formatting a document. Successful candidates generally have six or more months of experience with the application, including either formal instructor-led training with a MOUS Authorized Instructor or self-study using MOUS-approved books, guides, or interactive computer-based materials.

Candidates for expert-level certification, by comparison, are expected to complete more complex business-oriented assignments utilizing the application's advanced functionality, such as importing data and recording macros. Successful candidates generally have two or more years of experience with the application, again including formal instructor-led training with a MOUS Authorized Instructor or self-study using MOUS-approved materials.

# MOUS Exam Objectives

Every MOUS certification exam is developed from a list of exam objectives, which are derived from studies of how the Office application is actually used in the workplace. Because these objectives dictate the scope of each exam, they provide you with critical information on how to prepare for MOUS certification.

## Tip

See the previous section, "MOUS Objectives," for a complete list of objectives for FrontPage.

MOUS Approved Courseware, including Microsoft Press's Step by Step series, is reviewed and approved on the basis of its coverage of the MOUS exam objectives.

# The Exam Experience

The MOUS certification exams are unique in that they are performance-based examinations that allow you to interact with a "live" version of the Office application as you complete a series of assigned tasks. All the standard menus, toolbars, and keyboard shortcuts are available—even the Help menu. MOUS exams for Office XP applications consist of 25 to 35 questions, each of which requires you to complete one or more tasks using the Office application for which you are seeking certification. For example:

Prepare the document for publication as a Web page by completing the following three tasks:

1    Convert the memo to a Web page.
2    Title the page **Revised Company Policy**.
3    Name the memo **Policy Memo.htm**.

The duration of MOUS exams ranges from 45 to 60 minutes, depending on the application. Passing percentages range from 70 to 80 percent correct.

## The Exam Interface and Controls

After you fill out a series of information screens, the testing software starts the exam and the respective Office application. You will see the exam interface and controls, including the test question, in the dialog box in the lower right corner of the screen.

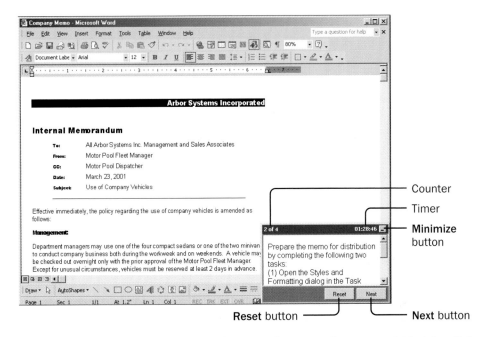

- If the exam dialog box gets in the way of your work, you can hide it by clicking the **Minimize** button in the upper right corner, or you can drag it to another position on the screen.

- The timer starts when the first question appears on your screen and displays the remaining exam time. If the timer and the counter are distracting, click the timer to remove the display.

**Important**

The timer will not count the time required for the exam to be loaded between questions. It keeps track only of the time you spend answering questions.

- The counter tracks how many questions you have completed and how many remain.

- The **Reset** button allows you to restart work on a question if you think you have made an error. The **Reset** button will *not* restart the entire exam or extend the exam time limit.

- When you complete a question, click the **Next** button to move to the next question.

**Important**

It is not possible to move back to a previous question on the exam.

## Test-Taking Tips

- Follow all instructions provided in each question completely and accurately.

- Enter requested information as it appears in the instructions but without duplicating the formatting. For example, all text and values that you will be asked to enter will appear in the instructions as **bold** and **underlined**; however, you should enter the information without applying this formatting unless you are specifically instructed to do otherwise.

- Close all dialog boxes before proceeding to the next exam question unless you are specifically instructed otherwise.

- There is no need to save your work before moving on to the next question unless you are specifically instructed to do so.

- Do not cut and paste information from the exam interface into the application.

- For questions that ask you to print a document, spreadsheet, chart, report, slide, and so forth, nothing will actually be printed.

- Responses are scored based on the result of your work, not the method you use to achieve that result (unless a specific method is explicitly required), and not the time you take to complete the question. Extra keystrokes or mouse clicks do not count against your score.

- If your computer becomes unstable during the exam (for example, if the application's toolbars or the mouse no longer functions) or if a power outage occurs, contact a testing center administrator immediately. The administrator will then restart the computer, and the exam will return to the point before the interruption occurred.

## Certification

At the conclusion of the exam, you will receive a score report, which you can print with the assistance of the testing center administrator. If your score meets or exceeds the minimum required score, you will also be mailed a printed certificate within approximately 14 days.

# For More Information

To learn more about becoming a Microsoft Office User Specialist, visit *www.mous.net*

To purchase a Microsoft Office User Specialist certification exam, visit *www.DesktopIQ.com*

To learn about other Microsoft Office User Specialist approved courseware from Microsoft Press, visit *mspress.microsoft.com/certification/mous/*

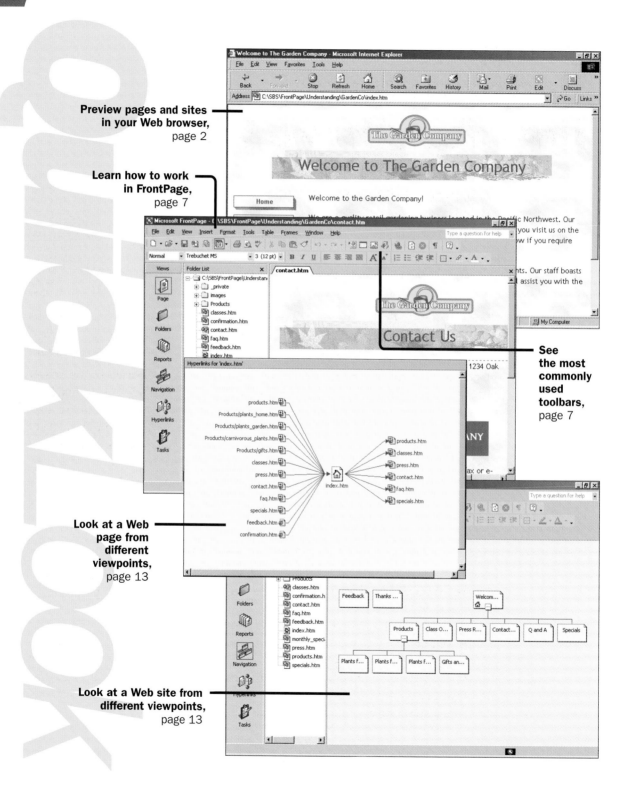

**Preview pages and sites in your Web browser,** page 2

**Learn how to work in FrontPage,** page 7

**See the most commonly used toolbars,** page 7

**Look at a Web page from different viewpoints,** page 13

**Look at a Web site from different viewpoints,** page 13

# Chapter 1
# Understanding
# How FrontPage Works

**After completing this chapter, you will be able to:**

✔ **Open and preview a FrontPage-based Web site.**

✔ **Open and preview an individual Web page.**

✔ **Look at a Web site from a variety of viewpoints.**

✔ **Look "behind the scenes" at the HTML code that does all the work.**

Microsoft FrontPage 2002 is a comprehensive application that you can use to develop Web sites. This sophisticated program provides everything you need to create Web sites ranging from a simple Web-based résumé to a complex Web-based retail store.

In spite of its sophistication, FrontPage is easy to use. As a member of the **Microsoft Office XP** suite of applications, it works pretty much the same way the other Office applications do. If you've avoided trying to create Web sites because you didn't want to learn how to program in **Hypertext Markup Language (HTML)**, FrontPage might well be the answer you've been waiting for. With FrontPage, you can easily create good-looking, interesting Web sites that incorporate complex elements, without typing a single line of programming code. But if you have some HTML programming experience or want to feel more in control, FrontPage gives you easy access to the code that it creates behind the scenes. You can view and edit the underlying HTML code at any time; but the great thing is that you don't have to. No programming experience is necessary to become a successful FrontPage developer.

This chapter introduces FrontPage and explains the concept of a FrontPage-based Web site. You will learn how to open an existing Web site, how to navigate between Web pages, and how to view the pages in different ways. You will then look at various ways of working in FrontPage and learn how to locate and control the FrontPage features you are likely to want to use in your own Web sites. In addition, you will learn how to view the underlying HTML code that makes all Web sites work. You will also get an overview of the different types of Web sites you can create with FrontPage and of the decision-making tools and resources that are necessary to create, manage, and maintain a personal or commercial Web site.

The exercises in this chapter and throughout the book are built around a Web site created for a fictitious garden and plant store called *The Garden Company*. This Web site, which is named *GardenCo*, contains realistic examples of content and structure that serve to demonstrate the concepts covered in each chapter. In this particular chapter, you will be working with the sample Web site that is stored in the *SBS\FrontPage\Understanding* folder.

## Tip

To follow along with the exercises in this book, you need to install the practice files from the companion CD-ROM. (You cannot just copy the files.) You'll find instructions for installing the files in the "Using the Book's CD-ROM" section at the beginning of the book.

# Exploring an Existing Web Site

FP2002-1-2
FP2002-1-3

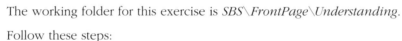 When you work with other Office XP applications, you create self-contained documents that can be individually opened from within Windows Explorer. When you work with FrontPage, you create a group of interconnected files that collectively make up each FrontPage-based Web site. As a result, Web sites must be opened from within FrontPage; clicking a single file name in Windows Explorer might open that file, but it won't open the Web site that the file belongs to.

In this exercise, you will start FrontPage and open a sample FrontPage-based Web site. You will then preview the Web site.

GardenCo

 The working folder for this exercise is *SBS\FrontPage\Understanding*.

Follow these steps:

1   At the left end of the taskbar at the bottom of your screen, click the **Start** button. Then on the **Start** menu, point to **Programs**, and click **Microsoft FrontPage**.

## Tip

Depending on your system resources, you might see a message box notifying you of additional system requirements for using certain Office XP features, such as Speech Recognition. If you see this message box, click **OK** to continue.

When FrontPage opens for the first time, you see a new page file called *new_page_1.htm* in the Page view editing window, as shown here:

The Standard toolbar — The New Page or Web task pane —

The
Formatting
toolbar

The **Views**
bar

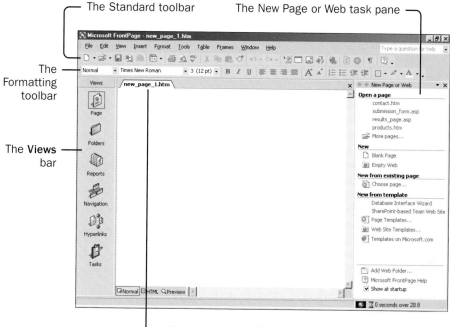

The name of the file is shown on the page tab.

Office task
panes
new for
**Office**XP

The **New Page or Web** task pane opens when FrontPage starts with no Web site open. If you don't want the task pane to be shown by default, clear the **Show at startup** check box on the bottom of the task pane.

**2** On the **File** menu, click **Open Web** to open this dialog box:

The icons in
the **Views** bar
represent
frequently
used folders.

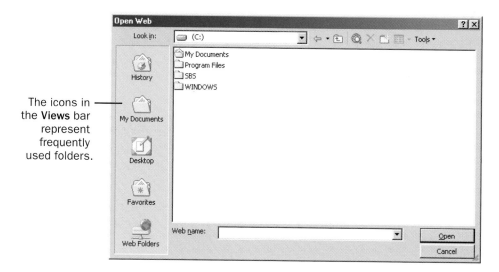

**3** In the **Open Web** dialog box, browse to the *SBS\FrontPage\Understanding* folder.

Web site icon

A FrontPage-based Web site called *GardenCo* is located here, indicated by the Web site icon preceding the name.

**4** Click **GardenCo** to select the Web site, and then click **Open**.

The **New Page or Web** task pane closes, the new_page_1.htm file closes, and the **Folder List** opens with the folders and files that make up the GardenCo Web site displayed, like this:

The **Folder List** displays the visible structure of the web site.

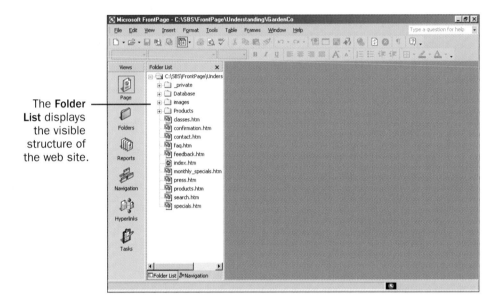

The **Folder List** displays the visible folders and files that you can access in the Web site. You can open files of all types from the **Folder List** by double-clicking them.

**Important**

A FrontPage-based Web site includes hidden folders and files generated by FrontPage for behind-the-scenes operations. Deleting or changing these files and folders might "break" the site by damaging the navigation structure, rendering links invalid, or worse; so FrontPage designates them as hidden. Provided your computer is not set to show hidden files and folders (this setting is on the **View** tab of the Microsoft Windows **Folder Options** dialog box), you will not see these files, and there will be no danger that you might accidentally delete or alter them.

**5** Click the plus sign preceding each of the folders to view the folder contents.

Different icons designate the various types of files that make up this site. For example, the Web page icon precedes the **file name** of each page of the FrontPage-based Web site, and the home page icon indicates the **home page** of the site.

**Toggle Pane**

The **Toggle Pane** button on the Standard toolbar is selected, indicating that you can click it to toggle the current pane between open and closed.

**6** Click the **Toggle Pane** button to close the **Folder List**, and click it again to open the list.

**7** At the bottom of the **Folder List,** click the **Navigation** button to switch to the **Navigation Pane**.

**8** Drag the right border of the **Navigation Pane** to the right until all the **page titles** are visible, like this:

The **Navigation Pane** displays the page titles of all of the files that have been added to the **navigational structure** of the Web site. This view of the navigational structure is essentially a hierarchical map of how pages are connected within the site and what routes you can take to get from one page to another. As with the **Folder List**, you can open each of these files by double-clicking the page icon or title in the **Navigation Pane**.

**9** Click the **Toggle Pane** button to close the **Navigation Pane**, and click it again to open the pane.

**10** Click the **Toggle Pane** button's down arrow, and select **Folder List** from the drop-down list to switch back to the **Folder List**.

**11** In the **Folder List**, click **index.htm** to select the file.

**12** To see how the site looks in your Web browser, click **Preview in Browser**, on the **File** menu.

The **Preview in Browser** dialog box opens:

Installed Internet browsers are shown in the **Browser** list. ———

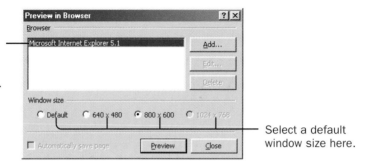

——— Select a default window size here.

**13** Select your preferred browser and window size (800 x 600 is recommended), and click **Preview**.

The GardenCo Web site opens in your selected browser, like this:

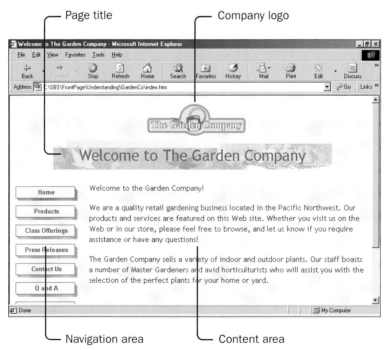

— Page title          — Company logo

— Navigation area          — Content area

**14** Click each of the navigation links to move between pages.

Close

**15** When you're done, click the **Close** button to close the browser.

**16** On the FrontPage **File** menu, click **Close Web** to close the Web site.

## Optimizing Your Screen Display Properties

The width and height of your screen area is measured in pixels. When personal computers first became popular, most computer monitors were capable of displaying a screen area of only 640 pixels wide by 480 pixels high (more commonly known as *640 x 480*). Now most computer monitors can also display at 800 by 600 pixels and 1024 by 768 pixels. Some monitors can even display a screen area of 1152 by 864 pixels, or larger.

Most computer users have the choice of at least two different screen area sizes. Some people prefer to work in the 640 by 480 area because everything on screen appears larger. Others prefer being able to fit more information on their screen with a 1024 by 768 display.

When designing a Web page that consists of more than free-flowing text, it is important to consider the likely screen area of your Web visitors. It is currently common practice to design Web sites to look their best when the visitor's screen area is set to 800 by 600 pixels. This means that visitors who view your site with a 640 by 480 area will have to scroll to display the entire page.

To determine your current screen area settings on a Windows 98 computer:

1   Click **Start**, point to **Settings**, and then click **Control Panel**.

2   In the Control Panel window, double-click **Display** to open the **Display Properties** dialog box.

3   On the **Settings** tab, look at the **Screen area** slider. The current screen area appears beneath the slider.

4   Click **Less** or **More** to move the slider and change the screen area.

## Exploring an Existing Web Page

FP2002-1-2
FP2002-1-3

**Web pages** are the building blocks of every Web site. When you view a Web site in a browser, you are usually viewing Web pages. When you are developing a Web site, you are also working with pages. When you want to edit a Web page that is part of a FrontPage-based Web site, you first open the site in FrontPage and then open the individual page. Opening the page in FrontPage, rather than as an individual file in another program, avoids the possibility that you might damage the site. It also ensures that changes made on an individual page are reflected across the entire site, as appropriate.

## Important

If FrontPage is your default HTML editor, you can open individual Web pages from outside FrontPage by double-clicking the page file in Windows Explorer. However, if FrontPage is not your default editor, accessing and changing files individually from outside FrontPage could result in damage to the Web site.

In this exercise, you will open an individual Web page, view the HTML code generated by FrontPage, and preview a Web page both in FrontPage and in a browser.

GardenCo

The working folder for this exercise is *SBS\FrontPage\Understanding*.

Follow these steps:

**1** On the **File** menu, click **Open Web**.

**2** In the **Open Web** dialog box, browse to the *SBS\FrontPage\Understanding* folder, select **GardenCo**, and click **Open**.

The Web site opens in FrontPage with the **Folder List** displayed, like this:

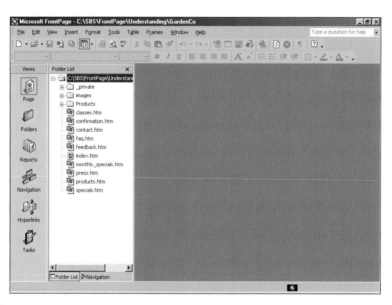

## Tip

If the **Folder List** is not displayed, click **Folder List** on the **View** menu to display it.

**3** In the **Folder List**, right-click the **contact.htm** file, and click **Open** on the shortcut menu.

The file icon changes to an open Web page icon, and the file opens in the **Page view editing window**, like this:

Files open in Page view — Page view editing window

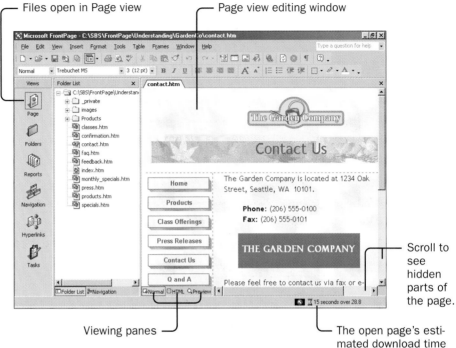

Scroll to see hidden parts of the page.

Viewing panes — The open page's estimated download time

**4**   Use the scroll bars to look at the entire page.

This page has **shared borders** at the top and left side of the page, delineated by the dotted lines, as shown here:

Top shared border

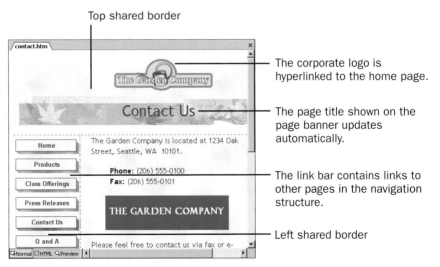

The corporate logo is hyperlinked to the home page.

The page title shown on the page banner updates automatically.

The link bar contains links to other pages in the navigation structure.

Left shared border

The shared borders appear on every page of the Web site and contain the same information, giving the site a consistent look. The top shared border of this site contains a corporate logo and a title, or **page banner**. The left shared border contains a **link bar** displaying **hyperlinks** that you can click to jump to other pages in the site.

The content area in the center of the page contains text, a graphic (not visible below), a table, and two **e-mail links**, as shown here:

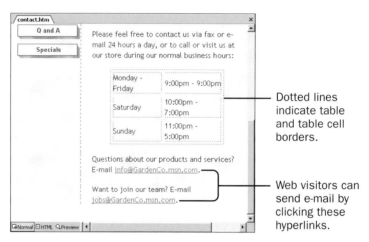

Dotted lines indicate table and table cell borders.

Web visitors can send e-mail by clicking these hyperlinks.

**5** Now that you've seen the outside, let's look at the inside. Click the **HTML** button at the bottom of the Page view editing window to switch to the **HTML pane**.

The HTML code making up this page looks like this:

```html
<html>

<head>
<meta http-equiv="Content-Language" content="en-us">
<meta name="GENERATOR" content="Microsoft FrontPage 5.0">
<meta name="ProgId" content="FrontPage.Editor.Document">
<meta http-equiv="Content-Type" content="text/html;
  charset=windows-1252">
<title>Contact Us</title>
<meta name="Microsoft Theme" content="modified-nature-theme 011,
  default">
<meta name="Microsoft Border" content="tl, default">
</head>

<body>
```

```
<p>The Garden Company is located at 1234 Oak Street, Seattle, WA 
   10101.</p>
<blockquote>

<p><b>Phone:</b> (206) 555-0100<br>
<b>Fax:</b> (206) 555-0101</p>
</blockquote>

<p align="center">
<applet code="fprotate.class" codebase="images/" width="264"
   height="72">
  <param name="image1" valuetype="ref" value="images/banner1.gif">
  <param name="image2" valuetype="ref" value="images/banner2.gif">
  <param name="image3" valuetype="ref" value="images/banner3.gif">
  <param name="rotatoreffect" value="blindsHorizontal">
  <param name="time" value="2">
</applet></p>

<p>Please feel free to contact us via fax or e-mail 24 hours a day, or
   to call or visit us at our store during our normal business
   hours:</p>
<div align="left">
  <blockquote>
  <table border="0" cellpadding="0" cellspacing="6" style="border-
    collapse: collapse" id="AutoNumber1" height="57">
    <tr>
      <td height="19">Monday - Friday</td>
      <td height="19">9:00pm - 9:00pm</td>
    </tr>
    <tr>
      <td height="19">Saturday</td>
      <td height="19">10:00pm - 7:00pm</td>
    </tr>
    <tr>
      <td height="19">Sunday</td>
      <td height="19">11:00pm - 5:00pm</td>
    </tr>
  </table>
  </blockquote>
</div>

<p>Questions about our products and services? E-mail
<a href="mailto:info@GardenCo.msn.com">info@GardenCo.msn.com</a>.</p>
<p>Want to join our team? E-mail <a href="mailto:
   jobs@GardenCo.msn.com">jobs@GardenCo.msn.com</a>.</p>

</body>

</html>
```

**6** Find each section of text within the page code and study the surrounding HTML code. Try to identify the code that creates each page element.

**7** Click the **Normal** button at the bottom of the Page view editing window to switch back to the **Normal pane**.

**8** Now see how the page will look to **Web visitors**. Click the **Preview** button at the bottom of the Page view editing window to switch to the **Preview pane**, where FrontPage displays the page like this:

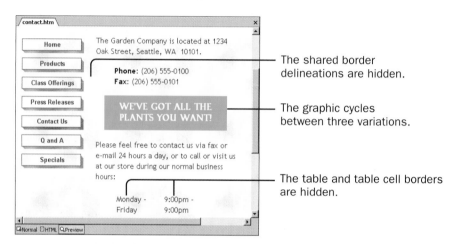

- The shared border delineations are hidden.
- The graphic cycles between three variations.
- The table and table cell borders are hidden.

Preview in Browser

**9** Preview the page in your default Web browser. On the Standard toolbar, click the **Preview in Browser** button.

Although you've chosen to preview only this page, you can still open the other pages of the site by clicking the hyperlinked buttons on the link bar.

Close

**10** When you're done previewing the Web site, click the **Close** button to close the browser and return to FrontPage.

**11** Use the buttons at the bottom of the Page view editing window to switch between the Normal, HTML, and Preview panes as much as you like. When you're done looking at the page, click the **Close** button in the upper right corner of the Page view editing window to close the file.

**12** On the **File** menu, click **Close Web** to close the Web site.

# Looking at a Web Site in Various Ways

FP2002-1-3
FP2002-5-1

FrontPage 2002 provides six different **views** of a Web site:

Page tabs
new for
**Office**XP

- **Page view** displays the open page or pages in the Page view editing window. A tab at the top of each page shows the file name. If multiple pages are open, you can switch to another page by clicking its tab or by clicking its file name on the **Window** menu.

- **Folders view** displays the visible files and folders that are part of the open Web site. For each file, this view shows the file name, page title, file size, file type, the date the file was last modified and by whom, and any comments that have been added to the file information.

- **Reports view** displays any of 27 reports about the open Web site. Reports view defaults to the last opened report. If no other report has been open during the current FrontPage session, the default is a Site Summary report that collates the results of the other reports. The various reports can be chosen from the **View** menu or from the Reporting toolbar.

- **Navigation view** graphically displays a hierarchical view of all the files that have been added to the navigation structure of the open Web site. To add a file to the navigation structure, you simply drag the file into the Navigation view window and drop it in the appropriate location. To fit the site content into the window, you can switch between Portrait mode (vertical layout) and Landscape mode (horizontal layout) or zoom in or out using the buttons on the Navigation toolbar.

- **Hyperlinks view** displays the hyperlinks to and from any selected page in the open Web site. Internal hyperlinks are shown as well as external hyperlinks and e-mail hyperlinks. You select a file in the **Folder List** to see the hyperlinks to and from that file, and then select the plus sign next to any file name to further expand the view.

- **Tasks view** displays a list of tasks to be completed in the open Web site. FrontPage creates these **tasks** when you use a wizard to create a Web site, or you can create your own tasks. For each task, you see the status, name, and description. You are also told to whom the task is assigned; whether the task has been categorized as High, Medium, or Low priority; and when the task was last modified. Tasks are a useful way of tracking the readiness status of a site.

You can switch between views by clicking the desired view on the **View** menu or on the **Views** bar.

GardenCo

In this exercise, you will look at Web pages in each of the FrontPage views to get an idea of what information is available to you in each view.

The working folder for this exercise is *SBS\FrontPage\Understanding*.

Follow these steps:

Open

**1** On the Standard toolbar, click the down arrow to the right of the **Open** button, and then click **Open Web** on the drop-down list.

**2** In the **Open Web** dialog box, browse to the *SBS\FrontPage\Understanding* folder, select **GardenCo**, and click **Open** to open the Web site located in the working folder.

**3** In the **Folder List**, double-click **classes.htm** to open the file in the Page view editing window.

On the **Views** bar, the **Page** icon is selected to indicate that you are working in Page view.

Folders

**4** On the **Views** bar, click the **Folders** icon.

FrontPage displays the contents of the Web site in Folders view, like this:

| Contents of 'C:\SBS\FrontPage\Understanding\GardenCo' | | | | |
|---|---|---|---|---|
| Name | Title | Size | Type | Modified Date |
| _private | | | | |
| images | | | | |
| Products | | | | |
| classes.htm | Class Offerings | 16KB | htm | 3/15/01 12:2? |
| confirmation.... | Thanks for Your Feedback! | 9KB | htm | 3/15/01 9:38 |
| contact.htm | Contact Us | 8KB | htm | 3/15/01 12:2? |
| faq.htm | Q and A | 12KB | htm | 3/26/01 4:31 |
| feedback.htm | Feedback | 11KB | htm | 3/15/01 9:30 |
| index.htm | Welcome to The Garden Company | 8KB | htm | 3/26/01 4:57 |
| monthly_spec... | monthly_specials.htm | 1KB | htm | 3/15/01 2:47 |
| press.htm | Press Releases | 8KB | htm | 3/15/01 12:2? |
| products.htm | Products | 8KB | htm | 3/26/01 4:30 |
| specials.htm | Specials | 7KB | htm | 3/15/01 2:47 |

**5** Use the scroll bars to view the entire screen.

Reports

**6** On the **Views** bar, click the **Reports** icon.

FrontPage opens the Reporting toolbar and displays the Site Summary report for the open Web site, like this:

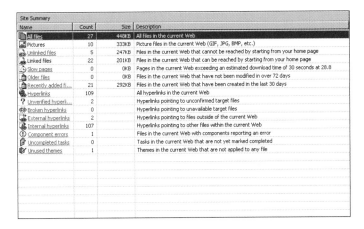

To see the individual reports that are collated into the Site Summary report, you can click the hyperlinked report names in the Site Summary or select the desired report from the **Reports** drop-down list on the Reporting toolbar.

Navigation

**7** On the **Views** bar, click the **Navigation** icon.

FrontPage displays the Navigation toolbar and the navigational structure of the open Web site.

**8** On the Navigation toolbar, select a percentage display size from the **Zoom** drop-down list so that the entire site fits in the window. (For example, for an 800 x 600 display, you might want to select **75**.)

Your screen now looks like this:

Change the **Zoom** setting to see the entire navigation structure.

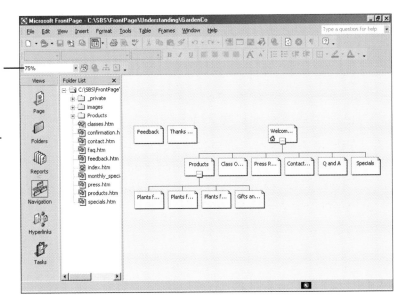

The home page icon indicates the home page of the site. Each page displays its page title rather than its file name.

**9**   On the Navigation toolbar, click the **Portrait/Landscape** button to change the orientation of the navigation structure.

**10**   Click the **Products** page to select it.

**11**   On the Navigation toolbar, click the **View Subtree Only** button.

If you are working with a particularly large Web site you can use this technique to single out one section of the navigation structure.

**12**   Click the **View Subtree Only** button again to see the entire site map.

**13**   On the **Views** bar, click the **Hyperlinks** icon.

Because no specific page is selected, the screen reads *Select a page from the Folder List to view hyperlinks to and from that page.*

**14**   In the **Folder List**, click **index.htm**, the home page.

All the hyperlinks to and from the home page are displayed, like this:

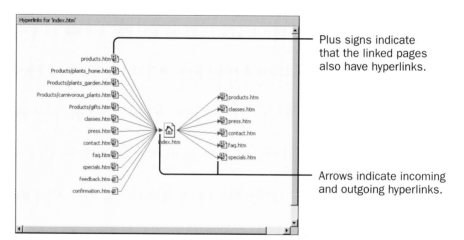

Plus signs indicate that the linked pages also have hyperlinks.

Arrows indicate incoming and outgoing hyperlinks.

**15**   Right-click **contact.htm**, and click **Move to Center** on the shortcut menu to move that file to the center point of the hyperlink structure.

Notice that different icons represent different types of links.

**16**   Click the plus sign next to any file icon to see the other hyperlinks from that file's page.

**17**   Click the minus sign to collapse the hyperlink view.

**18**   On the **Views** bar, click the **Tasks** icon.

Tasks view shows you a reminder list of the things that need to be done in the open Web site. Tasks are automatically created when you use a FrontPage wizard to create a Web site. Tasks can also be created manually by anyone working on the Web site. The tasks that have been assigned to this Web site are shown here:

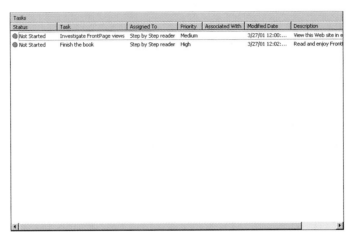

**19**  Use the scroll bars to view the entire list.

**20**  Double-click the task titled *Investigate FrontPage views* to open it. Read the description and study the task details, and then click **OK** to close the task.

**21**  Right-click the task titled *Investigate FrontPage views*, and click **Mark Complete** on the shortcut menu.

The task's **Status** setting changes from *Not Started* to *Completed*.

**22**  Double-click the task titled *Finish the book* to open it. Read the description and study the task details, and then click **OK** to close the task.

**23**  On the **File** menu, click **Close Web** to close the Web site.

## Looking Around in FrontPage 2002

For those of you who are learning FrontPage without having much experience with the other applications in the Office XP suite, here is a summary of some of the basic techniques you will use to work with FrontPage.

FrontPage 2002 commands are available from 10 separate **menus**. Office XP applications feature the same expanding, dynamic menus that were first made available in Office 2000. The menu commands you use most often move to the top of each menu, making them easier to access. The menu commands you don't use are tucked out of sight, but can be easily accessed by clicking the double chevron at the bottom of the menu. Menu commands that are followed by an arrowhead have submenus. Menu commands that are followed by an ellipsis (...) open dialog boxes where you provide the information necessary to carry out the command.

Most of the menu commands are also represented graphically on 12 **toolbars**, all of which are customizable. The graphic on the toolbar buttons corresponds to the graphic next to the same command on the menu. Each of the buttons has a **Screen-Tip** to tell you the name of the command.

Menu and toolbar options are unavailable when the option can't be applied either to the environment you're working in or to the specific object that is selected. Available menu commands are displayed in black; unavailable commands are **dimmed**, or displayed in a gray font.

The FrontPage 2002 Help file contains information that will assist you when you have questions about FrontPage. The opening screen of the Help file features the latest topics, such as *What's New* and *Get Started*, as well as a link to the Microsoft Office Web site and other resources. The tabs across the top of the Help file give you three different ways to access information:

■ The **Contents** tab displays the Help file topics in a traditional table of contents view.

More convenient access to Help
new for
**Office**XP

■ The **Answer Wizard** tab accepts questions in plain language and then matches your question up with topics that contain possible answers. The Answer Wizard is also accessible through the Ask A Question box at the right end of the FrontPage menu bar.

■ The **Index** tab lists topic keywords for the entire Help file. You can either scroll through the list or type the word or words that you're looking for into the **Type keywords** box to search for them.

In this exercise, you will look at the commands that are available on the FrontPage 2002 menus and toolbars. You will also look at the Help file to learn about the types of information that are available to you when you need additional help.

There is no working folder for this exercise. Follow these steps:

Create a new
normal page

**1** On the Standard toolbar, click the **Create a new normal page** button.

A new page called *new_page_1.htm* opens in the Page view editing window.

**2** Click the **File** menu to open it, and then click the double chevron at the bottom of the menu to expand the complete menu.

**3** Study the commands available on the menu, and think about how you might use each one.

The **Close Web**, **Publish Web**, and **Export** commands are dimmed because they are unavailable at this time—in this case, because they apply to Web sites rather than Web pages, and no Web site is open at the moment.

**4** Arrowheads follow the **New**, **Recent Files**, and **Recent Webs** commands to indicate that each has a submenu. Point to the **New** command to see its submenu, like this:

**5** Repeat steps 2 through 4 for each of the remaining menus: **Edit**, **View**, **Insert**, **Format**, **Tools**, **Table**, **Frames**, **Window**, and **Help**. Study the available and unavailable options, and expand the submenus.

**6** Click any command that is followed by an ellipsis to open the command's dialog box, and then click **Cancel** to close it.

**7** When you get to the **Help** menu, click **Microsoft FrontPage Help**.

The Help file opens.

**8** Click each of the three tabs to see the types of information that are available and the different ways that information can be accessed.

Close

**9** Click the **Close** button to close the Help file.

**10** Right-click anywhere in the menu and toolbar area at the top of the window to open the toolbar shortcut menu, as shown on the next page.

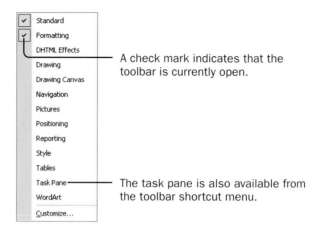

A check mark indicates that the toolbar is currently open.

The task pane is also available from the toolbar shortcut menu.

Check marks indicate that the Standard and Formatting toolbars are currently turned on. FrontPage automatically turns on these two toolbars because they include buttons for the most commonly used page and file commands.

**11** Point to each of the buttons on the Standard and Formatting toolbars to read their command names.

Each available button is highlighted as you point to it.

**12** Click the top, left, bottom, or right border of the Formatting toolbar, and when the pointer turns into a four-headed arrow, drag the toolbar to the center of the screen, like this:

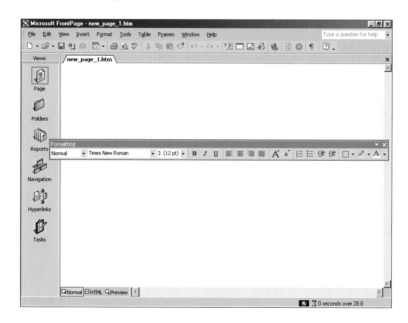

**13** Now drag the Formatting toolbar by its title bar to the left edge of the screen so that it changes from horizontal to vertical orientation.

Moving a toolbar to one edge of the window is called **docking** the toolbar. You can dock the FrontPage toolbars at the top, left, bottom, or right edge of the window. The toolbar's orientation changes as it is moved. Toolbars docked on the left or right are vertically oriented; toolbars docked on the top or bottom and undocked toolbars are horizontally oriented.

**14** Right-click the toolbar to open the toolbar shortcut menu. On the toolbar shortcut menu, click **Drawing**.

The Drawing toolbar opens in its default location at the bottom of the screen.

The Formatting toolbar

The Drawing toolbar

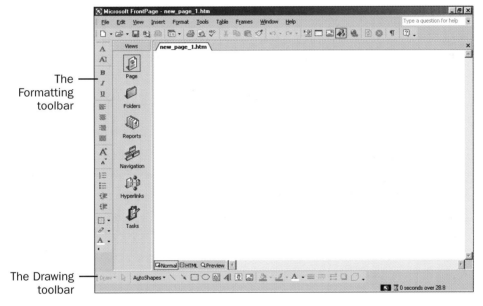

**15** Click the down arrow at the right end of the Drawing toolbar to display the **Add or Remove Buttons** command. Point to **Add or Remove Buttons**, and then click **Drawing** to open the list of the commands that are available from the Drawing toolbar, as shown on the next page.

A similar list is available for each of the toolbars.

**16**  Click the **AutoShapes**, **Line**, and **Arrow** buttons to remove them from the Drawing toolbar.

**17**  Click **Reset Toolbar** to return the toolbar to its original state, and then close the list.

**18**  Click the **Close** button to close FrontPage.

**19**  Reopen FrontPage by clicking **Start**, pointing to **Programs**, and then clicking **Microsoft FrontPage**.

When FrontPage reopens, notice that the changes you made are still in effect; the Formatting toolbar is still docked at the left side of the window.

**20**  Move the Formatting toolbar back to its original location below the Standard toolbar at the top of the window.

**21**  Right-click the toolbar, and click **Drawing** to close the Drawing toolbar.

**22**  On the **File** menu, click **Close Web** to close the Web site.

**23**  If you are not continuing on to the next chapter, quit FrontPage.

## Understanding FrontPage Concepts

This section discusses the types of sites that can be developed with FrontPage and the system requirements that are necessary to take full advantage of the FrontPage 2002 development environment.

There are two kinds of Web sites: **disk-based Web sites** and **server-based Web sites**. A disk-based Web site can be run on any kind of computer, or even from a floppy disk or CD-ROM. Disk-based Web sites support only basic HTML functionality. Many of the more interesting **Web components** that FrontPage supplies won't work on a disk-based site.

Server-based Web sites run on a Web server—a computer that is specifically configured to **host** Web sites. On a small scale, a Web server might be a local computer such as your own, or it might be an intranet server within your company. On a larger scale, Web servers that host corporate Internet sites are usually located at professional **server farms** run by an **Internet service provider (ISP)** or **Web hosting company**.

Most Web sites are initially developed as disk-based sites; that is, you develop them on your local computer. You then publish them to a Web server, either within your organization or at your hosted Web location.

FrontPage 2002 makes it easy to develop both disk-based and server-based Web sites. However, a variety of factors, such as what capabilities you can add to your site and whether those capabilities can be previewed in FrontPage or in the browser, depend on the type of site you are working with. For instance:

- Some FrontPage **Web components**—ready-made elements that provide capabilities such as link bars and tables of contents—work only when they are placed on a page that is part of a FrontPage-based Web site.
- Some components require that the Web page or site be located on a Web server running SharePoint Team Services from Microsoft.
- Other common Web components work only in a server-based Web site located on a Web server running the FrontPage Server Extensions.
- Some components pull their content directly from other Web sites, so they require an Internet connection to be visible.
- Server administration features are available only for server-based Web sites stored on Web servers running SharePoint Team Services or the FrontPage Server Extensions 2002.
- To display database information, your site must be hosted on a Web server that supports Active Server Pages (ASP) and ActiveX Data Objects (ADO).

FrontPage-based Web sites can run on any kind of Web server, but the full functionality of your Web site might not be available unless your site is hosted on a Web server with the FrontPage Server Extensions 2002 installed. If you maintain your own Web server, installing the server extensions is a simple exercise; they are available on the Office XP installation CD-ROM. If you are looking for a company to host your Web site, or if you already have an ISP but you have never asked it to host a FrontPage–based Web site before, be sure to ask whether its servers have the FrontPage Server Extensions 2002 installed.

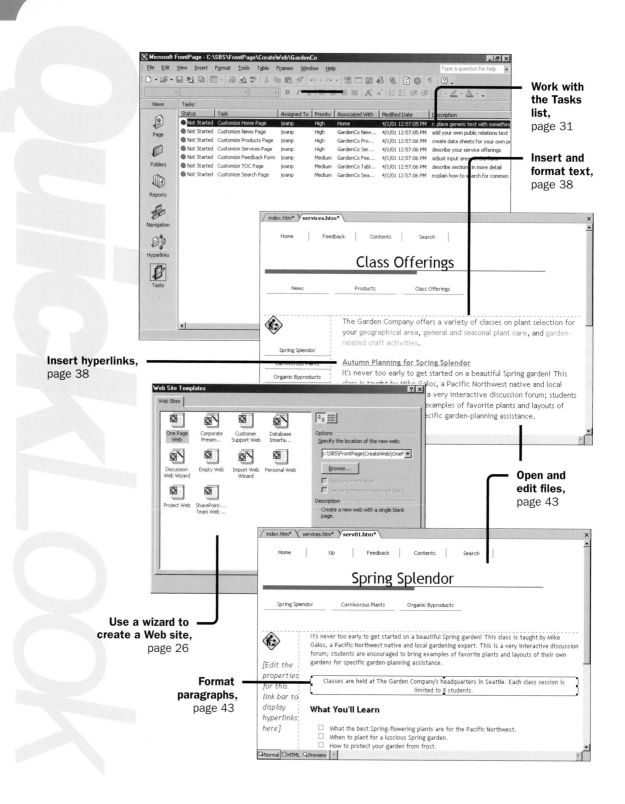

**Work with the Tasks list,** page 31

**Insert and format text,** page 38

**Insert hyperlinks,** page 38

**Open and edit files,** page 43

**Use a wizard to create a Web site,** page 26

**Format paragraphs,** page 43

# Chapter 2
# Creating a Web Site to Promote Yourself or Your Company

**After completing this chapter, you will be able to:**

✔ Create a Web site using a template or a wizard.

✔ Keep track of the tasks necessary to complete a Web site.

✔ Insert, edit, and format content from a variety of sources.

✔ Insert hyperlinks.

✔ Preview a Web site in FrontPage and in a browser.

✔ Delete a Web site.

All Microsoft Office XP applications provide tools for jump-starting the creation of common types of files. In the case of Microsoft FrontPage, you can use templates and wizards to set up the structure for basic types of Web pages and even entire Web sites. When you use one of these tools, FrontPage does most of the structural work for you, leaving you free to concentrate on the site's content.

You can use the FrontPage templates and wizards to create everything from a bare-bones Web page to a complex, multi-page, interactive site. These are great tools to use if you are new to Web design and want to explore the possibilities, or if you are looking for a quick way to get started on the creation of a real Web site.

In this chapter, you walk through the steps for creating a couple of Web sites, including a corporate site that we will work with throughout most of the book. You learn how to enter and format text, how to preview a Web site, and how to delete a site you no longer need.

You will be working with files that are stored in the following subfolders of the *SBS\FrontPage\CreateWeb* folder: *TasksList*, *InsertText*, *InsertExist*, *FormatText*, *InsertHype*, and *PreviewPages*.

# Creating a New Web Site Using a Template

FP2002-1-1

The easiest way to create a new Web site is by using one of FrontPage's **templates**. Templates create the layout for a specific type of Web page or Web site, designating with placeholders the type of content you should put in each location. All you have to do is replace the placeholders with your own content, and you have a finished page or site to show off.

To create a Web site using a template, you simply select the template and specify the location where the site should be created. FrontPage then creates the new Web site and applies the template's structure to it, leaving it up to you to fill in the content and customize the look of the site to suit your needs.

In this exercise, you will create two different types of Web sites using templates: a simple one-page site and a personal Web site.

There is no working folder for this exercise.

Follow these steps:

**1**    If FrontPage is not already open, start it now.

**2**    If the **New Page or Web** task pane is not open, point to **New** on the **File** menu, and then click **Page or Web**.

Your screen now looks like this:

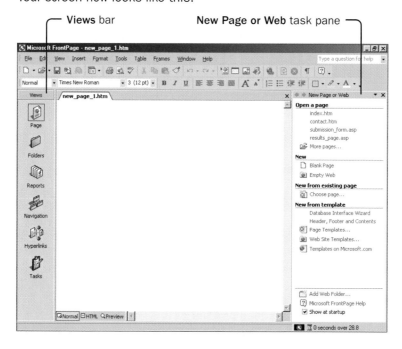

# New Page or Web Task Pane

The **New Page or Web** task pane contains convenient links to the Web sites and individual pages that you have created or worked with in FrontPage. It also contains links to templates and wizards you can use to create new Web pages or sites. If this task pane is not already open, you can open it using one of the following three methods:

■ On the **File** menu, point to **New**, and then click **Page or Web**,

■ On the **View** menu, click **Task Pane**. If a different task pane is displayed, click the down arrow at the right end of the task pane's title bar, and click **New Page or Web** in the drop-down list.

■ Right-click the toolbar, and click **Task Pane** on the toolbar shortcut menu. If a different task pane is displayed, click **New Page or Web** in the task pane's drop-down list.

To open the task pane every time you start FrontPage:

■ On the **Tools** menu, click **Options**, and then select the **Startup Task Pane** check box.

3 In the **New from template** area of the **New Page or Web** task pane, select **Web Site Templates**.

This **Web Site Templates** dialog box opens:

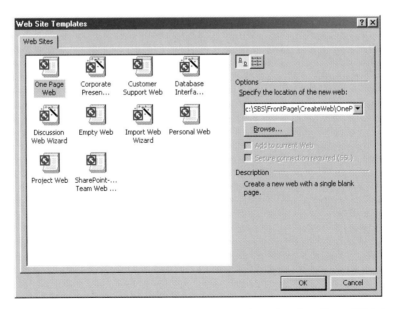

4 In the **Web Site Templates** dialog box, select the **One Page Web** icon.

**5**   Under **Options**, specify what you want to call your Web site and where you want to store it. In this case, type **C:\SBS\FrontPage\CreateWeb \OnePage** in the **Specify the location of the new web** box to create a disk-based Web site in the working folder for this exercise.

## Tip

If you installed the practice files to a drive other than drive C, substitute that drive letter in the above path.

**6**   Click **OK**.

In about three seconds, you have created a new one-page Web site.

**7**   If the **Folder List** is not open, click **Folder List** on the **View** menu to open it.

**8**   In the **Folder List**, double-click **index.htm** to open it.

Your screen now looks like this:

Newly created one-page Web site files

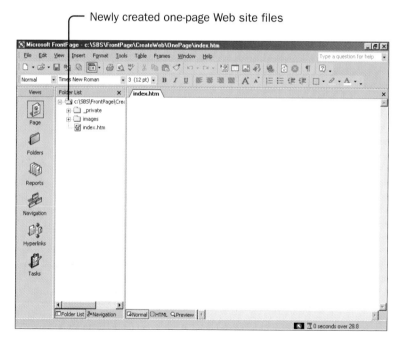

## Tip

FrontPage opens your new Web site in the view that was last active. If your screen doesn't look like our graphic, check the **Views** bar and make any adjustments necessary to make your view the same as ours.

In FrontPage, it appears that your one-page Web site consists of a single file called *index.htm* and two empty folders called *_private* and *images*. However, as you can see from this view of the site in Windows Explorer, many files and folders (some of them hidden) support this single page:

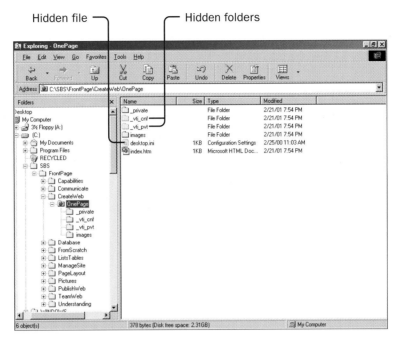

When index.htm is displayed in Page view, the page is completely empty—a blank canvas upon which you can create a veritable work of art. By the time you finish this book, you will know enough to be able to create a fairly sophisticated page from scratch, but until then, it is a good idea to lean on FrontPage to give you a little more of a starting framework. Now you will test another template by creating a personal site to showcase your new skills.

Create a new
normal page

**9** Click the down arrow to the right of the **Create a new normal page** button, and then click **Web**.

The **Web Site Templates** dialog box opens.

**10** In the **Web Site Templates** dialog box, click the **Personal Web** icon, specify the location as **C:\SBS\FrontPage\CreateWeb\Personal**, and click **OK**.

## Tip

FrontPage suggests a location for your new Web site based on the location of the last Web site you created.

A second FrontPage window opens, and FrontPage creates the personal Web site in the second window. You now have two instances of the program running on your computer at the same time.

**11** In the **Folder List**, double-click the **index.htm** file to open the personal Web site in Page view.

The home page of the site is shown here:

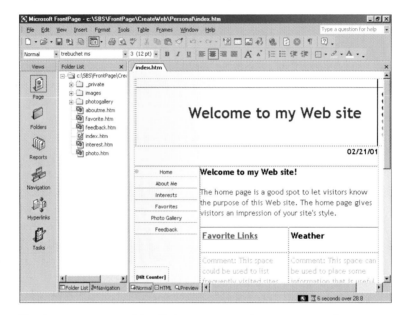

The home page provides links to pages about you, your interests, and your favorite Web sites. You can display photos of yourself, your family, your friends, your dog, and your vacations (real or imagined) in the photo gallery, and Web visitors can contact you by using the feedback page.

Placeholders currently represent all the information in this Web site. By replacing the placeholders with your own information, you can have an attractive site ready to publish in no time at all.

**12** On the **File** menu, click **Close Web** to close the personal Web site.

Close

**13** Click the **Close** button to close the second instance of FrontPage and return to the first instance.

**14** On the **File** menu, click **Close Web** to close the one-page Web site.

# Creating a New Web Site Using a Wizard

FP2002-1-1

Now let's create something a little more complex using one of FrontPage's **wizards**. Wizards are similar to templates, but even better. A wizard not only creates the layout of a page or site for you, but it also leads you through the process of personalizing the content and the appearance of the final product.

In this exercise, you will create a corporate Web site for a fictitious plant and garden store called The Garden Company. To provide some context for the sample site, imagine that The Garden Company has a small store located in Seattle, Washington. The owner of the company is Catherine Turner, who would like to communicate with her existing customers and expand her customer base by having a corporate presence on the Internet. If maintaining a Web site meets these modest goals, she may later choose to expand the site's capabilities to permit online retailing. You will use the **Corporate Presence Wizard** to create the basic corporate Web site.

# Online Retailing

On the surface, expanding your business by selling goods or services via the Internet seems like a good idea. However, this decision should not be made without a good deal of analysis and planning. First, what you have to offer has to be so compelling that people will want to buy it, and second, you have to offer it under terms and conditions that will make people want to buy it from you, rather than from someone else. Unless you have an exclusive right to sell your particular product, you are going to be competing on many fronts, including price, cost and speed of delivery, and customer service. You must also consider how you will provide a secure environment for the handling of other people's money. All these topics are beyond the scope of this book, but if you are interested in learning more about online retailing, you might want to check out *Small Business Solutions for E-Commerce* by Brenda Kienan (Microsoft Press, 2000).

There is no working folder for this exercise.

Follow these steps:

1   Click the down arrow to the right of the **New** button, and then click **Web**.
    The **Web Site Templates** dialog box opens.

2   In the **Web Site Templates** dialog box, click the **Corporate Presence Wizard** icon, specify the location and name of your Web site as **C:\SBS\FrontPage \CreateWeb\GardenCo**, and click **OK**.

The first of a series of **Corporate Presence Wizard** dialog boxes, called *pages*, opens. The wizard uses these pages to prompt you to make choices and enter basic corporate information.

**3** Read the information on the first page, and then click **Next** to move to the second page.

**4** Continue reading the information and clicking **Next** to accept all the default selections in each of the **Corporate Presence Wizard** pages, until you come to the one that requests the name and address of the company.

**5** Enter the information shown here (or your own personalized information), and click **Next**:

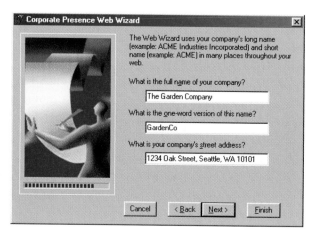

**6** Enter the corporate contact information shown here (or your personalized information), and click **Next**:

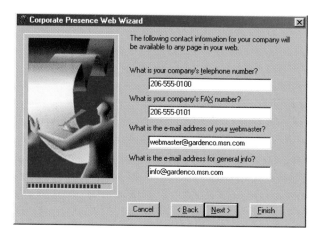

## Generic E-Mail Addresses

It's wise to use generic e-mail addresses in your contact information instead of specific people's addresses so that the address can stay the same no matter who is actually assigned to respond to the inquiry. For example, if The Garden Company listed its information contact address as that of Catherine Turner and then Catherine was away for an extended period of time, messages might build up in her mailbox with no one to answer them. Using a generic address and then forwarding all e-mail sent to that address to one or more individuals ensures that customers' questions are always answered promptly.

**7**  Most sites created by wizards come with a default graphic theme that gives all the Web pages in the site a consistent look. You can change the default theme, but you won't do so at this time, so click **Next**, and then click **Finish.**

FrontPage creates your site using the information you have provided and then displays this list of the tasks that need to be completed to finish the site:

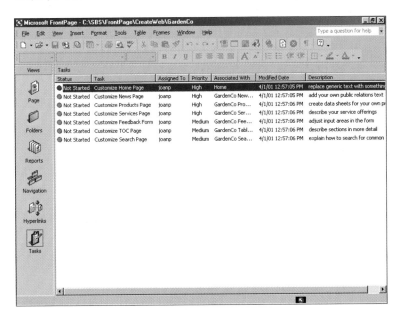

## Tip

If you have previously created sites in FrontPage, the program knows who you are because of information saved in your user profile. In that case, FrontPage assigns the tasks to you. If this is the first time you have created a Web site, FrontPage assigns the tasks to "nobody."

**8**  On the **File** menu, click **Close Web** to close the current Web site.

# Working with the Tasks List

FP2002-5-1
FP2002-5-4

All of the tasks listed for the corporate presence site relate to customizing the content provided by the **Corporate Presence Wizard** to meet the needs of a particular company. The tasks are listed in order of priority. The first high-priority task is to customize the home page by replacing its generic text with something more specific to your company, so let's tackle that task now.

GardenCo

The working folder for this exercise is *SBS\FrontPage\CreateWeb\TasksList*.

Follow these steps:

**1**   On the **File** menu, click **Open Web**.

**2**   Browse to the **GardenCo** Web site that is located in the working folder, and click **Open** to open the Web site.

Tasks

**3**   If you are not already in Tasks view, click the **Tasks** icon on the **Views** bar.

**4**   Double-click **Customize Home Page**, the first high-priority task, to open a **Task Details** dialog box like this:

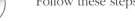

Your personal information appears here.

| Task Details | ? X |
|---|---|

Task name: Customize Home Page

Priority
◉ High
○ Medium
○ Low

Assigned to: me ▼

Associated with:   index.htm

Completed:   No

Modified by:   (Has not been modified)

Created by:   joanp (Corporate Presence Wizard) on 2/21/01 at 8:28:38 PM

Description:
replace generic text with something more specific to your company

Start Task | OK | Cancel

**5**   In the **Assigned to** box, double-click or drag to select the current entry. Assign the task to yourself by typing your name, user name, or initials, and then click the **Start Task** button.

The home page (index.htm) opens in Page view, ready for you to replace the comments that have been inserted by the **Corporate Presence Wizard** with your own content.

**6**   You won't actually edit this page now, so click **Close Web** on the **File** menu to close the current Web site.

# Inserting and Editing Comments

You can use comments to make notes to yourself or to communicate with other people working on a Web site. Comments don't show up in the published version of a Web page.

To insert a comment, click **Comment** on the **Insert** menu. Then type your notes in the text box, and click **OK**.

To edit a comment, double-click anywhere in the comment's text block to open an editing window. Make your changes, and click **OK**. To delete a comment, click it once to select it, and then press the [Del] key.

# Inserting and Editing Text

FP2002-2-1
FP2002-5-1

You can enter new text in a Web page by typing it directly in each page. When you use a FrontPage wizard to create a new Web site, the wizard uses **comments** as placeholders for the text that you need to personalize. The comments inserted by the wizard suggest the type of information you should enter in each area.

In this exercise, you will replace each of the three main blocks of placeholder text on the home page of a Web site created by the **Corporate Presence Wizard**.

GardenCo

The working folder for this exercise is *SBS\FrontPage\CreateWeb\InsertText*.

Follow these steps:

Open

1   On the Standard toolbar, click the **Open** button's down arrow, and then click **Open Web** in the drop-down list.

2   In the **Open Web** dialog box, browse to the **GardenCo** Web site that is located in the working folder, and click **Open** to open the Web site in FrontPage.

Close

3   In the **Folder List**, double-click **index.htm** to open the home page in the Page view editing window, and then click the **Close** button to close the **Folder List** and enlarge your work area.

4   In the body of the home page, click the introductory comment, and press the [End] key to position the insertion point at the end of the paragraph.

## Tip

Although you can delete the comments before typing new text, you don't have to. The comments will not be visible to your Web visitors.

**5** Type the following text:

**Welcome to The Garden Company. We are a quality retail gardening business located in the Pacific Northwest. Our products and services are featured on this Web site. Whether you visit us on the Web or in our store, please feel free to browse, and let us know if you require assistance or have any questions!**

**6** Position the insertion point at the end of the comment under the Our Mission heading, and then enter the following text:

**At The Garden Company, we take pride in offering only the highest-quality plants and garden-related products to our customers.**

**7** After the comment under the Contact Information heading, enter the following text:

**Please feel free to contact us via fax or e-mail 24 hours a day, or to call or visit us at our store during our normal business hours: Monday - Friday 9:00 am - 9:00 pm, Saturday and Sunday 10:00 am - 5:00 pm.**

Your screen looks something like this:

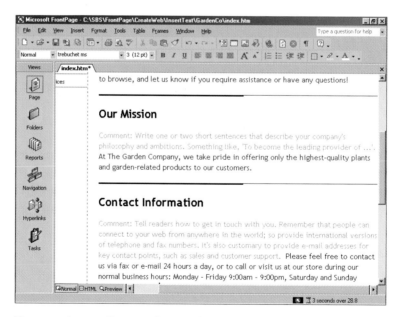

You can change the text that you've entered or add more text at any time.

**8** Position the insertion point at the end of the paragraph under the Our Mission heading.

**9** Press [Enter] to create a new paragraph, and then type the following text:

**We also offer a variety of classes on plant selection for rainy regions, general and seasonal plant care, and garden-related craft activities.**

**10** Now you'll place an e-mail icon next to the Electronic mail heading in the Contact Information area of the page. Position the insertion point to the left of the *E* in *Electronic mail*.

**11** On the **Insert** menu, click **Symbol** to display the **Symbol** dialog box.

**12** In the **Font** drop-down list, select **Webdings**.

**13** Scroll down until you see the three mail icons, and click the first mail icon to select it, like this:

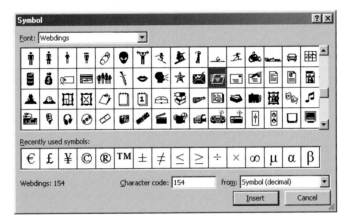

**14** Click **Insert**, and then click **Close**.

In the Normal pane, your contact information now appears as shown here:

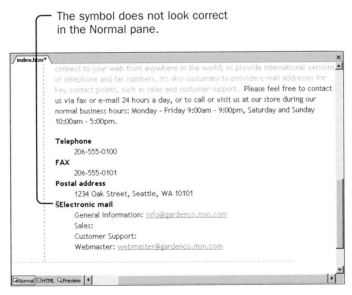

The symbol does not look correct in the Normal pane.

That sure doesn't look like the mail icon you just inserted!

**15** Switch to the Preview pane by clicking the **Preview** button at the bottom of the Page view editing window.

Now you can see the symbol as your Web visitors will see it:

The symbol looks correct in the Preview pane.

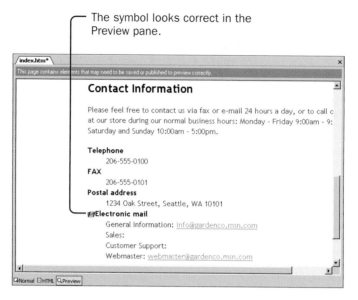

Save

**16** On the Standard toolbar, click the **Save** button to save your Web page.

**17** On the **Views** bar, click the **Tasks** icon to open Tasks view.

**18** Right-click the first task, and select **Mark Complete** from the shortcut menu to mark the task as completed.

**19** On the **File** menu, click **Close Web** to close the current Web site.

# Inserting Existing Text

FP2002-1-4
FP2002-1-5
FP2002-2-1
FP2002-5-1

If you have already created material for another purpose, such as a press release or company brochure, you probably don't want to have to create it all over again in your Web site. And you don't have to.

FrontPage makes it quite simple to copy and paste text into a template-based Web site in order to personalize it to your own taste. You can insert chunks of text, graphics, spreadsheets, or drawings cut or copied from other Office applications. You can even insert entire files.

**Office Clipboard** task pane

new for **Office**XP

You can copy or cut multiple pieces of content from Office programs and then paste the content into your Web pages. The **Office Clipboard** task pane stores text, tables, graphics, and other file elements in a convenient and accessible location and can archive up to 24 different elements across all the Office applications.

Paste the way
you want
new for
**Office**XP

Each time you paste content from the Clipboard into FrontPage, the floating **Paste Options** button appears, allowing you to choose to apply the destination styles, keep the source formatting, or keep only the text for your pasted selection. The default option is to keep the source formatting. You can ignore the **Paste Options** button if you do not want to select something other than source formatting.

Paste Options

To stop the **Paste Options** button from appearing, click **Options** on the **Tools** menu, and clear the **Show Paste Options button** check box.

In this exercise, you will insert text from external files into two existing Web pages of the GardenCo Web site: News and Services. In this site, the second high-priority task is to add public relations text to the News page. The text on this page currently consists of a Web Changes heading and a discussion of site updates. Because you have decided that site updates won't be of interest to patrons of The Garden Company, you will change this page to one that contains press releases. You will also modify the Services pages, using text contained in a Microsoft Word document. You will then update the page title of each page to reflect its new content.

GardenCo
PR2.doc
Classes.doc

The working folder for this exercise is *SBS\FrontPage\CreateWeb\InsertExist*.

Follow these steps:

1   Open the **GardenCo** Web site located in the working folder.

2   Switch to Tasks view.

**Important**

> You can display previously completed tasks by right-clicking the background of the Tasks list, and then clicking **Show History** on the shortcut menu.

3   Double-click **Edit the Customize News Page** task to open it. Assign the task to yourself, and then click **Start Task** to open news.htm.

4   Double-click the **Web Changes** heading to select it, and type **Press Releases**.

The text of the heading is replaced, but its formatting is retained.

5   Replace the default opening paragraph text with the following:

**Keep up with the news! Recent press releases and links to archived press releases are available here.**

6   Select the comment below the paragraph you just typed.

**7** On the **Insert** menu, click **File** to open the **Insert File** dialog box.

**8** Browse to the *SBS\FrontPage\CreateWeb\InsertExist* folder.

**9** In the **Files of type** drop-down list, select **Word 97-2002 (\*.doc)**.

**10** Select **PR2.doc** from the list of available files, and then click **Open** to insert the full text of the document in your Web page.

The text of the document is converted to rich text format and then to HTML and inserted into the News page, just as if you had created it there originally. The original formatting is retained.

## Tip

Don't spend time making a document perfect before you import it. You can always make adjustments to the text of the document after it is imported into your Web page.

The contact information at the top of the imported text is contained in a table. The table and cells are indicated by dotted lines.

**11** Click in the table. On the **Table** menu, point to **Select**, and then click **Table**.

The table and its contents are selected.

**12** Right-click the selection, and click **Delete Cells** on the shortcut menu to delete the table.

**13** Triple-click the **Press Release** heading to select the entire paragraph, and press the ⌨Del⌨ key to remove it from the Web page.

**14** Click the **Save** button to save your Web page.

FrontPage prompts you to update your Tasks list.

Close

**15** Click **Yes**, and then click the **Close** button in the top right corner of the work area to close the page file.

Tasks

**16** On the **Views** bar, click the **Tasks** icon to open Tasks view.

The Customize Home Page and Customize News Page tasks are now shown as Completed.

**17** Next you will add text to the Services page. Assign the Customize Services Page task to yourself and start the task.

The Services page opens.

**18** Now you'll customize the page banner. Right-click the **Services** page banner, and select **Page Banner Properties** from the shortcut menu, as shown here:

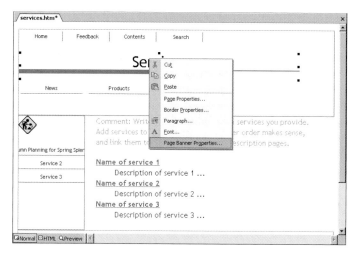

The **Page Banner Properties** dialog box opens.

**19** In the **Page banner** box, select and delete the current text, and then type **Class Offerings**, like this:

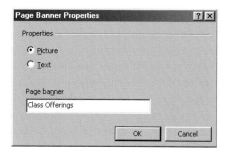

**20** Click **OK** to close the dialog box and change the page title.

This change affects the page title shown both on the page banner and in Navigation view.

**21** In Windows Explorer, browse to the *SBS\FrontPage\CreateWeb\InsertExist* folder, and double-click **Classes.doc** to open it in Word.

**22** Triple-click anywhere in the introductory paragraph to select it, and press `Ctrl`+`C` to copy the text to the Office Clipboard.

**23** On the services.htm page, click the comment text to select it, and then press `Ctrl`+`V` to paste the overview text of the Class Offerings document from the Office Clipboard.

The copied text replaces the comment.

**24** Select and delete the extra (empty) paragraph inserted with the text.

**25** From the **Folder List**, open **serv01.htm**, **serv02.htm**, and **serv03.htm** (the three individual service files) for editing.

**26** In each file, repeat steps 18 and 19 to change the page title to these short versions of the class names described in the Class Offerings document:

■ Change *Service 1* to **Spring Splendor**.

■ Change *Service 2* to **Carnivorous Plants**.

■ Change *Service 3* to **Organic Byproducts**.

As you update each page banner, the navigational links under the page banners and the Navigation view page titles are updated simultaneously.

**27** Return to the services.htm file, and note that the vertical navigation links along the left have also been updated to reflect the new page titles.

**28** For each of the three *Name of service* links, double-click the link to select it, and type the full name of the corresponding course from the Class Offerings document, as follows:

■ Replace *Name of service 1* with **Autumn Planning for Spring Splendor**.

■ Replace *Name of service 2* with **Carnivorous Plants: Vicious or Delicious?**

■ Replace *Name of service 3* with **Organic Byproducts: Use Them or Lose Them!**

Because these are hyperlinks, it is preferable to retype the link than to copy and paste it, to ensure that the link remains active.

**29** Now copy and paste the first descriptive paragraph for each class from the Class Offerings document into services.htm, replacing the corresponding service description.

When you're done, your page looks something like this:

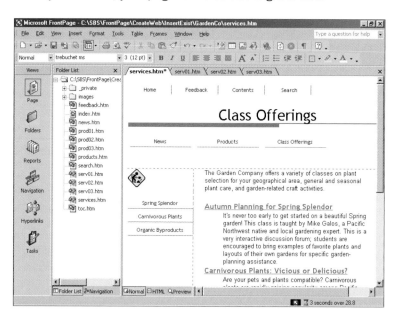

**30** On each of the three individual class description pages (serv01.htm, serv02.htm, and serv03.htm), click anywhere in the body of the page, press `Ctrl`+`A` to select all the content, and then press the `Del` key.

**31** In the Class Offerings document, select and copy the descriptive text, learning objectives, and class schedule for each class to the Office Clipboard, and then paste the Clipboard contents into the appropriate service page.

**32** On the **File** menu, select **Save All** to save your changes, and mark the task as completed when prompted to do so.

**33** On the **File** menu, click **Close Web** to close the Web site.

# Formatting Text

FP2002-3-1

Web sites and Web pages created by FrontPage wizards are already formatted to look terrific without any additional effort from you. However, there are times when you will want to give a word or two a special look or to make a paragraph stand out in some way. Most of the techniques you use in FrontPage to format text are the same as those you use in the other Office applications, so in this section, you will quickly review the types of formatting you are most likely to want to apply to your text, without much explanation.

In this exercise, you will format text and paragraphs using common Office formatting techniques.

GardenCo

The working folder for this exercise is *SBS\FrontPage\CreateWeb\FormatText*.

Follow these steps:

**1** Open the **GardenCo** Web site that is located in the working folder.

**2** Open **index.htm** (the home page) in the Page view editing window.

**3** Select and delete the three comment blocks to make the page easier to read.

**4** In the first paragraph, select the company name.

Increase Font Size

**5** On the Formatting toolbar, click the **Increase Font Size** button.

Note that the font size shown in the **Font Size** drop-down list box changes from *3 (12 pt)* to *4 (14 pt)* as the text size increases.

Italic

**6** Select the last sentence in the first paragraph (beginning with *Whether you visit us*), and click the **Italic** button to italicize the text.

**7** Click the **Preview** button at the bottom of the Page view editing window to switch to the Preview pane, and locate the mail icon in the Contact Information section.

Notice that at its current size, the icon is not very legible.

**8** Switch back to the Normal pane, and select the representation of the mail icon.

**9** On the Formatting toolbar, click the down arrow to the right of the **Font Size** box, and click **6 (24 pt)** in the drop-down list to increase the size of the mail icon.

## Tip

Font sizes are expressed in FrontPage in two ways: in **points** (as you are used to seeing in other applications, such as Word and Microsoft Excel) and in **sizes** of 1 through 7. Eight options are given in the **Font Size** drop-down list: **Normal**, **1 (8 pt)**, **2 (10 pt)**, **3 (12 pt)**, **4 (14 pt)**, **5 (18 pt)**, **6 (24 pt)**, and **7 (36 pt)**.

**10** Insert a space between the icon and the adjacent text for tidiness, and then switch to the Preview pane to see the effects of the change.

Your page looks something like this:

**11** Open **services.htm** (the Class Offerings page) in Page view.

Notice that the text on this page is a different font than the default font on the home page.

**12** Select the first paragraph.

**13** Click the down arrow to the right of the **Font** box, and click **Trebuchet MS** in the drop-down list.

Notice that the font size is still different from that on the home page.

**14** With the first paragraph still selected, press Ctrl + Space to restore the original page formatting. Repeat this step with each of the three class description paragraphs.

**15** For each paragraph, position the insertion point at the end of the paragraph, and press ⌨ Enter to insert a line break.

**16** In the introductory paragraph, select the words **geographical area**.

Font Color
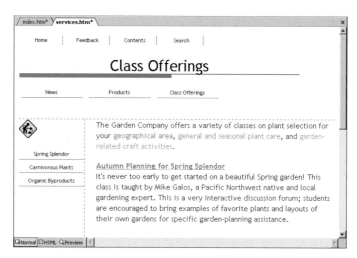

**17** On the Formatting toolbar, click the **Font Color** button's down arrow, and change the font color to **Blue**. Repeat this procedure to change the words *general and seasonal plant care* to **Green** and *garden-related craft activities* to **Red**.

Your page looks like this:

**18** Open **serv01.htm** (the Spring Splendor page) in the Page view editing window.

Notice that the font on this page does not match the default site font on the home page.

**19** Click ⌨Ctrl+⌨A to select all the page content. In the **Font** box's drop-down list, click **(default font)**.

The font of each of the page elements changes to the default font, Trebuchet MS.

**20** Select the paragraph that gives details about the class location and size.

Borders

**21** On the Formatting toolbar, click the **Borders** button's down arrow to display the **Borders** toolbar.

This toolbar can be detached and docked elsewhere, or it can float independently.

**22** Click the **Outside Borders** option to apply a border to the paragraph.

**23** With the paragraph still selected, click **Paragraph** on the **Format** menu.

**24** In the **Paragraph** dialog box, do the following:

- In the **Alignment** drop-down list, click **Center**.

■ In the **Indentation** section, set **Before text** and **After text** to **15**.

■ In the **Spacing** section, set **Before** and **After** to **0**.

The dialog box now looks like this:

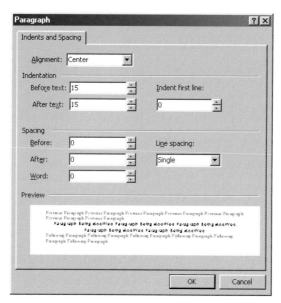

**25** Click **OK** to apply the paragraph formatting.

Your page looks as shown here:

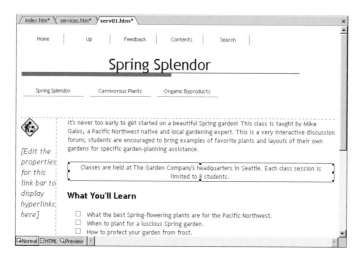

**26** Repeat steps 18 through 25 to reformat serv02.htm (the Carnivorous Plants page) and serv03.htm (the Organic Byproducts page).

**27** On the **File** menu, click **Save All** to save all the open files.

**28** On the **File** menu, click **Close Web** to close the Web site.

# Cascading Style Sheets

Cascading style sheets (CSS) are documents defining formats and styles for different page elements (headings, paragraphs, tables, lists, and so forth) in a central location, either as an **embedded cascading style sheet** within a Web page or as an **external cascading style sheet**. External style sheets can be referenced by multiple documents to provide a consistent look across pages and sites.

Cascading style sheets also allow a Web author to stipulate how page elements are to be displayed by different browsers. Many Web sites utilize a **browser sniffer** that detects the Web browser and version used by each Web visitor and attaches the appropriate cascading style sheet to the site at that time.

To create an embedded cascading style sheet in FrontPage, click **Style** on the **Format** menu, and then define your own styles. The definitions are saved in the HTML code of the page.

To create an external cascading style sheet in FrontPage, select the CSS type from the options available on the **Style Sheets** tab of the **Page Templates** dialog box, click **OK** to create a CSS file, and then define your styles within the file.

To attach a style sheet in FrontPage, click **Style Sheet Links** on the **Format** menu, and browse to the CSS file on your computer or (if you have an Internet connection) anywhere on the Web.

Alternatively, you can select the **Apply using CSS** option in the **Themes** dialog box when applying a theme to your page or site.

The World Wide Web Consortium (W3C) originally developed cascading style sheets. For more information about current and future CSS specifications and how various browsers support CSS, visit *www.w3c.org*.

# Inserting Hyperlinks

FP2002-3-2

When you use a wizard to generate a Web site, the wizard creates hyperlinks between the pages of the Web site. However, you will often want to add hyperlinks of your own. These hyperlinks might be to specific items of information on the same page or on a different page, to other Web sites, or to documents that are not part of any Web site.

In this exercise, you will create hyperlinks from the News page of the GardenCo Web site to important press releases that are stored in an external Word document.

GardenCo PR1.doc

The working folder for this exercise is *SBS\FrontPage\CreateWeb\InsertHype*.

Follow the steps on the next page.

1 Open the **GardenCo** Web site that is located in the working folder.

2 Open **news.htm** in Page view, and press [Ctrl]+[End] to move the insertion point to the end of the document.

3 Press [Enter] to move to a new line. Type **Archived Press Releases**, and press [Enter].

4 On the **Insert** menu, click **Hyperlink**.

Browse for File

5 Click the **Browse for File** button, browse to the *SBS\FrontPage\CreateWeb \InsertHype* folder, select **PR1.doc**, click **OK** to select the file, and then click **OK** again.

A hyperlink to the press release is inserted at the insertion point, like this:

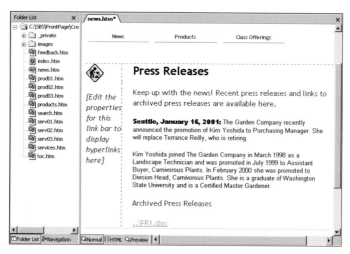

6 To view the contents of the linked file from within FrontPage, press the [Ctrl] key and click the link.

A press release dated September 23, 1998 opens in Word.

7 Close the press release to return to your Web site.

8 Save and close the open file.

9 On the **File** menu, click **Close Web** to close the current Web site.

## Seeing Your Web Pages as Visitors Will

FP2002-1-2

We've made a pretty good start at personalizing The Garden Company's Web site, and you are probably anxious to see the results of your work. There are two ways to view a Web site created with FrontPage before it is published: in FrontPage or in a browser.

Previewing your Web site in FrontPage is a good way to look at the basic layout and evaluate the overall presentation of the site, but it doesn't always represent the site as a visitor will experience it. Apart from the fact that you probably can't see as much of the page as you intend your visitors to see, none of the advanced controls that you might choose to add later will work in this view. To see an accurate preview of your Web site before it is published, you will want to preview it in a browser.

Viewing the Web site in a browser is a great opportunity to test its usability and functionality before exposing it to the scrutiny of the real world. Always be sure to take the time to test your site before publishing it.

In this exercise, you will look at the GardenCo Web site in the Preview pane, and then you will preview it in a Web browser.

GardenCo

The working folder for this exercise is *SBS\FrontPage\CreateWeb\PreviewPages*.

Follow these steps:

**1** Open the **GardenCo** Web site located in the working folder.

**2** Open the home page in Page view.

**3** Click the **Preview** button at the bottom of the screen to switch to the Preview pane.

The Web page is displayed in FrontPage as shown here:

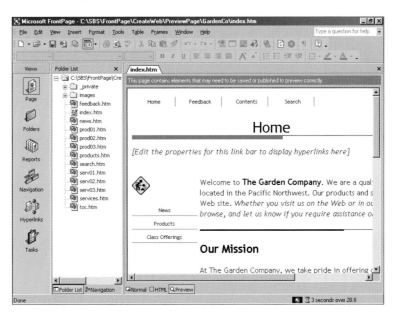

**4** Click the navigation link on the left to jump to the News page.

**5** Click **Home** at the top of the page to return to the home page.

At the top of the screen, a message tells you the page contains elements that might need to be saved or published to be previewed correctly.

Preview in
Browser

**6**   Click the **Preview in Browser** button.

**7**   The **Preview in Browser** dialog box opens. Select a browser and a window size, and click **Preview**.

The home page of the GardenCo site opens in your default browser and window size.

**8**   Browse through the site just as a visitor would, clicking various links to ensure that they work.

**9**   Close the browser and return to FrontPage.

## Troubleshooting

You cannot edit a file in FrontPage while you are previewing it in a browser. Attempting to do so causes an error called an **access violation**. Always close the browser, and then make any necessary changes to your site in FrontPage.

**10**   On the **File** menu, click **Close Web** to close the current Web site.

## Deleting a Web Site

When you first start creating Web sites with FrontPage, you will probably want to experiment. As a result, you will more than likely end up with Web sites on your hard disk drive that you no longer need. What's more, if you make a mess when creating a real Web site and decide to start over, because you already have a Web site with your chosen name stored on your hard disk drive, FrontPage will not allow you to overwrite the existing site with a new one. It will insist that you create a whole new set of files by appending a number to the name you want to use.

To solve these problems, you might be tempted to simply delete existing sites in Windows Explorer, but if you do, you risk leaving behind extraneous hidden files. Instead you must delete the sites from FrontPage. In this section, we show you how to delete the two Web sites you created with templates at the beginning of the chapter.

### Important

If you did not create the Web sites in the first two exercises of this chapter, you will obviously not be able to delete them in this exercise.

There is no working folder for this exercise.

Follow these steps:

1   On the **File** menu, click **Open Web**.

2   In the **Open Web** dialog box, browse to *C:\SBS\FrontPage\CreateWeb
    \OnePage*, and click **Open** to open the Web site.

3   Open the **Folder List** if it is not already open.

4   In the **Folder List**, right-click the top-level folder of the site, and click **Delete**
    on the shortcut menu to open this **Confirm Delete** dialog box:

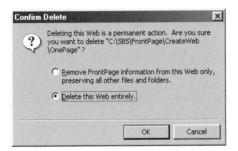

5   Select the **Delete this Web entirely** option, and click **OK** to delete the Web
    site.

    The Web site is deleted and the **Folder List** closes, because the displayed
    content no longer exists.

6   Repeat steps 1 through 5 to delete the Personal Web site created at the
    beginning of this chapter.

7   If you are not continuing on to the next chapter, quit FrontPage.

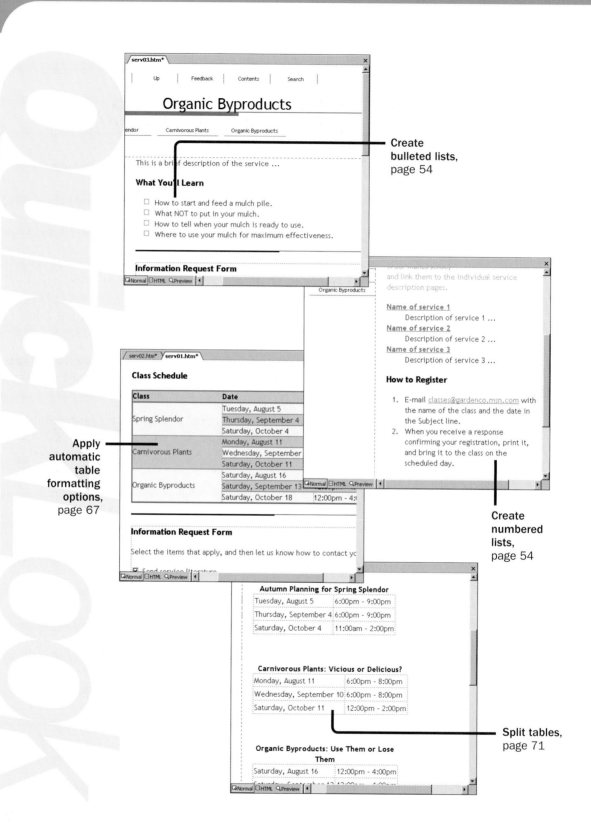

**serv03.htm***

Up | Feedback | Contents | Search |

# Organic Byproducts

endor | Carnivorous Plants | Organic Byproducts

This is a brief description of the service ...

**What You'll Learn**

☐ How to start and feed a mulch pile.
☐ What NOT to put in your mulch.
☐ How to tell when your mulch is ready to use.
☐ Where to use your mulch for maximum effectiveness.

**Information Request Form**

Normal | HTML | Preview

**Create bulleted lists, page 54**

---

Organic Byproducts

and link them to the individual service description pages.

**Name of service 1**
    Description of service 1 ...
**Name of service 2**
    Description of service 2 ...
**Name of service 3**
    Description of service 3 ...

**How to Register**

1. E-mail classes@gardenco.msn.com with the name of the class and the date in the Subject line.
2. When you receive a response confirming your registration, print it, and bring it to the class on the scheduled day.

Normal | HTML | Preview

**Create numbered lists, page 54**

---

serv02.htm* / serv01.htm*

**Class Schedule**

| Class | Date | |
|---|---|---|
| Spring Splendor | Tuesday, August 5 | |
| | Thursday, September 4 | |
| | Saturday, October 4 | |
| Carnivorous Plants | Monday, August 11 | |
| | Wednesday, September | |
| | Saturday, October 11 | |
| Organic Byproducts | Saturday, August 16 | |
| | Saturday, September 13 | |
| | Saturday, October 18 | 12:00pm - 4:1 |

**Apply automatic table formatting options, page 67**

**Information Request Form**

Select the items that apply, and then let us know how to contact yo

Normal | HTML | Preview

---

**Autumn Planning for Spring Splendor**

| | |
|---|---|
| Tuesday, August 5 | 6:00pm - 9:00pm |
| Thursday, September 4 | 6:00pm - 9:00pm |
| Saturday, October 4 | 11:00am - 2:00pm |

**Carnivorous Plants: Vicious or Delicious?**

| | |
|---|---|
| Monday, August 11 | 6:00pm - 8:00pm |
| Wednesday, September 10 | 6:00pm - 8:00pm |
| Saturday, October 11 | 12:00pm - 2:00pm |

**Split tables, page 71**

**Organic Byproducts: Use Them or Lose Them**

| | |
|---|---|
| Saturday, August 16 | 12:00pm - 4:00pm |

Normal | HTML | Preview

Quick Look

# Chapter 3
# Presenting Information in Lists and Tables

**After completing this chapter, you will be able to:**

✔ **Create bulleted and numbered lists.**

✔ **Create a table in various ways.**

✔ **Enter, edit, and format information in a table.**

✔ **Edit a table's structure.**

✔ **Create a table within a table.**

You are probably familiar with the kinds of lists and tables you can create in applications such as Microsoft Word and Microsoft PowerPoint. In Microsoft FrontPage, you use similar techniques to create lists and most kinds of tables.

Both lists and tables are traditionally used to present information in structured, easy-to-grasp formats. In Web pages, you use lists and tables for their traditional purposes, but you can also use tables to structure entire Web page layouts. Using tables to establish the look of an entire Web page minimizes browser display variations and gives you more control than if you depend on a non-structured presentation.

In this chapter, we'll first add a few lists to some of the pages of The Garden Company's Web site. Then we'll create tables using three simple methods:

■ By using the **Insert Table** button.

■ By using the **Insert Table** command.

■ By drawing lines to create the table's rows and columns.

 You will be working with files that are stored in the following subfolders of the *SBS\FrontPage\ListsTables* folder: *CreateList*, *CreateTable*, *TableText*, *TableStruct*, *FormatTable*, and *TableInTable*.

# Creating a List

FP2002-2-1
FP2002-3-1

You use **lists** to break out items of information that might otherwise be buried in a text paragraph. If the items don't have to appear in a particular order, they usually appear in **bulleted lists**; for example, a list of plants that are drought tolerant would be presented in a bulleted list. If the items do have to appear in a particular order, they usually appear in **numbered lists**; for example, instructions for repotting a particular houseplant would be presented in a numbered list.

In this exercise, you will personalize the content in a version of The Garden Company's Web site that was created using the **Corporate Presence Wizard** by adding some lists. To create bulleted and numbered lists in FrontPage, you use the same techniques you would use in Microsoft Word, so you'll move quickly through the exercise without going into a lot of detail.

GardenCo

The working folder for this chapter is *SBS\FrontPage\ListsTables\CreateList*.

Follow these steps:

**1** If FrontPage is not already open, start it now.

Open

**2** Click the **Open** button's down arrow, and click **Open Web** on the drop-down list to display this **Open Web** dialog box:

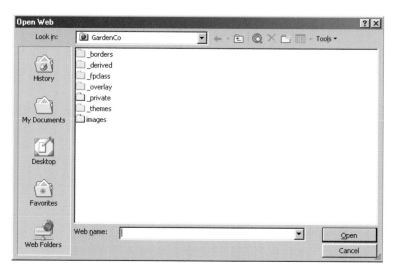

**3** Browse to the working folder, select **GardenCo**, and click **Open**.

The Garden Company's Web site opens in the view that was active when you last quit FrontPage. If you are in Page view, your work area is blank because none of the Web site's pages is open.

**4**   If the **Folder List** is not already open, click **Folder List** on the **View** menu. Then double-click **serv01.htm** to open the Spring Splendor page.

**5**   Select the Key Benefits heading and type What You'll Learn to replace the heading text.

**6**   Select and replace the three bulleted items with these:

- ◼ **Which Spring-flowering plants are best for the Pacific Northwest.**
- ◼ **When to plant for a luscious Spring garden.**
- ◼ **How to protect your garden from frost.**

Close

**7**   Click the serv01.htm file's **Close** button to close the Spring Splendor page, saving your changes when prompted.

**8**   In the **Folder List**, double-click **serv02.htm** to open the Carnivorous Plants page in the Page view editing window.

**9**   Repeat steps 5 and 6 on the Carnivorous Plants page, replacing the bulleted items with these:

- ◼ **What types of carnivorous plants thrive in the Pacific Northwest.**
- ◼ **Which plants are appropriate for indoor and outdoor locations.**
- ◼ **What risks pets and livestock face during periods of extreme growth.**

**10**   Click the serv02.htm file's **Close** button to close the Carnivorous Plants page, saving your changes when prompted.

**11**   In the **Folder List**, double-click **serv03.htm** to open the Organic Byproducts page in the Page view editing window.

**12**   Repeat steps 5 and 6 on the Organic Byproducts page, replacing the bulleted items with these:

- ◼ **How to start and feed a mulch pile.**
- ◼ **What NOT to put in your mulch.**
- ◼ **How to tell when your mulch is ready to use.**

**13**   To add a new bulleted item to the Organic Byproducts list, position the insertion point at the end of the third item, and press $\boxed{\text{Enter}}$.

A new, blank bulleted list line is created.

**14**   Type Where to use your mulch for maximum effectiveness. as the fourth bullet.

The bulleted list looks as shown on the next page.

# Changing Paragraphs to Lists

As in Word, to convert a series of regular paragraphs to a bulleted list, select the paragraphs and click the **Bullets** button on the Formatting toolbar. To convert the bulleted items back to regular paragraphs, select the items and click the **Bullets** button to toggle it off. Similarly, to convert regular paragraphs to a numbered list, select the paragraphs and click the **Numbering** button on the Formatting toolbar.

**15**  Click the serv03.htm file's **Close** button to close the Organic Byproducts page, saving your changes when prompted.

**16**  In the **Folder List**, double-click **services.htm** to open the Class Offerings page in the Page view editing window.

**17**  Press [Ctrl]+[End] to move the insertion point to the bottom of the page.

**18**  Type **How to Register**, and then hold down the [Shift] key and press [Home] to select the text.

**19**  In the **Style** drop-down list, click **Heading 3** to format the text as a third-level heading.

**20**  Press [End] to move the insertion point to the end of the heading, and then press [Enter] to start a new line.

Type **E-mail classes@gardenCo.msn.com with the name of the class and the date in the Subject line.** As you type, the e-mail address will automatically be formatted as a hyperlink.

Numbering

**21** Click the **Numbering** button on the Formatting toolbar to turn the paragraph into a numbered item, and then press [Enter] to create a new line.

FrontPage styles the next paragraph as a numbered item.

**22** Type **When you receive a response confirming your registration, print it, and bring it to the class on the scheduled day.**

**23** Press [Enter] to create a new line, and then click the **Numbering** button to turn off numbering and convert the new numbered item to a regular paragraph.

The numbered list looks like this:

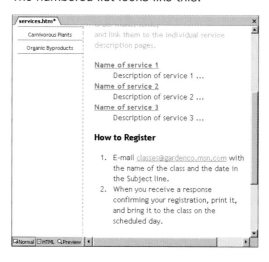

# Tip

If you're interested, you might want to click the **HTML** button to display the underlying source code for the numbered list in the HTML pane. As you will see, FrontPage designates the entire list as an **ordered list** by enclosing it in <ol> and </ol> tags. Each list item is enclosed in <li> and </li> tags. A bulleted list has a similar structure, except that the entire list is designated as an **unordered list** by enclosing it in <ul> and </ul> tags.

**24** Click the services.htm file's **Close** button to close the Class Offerings page, saving your changes when prompted.

**25** On the **File** menu, click **Close Web** to close the current Web site.

## No Tabular List?

Sometimes text or numbers would stand out better for your Web visitors if they were presented in columns and rows, but they don't need the structure of a table. In Word, you would use a tabular list—a set of pseudo columns and rows in which you use tabs to line everything up—instead of setting up a table structure. But FrontPage doesn't accommodate this type of list. When you want to put information in columns and rows, you need to create a real table.

## Creating a Table

FP2002-3-1
FP2002-3-4

A **table** consists of vertical **columns** and horizontal **rows**. A table might have an overall **table title** that appears either as a separate paragraph above the body of the table or in the table's top row. It usually has a **header row**, which contains a title for each column, and it might have a **header column**, which contains a title for each row.

In this exercise, you'll learn one way of creating a table as you set up the structure for a Class Schedules table. You will use this table to organize information about the gardening classes offered by The Garden Company.

GardenCo

The working folder for this chapter is *SBS\FrontPage\ListsTables\CreateTable*.

Follow these steps:

1   On the **File** menu, click **Open Web**.

2   In the **Open Web** dialog box, browse to the GardenCo Web site located in the working folder, and then click **Open**.

## Converting Existing Text to a Table

If you have an existing block of text with items separated by commas, tabs, or paragraph marks, you can convert the text to a table. Select the text you want to convert, and then on the **Table** menu, point to **Convert** and click **Text to Table**. The **Convert Text To Table** dialog box opens so that you can tell FrontPage how the elements of the selected text are separated. Make your selection, and click **OK**. FrontPage converts the text to a table, and because the table is selected, the Tables toolbar opens so that you can make any necessary adjustments.

You can also convert a table to text. Select the table, and on the **Table** menu, point to **Convert** and click **Table to Text**. Then in the **Convert Table to Text** dialog box, select the character you want to use to separate items, and click **OK**.

**3** In the **Folder List**, double-click the **serv01.htm** file to open the Spring Splendor page in the Page view editing window.

**4** Click the black horizontal rule about halfway down the page, and then press `Home` to position the insertion point at the beginning of the line.

**5** Type **Class Schedule**. Then hold down `Shift` and press `Home` to select the text.

**6** In the **Style** drop-down list, click **Heading 3** to format the text as a third-level heading.

**7** Press `End` to move the insertion point to the end of the heading, and then press `Enter` to start a new line.

Insert Table

**8** On the Standard toolbar, click the **Insert Table** button to display this grid:

**9** Point to the first **cell**—the intersection of the first row and the first column—and hold down the left mouse button. Drag the pointer until an area three cells wide by ten cells high is highlighted (the grid will expand as you drag the mouse to the edge), and then release the mouse button.

FrontPage inserts a table with the number of rows and columns you high-lighted, like this:

**10** Click the serv01.htm file's **Close** button to close the Spring Splendor page, saving your changes when prompted.

**11** In the **Folder List**, double-click **serv02.htm** to open the Carnivorous Plants page in the Page view editing window.

**12** Repeat steps 4 through 7 to create the Class Schedule heading and blank line.

**13** On the **Table** menu, point to **Insert**, and then click **Table** to display this dialog box:

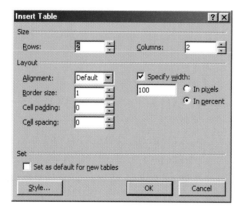

Unlike most corresponding menu commands and toolbar buttons in Microsoft Office XP, the **Insert Table** command and the **Insert Table** button work differently. The command displays a dialog box, whereas the button displays a grid.

**14** In the **Size** section, specify **9** rows and **4** columns for your table.

**15** In the **Layout** section, set **Border size** to **0** and **Cell padding** to **3**.

## Tip

**Cell padding** is space between the borders of the cells and the text inside them. This padding is similar to the margins of a page.

**16** Check that the width is set to **100** percent, and click **OK** to create this table:

**17**  Click the serv02.htm file's **Close** button to close the Carnivorous Plants page, saving your changes when prompted.

**18**  In the **Folder List**, double-click **serv03.htm** to open the Organic Byproducts page in the Page view editing window.

**19**  Repeat steps 4 through 7 to create the Class Schedule heading and blank line.

**20**  On the **Table** menu, click **Draw Table**.

The Tables toolbar opens, and the mouse pointer changes to a pencil.

## Toolbars, Toolbars Everywhere

In FrontPage, whenever you select a type of object that has a toolbar associated with it, the toolbar pops up on the screen because the buttons on the toolbar probably provide the quickest way of accomplishing most tasks you would want to perform with that object. Selecting something else automatically closes the toolbar, but if you want to close the toolbar while you are working with the object to reduce screen clutter, you can either click the **Close** button at the right end of the title bar of a floating toolbar, or right-click the toolbar and click its name on the shortcut menu. If you close a toolbar in this way, it may not pop up the next time you select the associated type of object. To display a hidden toolbar, right-click any visible toolbar and then click the name of the toolbar you want on the shortcut menu.

**21** Click where you want to position the top left corner of the table, and drag the pencil pointer to where you want to position the bottom right corner.

FrontPage creates a single-cell table.

**22** Using the pencil pointer, draw lines to create the table's rows and columns, ending up with a table three columns wide by ten columns high, something like this one:

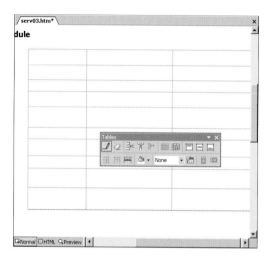

## Tip

Experiment with the locations of the lines separating columns and rows; you will find that the table expands to meet your needs.

**23** Press the [Esc] key to change the pointer back to its original shape.

Close

**24** Click the serv03.htm file's **Close** button to close the Organic Byproducts page, saving your changes when prompted.

**25** On the **File** menu, click **Close Web** to close the Web site.

# Entering and Editing Information in a Table

The Garden Company's Web site has the structures for three tables on three separate pages, but you need to fill the tables with information to make them useful. You enter information in FrontPage tables the same way you would enter it in Word tables.

In this exercise you will fill three existing tables with information. For The Garden Company's Web site, you'll place the same information in each table, but you would probably fill your own tables with different types of information.

The working folder for this chapter is *SBS\FrontPage\ListsTables\TableText*.

GardenCo
ClassList.doc

Follow these steps:

**1**  On the **File** menu, click **Open Web**.

**2**  In the **Open Web** dialog box, browse to the **GardenCo** Web site located in the working folder, and then click **Open**.

**3**  In the **Folder List**, click the **serv01.htm** file to select it, and then hold down the Ctrl key and click **serv02.htm** and **serv03.htm** so that all three files are selected.

**4**  Press Enter to open the three files in the Page view editing window.

**5**  On the Spring Splendor page, enter the column titles **Class**, **Date**, and **Time** in the cells of the first row of the table, thereby creating a header row.

**6**  Now enter the following information in the three columns of the table, under the respective headings:

| Class | Date | Time |
|---|---|---|
| Spring Splendor | Tuesday, August 5 | 6:00pm – 9:00pm |
| Spring Splendor | Thursday, September 4 | 6:00pm – 9:00pm |
| Spring Splendor | Saturday, October 4 | 11:00am – 2:00pm |
| Carnivorous Plants | Monday, August 11 | 6:00pm – 8:00pm |
| Carnivorous Plants | Wednesday, September 10 | 6:00pm – 8:00pm |
| Carnivorous Plants | Saturday, October 11 | 12:00pm – 2:00pm |
| Organic Byproducts | Saturday, August 16 | 12:00pm – 4:00pm |
| Organic Byproducts | Saturday, September 13 | 12:00pm – 4:00pm |
| Organic Byproducts | Saturday, October 18 | 12:00pm – 4:00pm |

## Tip

If you don't feel like typing, you can copy and paste this information from the ClassList.doc file stored in the *SBS\FrontPage\ListsTables\TableText* folder.

**7**  Click the **serv03.htm** page tab to switch to that file.

8    On the Organic Byproducts page, fill the hand-drawn table with the same header row and the same three columns of information.

9    Click the **serv02.htm** page tab to switch to that file.

10   For the table on the Carnivorous Plants page, ignore the header row, fill in the first two columns with the class and date information, and then fill in the fourth column with the time information.

11   On the **File** menu, click **Save All** to save the open files.

12   On the **File** menu, click **Close Web** to close the Web site.

# Editing the Structure of a Table

FP2002-3-4

Unless you are very skilled at creating tables, you will rarely create one that you don't have to later adjust in one way or another. Most likely, you will have to add or delete rows or columns and move information around until it is in the right place. Almost certainly, you will also have to adjust the size of rows and columns that are too big, too small, or unevenly spaced. Luckily, with FrontPage it is simple to fix all these structural problems.

## Tip

When columns are much wider than the information they contain, your Web visitors might have to scroll from side to side to see all of the information in a table. When columns are too narrow, your Web visitors might have to scroll up and down. Whenever possible, you want to avoid making them scroll by resizing one or more of the rows or columns in a table.

In this exercise, you will change the structure of an existing table in order to re-arrange the information it contains. On the Carnivorous Plants page of our sample Web site, the class schedule is currently presented in nine rows and four columns, one of which is blank. You will move the time information from the fourth to the third column and add a header row to this table.

GardenCo

The working folder for this exercise is *SBS\FrontPage\ListsTables\TableStruct*.

Follow these steps:

1    Open the **GardenCo** Web site located in the working folder.

2    In the **Folder List**, double-click **serv02.htm** to open the Carnivorous Plants page in the Page view editing window.

3    On the Carnivorous Plants page, click anywhere in the fourth column of the table.

4    On the **Table** menu, point to **Select**, and then click **Column**.

**5** Point to the selection, and drag the time information from the fourth column to the third column.

**6** Click anywhere in the top row of the table.

**7** On the **Table** menu, point to **Insert**, and then click **Rows or Columns** to display this dialog box:

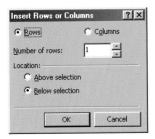

**8** Click **Above Selection** in the **Location** section, and click **OK**.

FrontPage inserts one new row at the top of the table.

**9** Now click anywhere in the fourth column of the table.

**10** On the **Table** menu, point to **Select**, and then click **Column**.

**11** Right-click the selection, and click **Delete Cells** on the shortcut menu to delete the blank column from the right side of the table.

**12** In the new header row, enter the same column headings as those in the other two tables: **Class**, **Date**, and **Time**.

The table on the Carnivorous Plants page now looks like those on the Spring Splendor and Organic Byproducts pages.

**13** Click the serv02.htm file's **Close** button to close the Carnivorous Plants page, saving your changes when prompted.

**14** In the **Folder List**, double-click **serv03.htm** to open the Organic Byproducts page in the Page view editing window.

**15** To adjust the size of the columns in the table on this page, start by pointing to the right border of the table's Date column.

The pointer changes to a double-headed arrow.

**16** Double-click the border.

FrontPage resizes the column so that it can hold all its entries on one line.

**17** Now click anywhere in the table, and on the **Table** menu, click **AutoFit to Contents**.

All the columns adjust to the exact width of their contents, as shown on the next page.

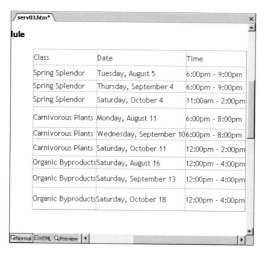

**18** Right-click anywhere in the table, and click **Table Properties** on the shortcut menu to display the **Table Properties** dialog box:

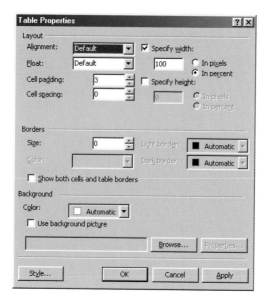

**19** In the **Table Properties** dialog box, do the following:

- In the **Alignment** drop-down list, click **Left**.
- Set **Cell padding** to **3**.

- In the **Specify width** box, type **100**, and then click **In percent**.
- In the **Borders** area, set **Size** to **0**.
- Click **OK** to close the dialog box and apply your changes.

**20** Next move the pointer to the top of the first column so that it changes to a down arrow. Hold down the left mouse button to select the column, and then drag to the right until all three columns are selected.

**21** On the **Table** menu, click **Distribute Columns Evenly** to make all the columns the same width.

Close

**22** Click the serv03.htm file's **Close** button to close the Organic Byproducts page, saving your changes when prompted.

**23** On the **File** menu, click **Close Web** to close the Web site.

# Formatting a Table

FP2002e-3-1
FP2002e-3-2
FP2002e-3-3

In FrontPage, as in Word, you have several options for formatting tables. You can choose from a large variety of pre-formatted table styles or create your own look. You can even merge two or more cells into one cell so that a table entry spans several columns or rows.

FrontPage 2002 now supports more of the standard Office table-formatting options, including the following:

More table
formatting
options

new for
**Office**XP

- **Fill right** and **fill down** allow you to quickly copy content from one table cell to several others.

- **Auto Format** provides a fast and easy way to create professional-looking tables by simply selecting a pre-formatted option from a list.

- The **border drop-down tool** button enables you to format table and cell borders as easily as you can in Word and Excel, by clicking your selection.

In this exercise, you'll format the tables in The Garden Company's Web site, first by doing things "the hard way"—and seeing just how easy that can be—and then by checking out a few of FrontPage's ready-made formats.

GardenCo

The working folder for this chapter is *SBS\FrontPage\ListsTables\FormatTable*.

Follow these steps:

**1** Open the **GardenCo** Web site located in the working folder.

**2** In the **Folder List**, double-click **serv02.htm** to open the Carnivorous Plants page in the Page view editing window.

**3** Scroll down to the table, and select the three cells of the header row.

**4** Right-click the selection, and click **Cell Properties** on the shortcut menu to display this dialog box:

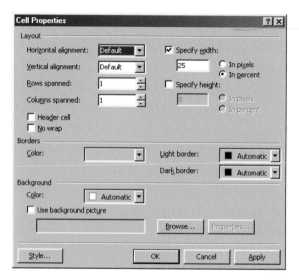

**5** In the **Cell Properties** dialog box, select the **Header cell** check box.

**6** In the **Background** area, click the **Color** box's down arrow to display the Standard and Theme color palettes.

The default color selections include the 16 standard colors of the "Web-safe" palette, as well as the colors that are currently used in the open document.

## Tip

When a theme is attached to a Web page, the default colors include those used in the theme. It is generally best to select colors from the theme to maintain a consistent look and feel throughout your Web site.

If you click **More Colors**, FrontPage opens a dialog box in which you can select from a palette of 127 colors or specify a custom color using the hexadecimal or RGB value. Your options are practically limitless!

**7** Select your favorite color from the default set, and then click **OK** to close the **Cell Properties** dialog box and apply your changes.

The background color is applied, and the words inside the header cells become bold and centered, as shown here:

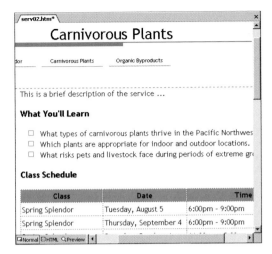

**8** In the **Folder List**, double-click **serv01.htm** to open the Spring Splendor page in the Page view editing window.

**9** Click anywhere in the table on that page.

**10** On the **Table** menu, click **Table AutoFormat**.

**11** In the **Table AutoFormat** dialog box, scroll through the **Formats** list on the left, clicking each format in turn.

When you select a format, a sample table with that format applied is displayed in the Preview window, like this:

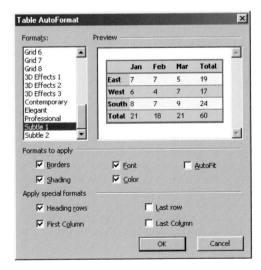

**12** Select the **Subtle 1** format.

**13** Because this table does not have a special first column, clear the **First Column** check box in the **Apply special formats** section.

**14** Click **OK** to apply the selected format to the table.

**15** Click the **Preview** button at the bottom of the Page view editing window to switch to the Preview pane.

When Web visitors view the table, it will look something like this:

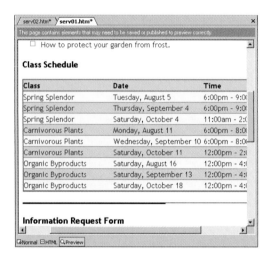

This table looks good, but notice that each class name in the first column is repeated three times. The table would look tidier if each class name appeared only once and spanned three rows.

**16** Click the **Normal** button at the bottom of the Page view editing window to switch to the Normal pane.

**17** In the first column, select the three cells containing the words *Spring Splendor*, and on the **Table** menu, click **Merge Cells**.

FrontPage merges the three cells into one cell that still contains three instances of *Spring Splendor*.

**18** Select and delete two instances of the class name, leaving just one.

**19** Repeat steps 17 and 18 for the Carnivorous Plants and Organic Byproducts classes.

The table now looks like this:

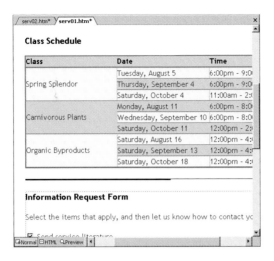

## Tip

To split one cell into multiple cells, right-click the cell and click **Split Cells** on the shortcut menu. In the **Split Cells** dialog box, specify the number of rows or columns you want to split the merged cell into, and click **OK**.

**20** On the **File** menu, click **Save All** to save the open pages.

**21** On the **File** menu, click **Close Web** to close the Web site.

# Creating a Table Within a Table

FP2002e-3-1
FP2002e-3-2

In the same way that you can split and merge individual cells, you can split and merge entire tables. You can also nest one table within another. These options might seem pretty complex for presenting straightforward information, but they offer wonderful possibilities, particularly when you want to organize an entire Web page with one table.

In this exercise you will split the Class Schedule table into three separate tables, one for each class, with each class name as the table title.

GardenCo

The working folder for this chapter is *SBS\FrontPage\ListsTables\TableInTable*.

Follow these steps:

**1** Open the **GardenCo** Web site located in the working folder.

**2** In the **Folder List**, double-click **serv02.htm** to open the Carnivorous Plants page in the Page view editing window.

**3** Scroll down to the table, and click in the first row containing the words *Carnivorous Plants*.

**4** On the **Table** menu, click **Split Table**.

FrontPage splits the table into two tables.

**5** Click in the first row containing the words *Organic Byproducts*, and split the table again.

You now have three distinct tables.

**6** Click in the row containing the words *Class*, *Date*, and *Time*.

**7** On the **Table** menu, point to **Select**, and then click **Row**.

**8** Right-click the selection, and click **Delete Cells** on the shortcut menu.

**9** Click anywhere in the Spring Splendor table, point to **Insert** on the **Table** menu, and then click **Caption**.

A centered caption row is inserted at the top of the table.

**10** Type **Autumn Planning for Spring Splendor** as the table caption.

**11** Select the caption, and make it bold.

**12** Select the first column. Right-click the selection, and click **Delete Cells** on the shortcut menu to delete the column.

**13** Click the anywhere in the table, and click **AutoFit to Contents** on the **Table** menu.

**14** Repeat steps 9 through 13 for the Carnivorous Plants and Organic Byproducts tables, using the following class titles as the table captions:

- **Carnivorous Plants: Vicious or Delicious?**

- **Organic Byproducts: Use Them or Lose Them!**

The results look something like this:

Close

**15** Click the serv02.htm file's **Close** button to close the Carnivorous Plants page, saving your changes when prompted.

**16** On the **File** menu, click **Close Web** to close the Web site.

**17** If you are not continuing on to the next chapter, quit FrontPage.

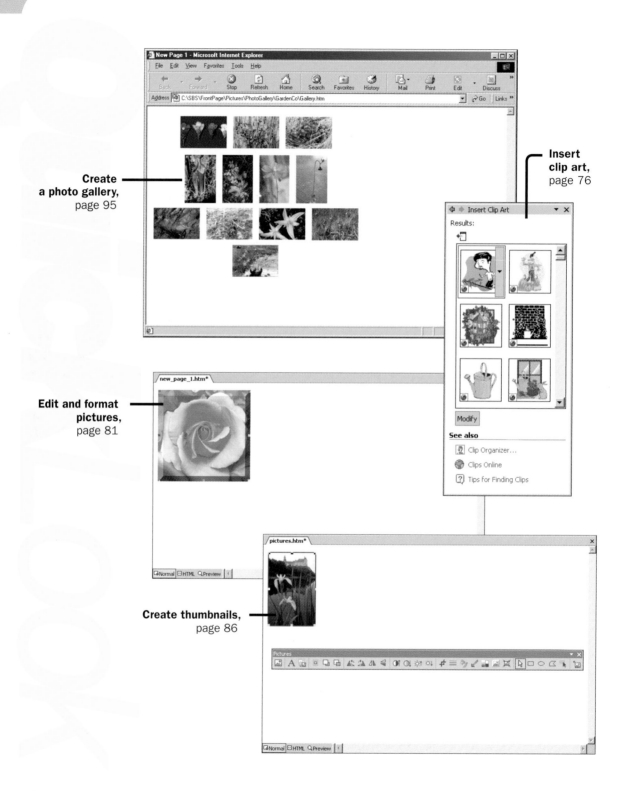

Insert
clip art,
page 76

Create
a photo gallery,
page 95

Edit and format
pictures,
page 81

Create thumbnails,
page 86

# Chapter 4
# Enhancing Your Web Site with Graphics

## After completing this chapter, you will be able to:

✔ Add clip art, pictures, and other graphic elements to a Web page.
✔ Change the size and look of pictures.
✔ Create picture thumbnails.
✔ Create a photo gallery.

You can do a lot to get your message across and increase the appeal of your Web pages by using well-crafted language and by formatting words and paragraphs in various ways. However, there are times when no matter how you format your text, it is not enough to grab the attention of your visitors and to make your Web site stand out from all the others.

At times like these, you need the pizzazz that pictures and other graphic images can add to your pages. With Microsoft FrontPage, you can insert a variety of graphic elements, including clip art, picture files, scanned images, drawings, shapes, WordArt objects, and videos.

It is safe to assume that a large part of the appeal of The Garden Company's Web site, which is used as the example for most of the exercises in this book, would be pictures of plants, "idea" shots of gardens to provide inspiration, garden bed designs, and other visually enticing elements. No amount of text will do the trick for a Web site that is about things you have to see to appreciate, just as no amount of text can possibly substitute for a music clip on a site dedicated to a particular band or genre of music.

To make The Garden Company's Web site visually appealing, you would need to use graphics judiciously, carefully selecting an appropriate style and exercising some restraint in order to avoid a confusing effect. Because you will be learning how to add a wide variety of graphic elements in this chapter, you will use the GardenCo Web site only when it's appropriate, practicing otherwise in a new page that you can discard later.

 In this chapter, you will be working with files that are stored in the following subfolders of the *SBS\FrontPage\Pictures* folder: *AddPicture*, *Thumbnail*, and *PhotoGallery*.

# Adding Clip Art

FP2002-2-1

FrontPage makes it easy to add all kinds of **media**, including graphics, pictures, videos, and even sound effects, into a Web page. When you're looking for a quick and simple graphic representation that won't cost you a licensing fee, an easy solution is to use **clip art**. A large "library" of clip art is supplied with Microsoft Office XP, and a seemingly endless selection is available on the Microsoft Design Gallery Live Web site at *dgl.microsoft.com*. If neither of these sources has what you need, you can find hundreds of small clip art galleries on the Web. You can also purchase clip art CD-ROMs, many of which focus on particular themes or on particular styles of clip art.

Office XP stores different clip art elements in different folders with the applications they are most often used with, and all of them are available to you in FrontPage. The first time you access the clip art feature, you will be prompted to create a catalog of all the clip art items on your computer. You have to run through this simple process only once.

Updated Clip
Organizer
new for
**Office**XP

The new and improved Clip Organizer (formerly known as the Clip Gallery) enables you to access and organize media files through an easy-to-use task pane interface. The Clip Organizer contains hundreds of new pieces of clip art and makes it easy to find additional digital art on the World Wide Web.

You can find, access, and insert a variety of media files from the **Insert Clip Art** task pane. In addition to traditional clip art, which usually consists of cartoon-like drawings, you can choose from photographs, movies, and sounds. This great resource area is a lot of fun to explore!

In this exercise, you will run through the initial configuration of the media files (if you haven't already done so), and then you will insert a piece of clip art on a practice page.

There is no working folder for this exercise.

Follow these steps:

**1**   If FrontPage is not already open, start it now.

Create a new
normal page

**2**   If a new page is not already open, click the **Create a new normal page** button on the Standard toolbar to open a new blank page to use as a canvas for your artwork.

**3**   On the **Insert** menu, point to **Picture**, and then click **Clip Art**.

If this is the first time you've opened the **Insert Clip Art** task pane, this **Add Clips to Organizer** dialog box appears:

**4** To catalog the media files, do the following:

▨ Click **Options** to access this listing of folders from which clip art will be imported:

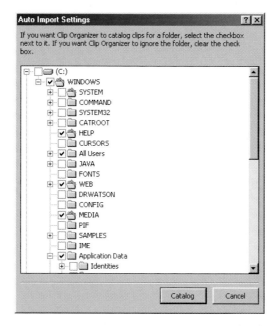

▨ Click **Cancel** to accept the default import folders and close the **Auto Import Settings** and **Add Clips to Organizer** dialog boxes.

▨ On the **Insert** menu, point to **Picture**, and click **Clip Art** again.

▨ This time, click **Now** to catalog all the media files available on your computer.

After the catalog process is finished, the **Insert Clip Art** task pane changes to look as shown on the next page.

**5** Make sure that **All media types** is displayed in the **Results should be** box, and then search for a piece of garden-related clip art by typing garden in the **Search text** box and clicking **Search**.

The results of your search are displayed in this **Results** box:

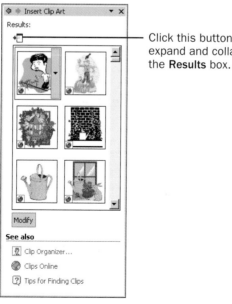

Click this button to expand and collapse the **Results** box.

You can expand and collapse the **Results** box by clicking the button above the window.

**6** Hover the mouse pointer over the graphics to display their descriptions, sizes, file sizes, and formats.

**7** Scroll through the search results until you find a graphic you like.

**8** Right-click the graphic, and click **Insert** on the shortcut menu.

FrontPage inserts the selected graphic in your page at the insertion point, like this:

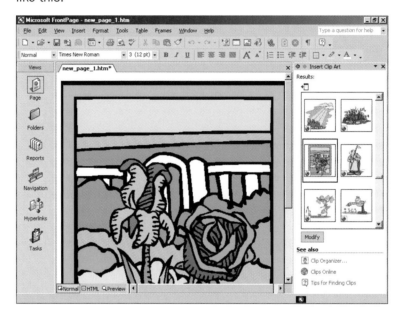

As you can see, the clip art is huge. Later in the chapter, you will practice resizing graphics.

Close

**9** Click the file's **Close** button to close the current file; click **No** when prompted to save your work.

# Adding a Picture

FP2002-2-1

Where Web pages are concerned, it's worth keeping in mind the well-worn saying "A picture is worth a thousand words." You will often find it beneficial to add photographs to your Web pages to illustrate or enhance the text or to demonstrate a difficult concept. You can obtain Web-ready pictures in a variety of ways: by taking photographs with a digital camera, by scanning existing photographs to create digital files, or by buying art files or downloading public-domain files from the Internet.

FrontPage 2002 can access picture files that are on your computer, on another computer on your network, or if you have an Internet connection, even on a Web site.

For the highest display quality, you should use pictures that have been saved as **Graphics Interchange Format (GIF)** or **Joint Photographic Experts Group (JPG)** files. Both display well over the Web. The GIF file format supports up to 256 colors. The JPG file format was specifically developed for photographs and is the best format to use for photos and other graphics with more than 256 colors. JPG files are usually smaller and therefore take less time to download over the Web.

## Tip

You can easily convert graphics of other file types to GIF or JPG format in FrontPage. In Page view, right-click the graphic, and then click **Picture Properties** on the shortcut menu. In the **Type** area of the **General** tab, click **GIF** or **JPG**.

In this exercise, you will insert a picture file on a practice page.

Garden4.gif

The working folder for this exercise is *SBS\FrontPage\Pictures\AddPicture.*

Follow these steps:

Create a new
normal page

**1** On the Standard toolbar, click the **Create a new normal page** button to create a new page.

The new page opens in the Page view editing window with the insertion point positioned at the top of the page.

**2** On the **Insert** menu, point to **Picture**, and then click **From File** to open the **Picture** dialog box.

**3** In the **Picture** dialog box, browse to the working folder.

The Garden4.gif file is selected because it is the only file in the directory.

Views

**4** If you don't see a preview of the graphic in the dialog box, click the **Views** button's arrow on the **Picture** dialog box's toolbar, and then click **Preview** on the drop-down menu.

The dialog box displays a preview of the selected graphic, as shown here:

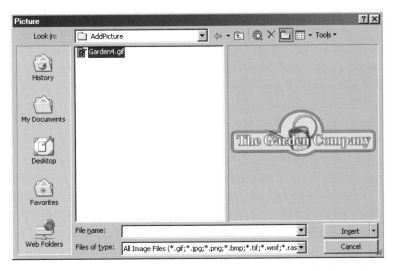

**5** Click **Insert** to insert the graphic in the Web page at the insertion point.

Close

**6** Click the file's **Close** button to close the current file; click **No** when prompted to save your work.

# Editing and Formatting Pictures

FP2002-4-1

Sometimes the picture you add to a Web page won't produce exactly the result you are looking for—perhaps it's too large or too small, or perhaps it includes a variety of elements that distract from the thing you're trying to draw the visitor's attention to. For really drastic changes, you will need to manipulate the picture in a graphics-editing program before adding it to the Web page. But for small modifications and for such enhancements as sizing, **cropping**, and adding a frame, you can do the job within FrontPage.

The commands used to edit and format pictures are contained on the Pictures toolbar, shown here:

■ Click **Insert Picture From File** to open the **Picture** dialog box, where you can search for and insert another picture.

■ Use the **Text** button to create a text box in the picture area into which you can insert your own text.

■ Click **Auto Thumbnail** to create a small preview version of your picture that is hyperlinked to the original. Viewers can click the thumbnail to view the full-size version.

- Use the **Position Absolutely**, **Bring Forward**, and **Send Backward** buttons to control the position of the picture on the page in relation to other elements; whether it is in front of or behind other objects; and whether it moves with the surrounding text.

- Click the **Rotate Left**, **Rotate Right**, **Flip Horizontal**, and **Flip Vertical** buttons to reverse and rotate your picture.

- Click the **More Contrast**, **Less Contrast**, **More Brightness**, and **Less Brightness** buttons to increase and decrease the brightness and contrast of the selected picture.

- Use the **Crop** button to cut the picture down to a smaller size; this will not shrink the picture, but will instead trim the picture as you indicate.

- Click the **Line Style** button to open the **Line Style** dialog box, in which you can change the width, length, color, and pattern of lines.

- Click the **Format Picture** button to open the **Format Picture** dialog box.

- Use the **Set Transparent Color** button to indicate that a particular color will be transparent when the graphic is viewed on a Web page. This is ideal when you want to display an irregularly shaped object (one without straight borders).

- Click the **Color** button to recolor your picture as a black and white, grayscale (black, white, and shades of gray), or washed out version of the original.

- Click **Bevel** to create a beveled self-framing effect.

- Use the **Resample** button to refine the focus of a picture that has been enlarged or shrunken.

- Click **Select** to change the insertion point to a pointer so that you can select a picture for editing. This button is selected by default when the Pictures toolbar is opened.

- Use the **Rectangular Hotspot**, **Circular Hotspot**, **Polygonal Hotspot**, and **Highlight Hotspots** buttons to select and view hotspots, or image maps, on your picture. These are areas that can be hyperlinked to jump to other graphics, other Web pages, or other Web sites. They can even generate e-mail messages!

- Click **Restore** to undo any changes that have been made to the picture since the Pictures toolbar was opened.

The Pictures toolbar opens automatically when you select a picture for editing, or you can open it at any time by right-clicking the toolbar area and then clicking **Pictures** on the shortcut menu.

In this exercise, you work with a photograph to practice using some of FrontPage's picture editing and formatting capabilities. First you size the picture and crop away the parts you don't want; then you convert the picture to black and white and give it a bevel frame.

There is no working folder for this exercise.

Follow these steps:

**Create a new normal page**

**1** On the Standard toolbar, click the **Create a new normal page** button to create a new page.

**2** If the **Insert Clip Art** task pane is not already open, click **Task Pane** on the **View** menu and select **Insert Clip Art** from the drop-down title bar.

**3** If the **Insert Clip Art** task pane still shows the results of your previous search, click **Modify** to start a new search.

**4** In the **Search text** box, type **roses**. In the **Results should be** drop-down list, clear the **Clip Art**, **Movies**, and **Sounds** check boxes, leaving only the **Photographs** check box selected. Then click away from the drop-down list to close it and click **Search** to look for pictures of roses.

**5** Click the first photo to insert it on the page.

**6** Close the **Insert Clip Art** task pane to give you more room to work.

**7** On the **View** menu, point to **Toolbars**, and then click **Pictures** to open the Pictures toolbar.

Your screen now looks like this:

**8** Drag the Pictures toolbar down until it docks at the bottom of the screen and is not covering the rose.

**Crop**

**9** Click the picture to select it, and then click the **Crop** button on the Pictures toolbar.

A dashed box appears in the picture, defining the edges of the area to be cropped.

**10**  Drag the handles of the crop box until the box contains just the central rose, like this:

The crop box is indicated by this dotted line.

**11**  Click the **Crop** button again to crop the picture to the specified shape and size.

**12**  Double-click the picture to display a **Picture Properties** dialog box like the one shown here:

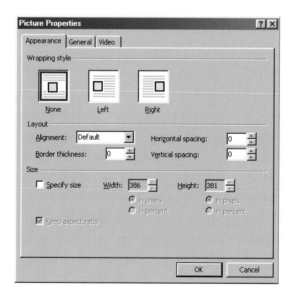

**13**  Select the **Specify size** check box, and set the **Width** to **200** pixels.

**14**  To prevent distortion, ensure that the **Keep aspect ratio** check box is selected.

The height will automatically resize to match the new width.

**15** Click **OK** to close the dialog box and apply your changes.

FrontPage resizes the graphic to your specified dimensions, as shown here:

Color

**16** On the Pictures toolbar, click the **Color** button.

**17** On the **Color** drop-down menu, click **Grayscale**.

The picture is converted to shades of gray, but retains the original quality of detail.

Bevel

**18** On the Pictures toolbar, click **Bevel**.

The colors at the edges of the picture change to make it appear that the center is raised, like this:

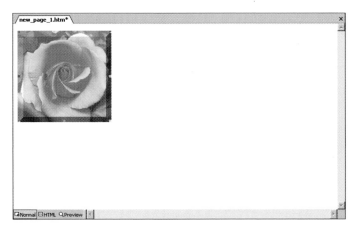

Close

**19** Click the file's **Close** button to close the current file; click **No** when prompted to save your work.

# Creating and Displaying Thumbnails

FP2002-2-1

**Thumbnails** are small versions of graphics that are hyperlinked to full-size versions. Thumbnails are often used on Web pages containing many graphics that Web visitors may or may not want to see (catalog items, for example). Because thumbnails are small, they download faster, so visitors are less likely to get impatient and move to another site.

In this exercise, you create a thumbnail of a picture and test it in FrontPage.

pictures.htm

The working folder for this exercise is *SBS\FrontPage\Pictures\Thumbnail*.

Follow these steps:

**1** Open the **pictures.htm** file located in the working folder.

**2** Click the picture on the page to select it and open the Pictures toolbar.

The Pictures toolbar opens.

Auto Thumbnail

**3** On the Pictures toolbar, click the **Auto Thumbnail** button.

The picture shrinks to thumbnail size and is now surrounded by a blue border that indicates the presence of a hyperlink, as shown here:

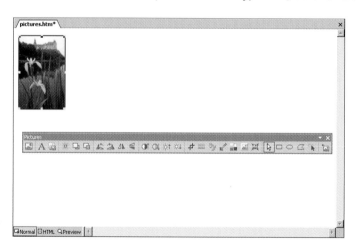

The hyperlink surrounding the graphic links the thumbnail version of the graphic to the original, which is no longer displayed on the page.

**4** Click the **HTML** button at the bottom of the Page view editing window to display the HTML code that links the thumbnail to the original graphic.

The code looks like this:

```
<img border="2" src="../../../WINDOWS/TEMP/FrontPageTempDir
    PH01245J[1]_small.jpg" width="100" height="151" xthumbnail-orig
    image="PH01245J[1].jpg">
```

**5** Click the **Normal** button at the bottom of the Page view editing window to return to the Normal pane.

**6** Drag the handles surrounding the selected thumbnail to make it bigger.

The thumbnail becomes blurry and grainy when you make it bigger, because it is not as detailed as the original picture.

Undo

**7** After you have seen the effect of enlarging the thumbnail, click the **Undo** button on the Standard toolbar to return the thumbnail to its original size.

**8** To test the thumbnail link, click the **Preview** button at the bottom of the Page view editing window to switch to the Preview pane, and then click the thumbnail to open the original picture in the Preview pane.

## Troubleshooting

Certain types of files, including Windows Metafile (WMF) files, won't open in the Preview pane. To preview these images, hold down the Ctrl key in the Normal pane and click the thumbnail to open the original picture in a separate window.

Preview in
Browser

**9** To experience the thumbnail link as your Web visitors will, click **Preview in Browser** on the Standard toolbar. Save the page and embedded graphics if prompted to do so.

Your Web page opens in your browser, with the thumbnail and hyperlink displayed.

**10** Click the thumbnail to display the full-size graphic, and then click the browser's **Back** button to return to the thumbnail.

**11** Close the browser to return to FrontPage.

**12** Close the page without saving your changes.

## Adding a Line, Shape, or Drawing

FP2002-2-2
FP2002-4-1

When it comes to dressing up your pages with graphic elements, you are not limited to images such as clip art, pictures, and photographs. You can also create designs with lines, squares, circles, and other shapes, and if you are artistically inclined, you can even create entire drawings from within FrontPage. For professional-quality art, you should use a dedicated graphics program, but you can use FrontPage to turn out simple, Web-ready artwork.

Cross-browser
enhanced
drawing tools
new for
**Office**XP

FrontPage 2002 includes enhanced drawing tools that make it easy to incorporate specially formatted lines, a wide variety of preformed shapes, WordArt objects, text boxes, and shadowing using the same techniques that are available in Microsoft Word and Microsoft PowerPoint. These lines, shapes, and drawings are collectively known as **Office Drawings**. Office Drawings can be copied from other Office applications and pasted directly into your FrontPage-based Web site.

The commands used to work with most graphics are represented as buttons on the Drawing toolbar and the Drawing Canvas toolbar. Both of these toolbars can be opened at any time by right-clicking the toolbar area and clicking their names on the toolbar shortcut menu. The Drawing toolbar opens automatically when you select an Office Drawing for editing. It contains these buttons:

■ Use the commands on the **Draw** menu to control the grouping, position, and movement of objects.

■ Click the **AutoShapes** button to display a menu of over 130 shapes ranging from basic geometric shapes and arrows to fully formed weather indicators. Special flowchart, banner, and call-out symbols are included. You can drag the **AutoShapes** menu away from the Drawing toolbar so that it functions as its own free-floating toolbar.

■ Use the **Line**, **Arrow**, **Rectangle**, and **Oval** buttons to draw these basic shapes in any size by clicking and dragging the shape onto the page.

■ Click the **Text Box** button to insert text frames within graphics.

■ Click the **Insert WordArt**, **Insert Clip Art**, and **Insert Picture From File** buttons to insert new graphic elements.

■ Use the **Fill Color**, **Line Color**, and **Font Color** buttons to control the colors of their respective elements.

■ Use the **Line Style**, **Dash Style**, and **Arrow Style** buttons to format the thickness, color, solidity, and end caps of line elements.

■ Apply shadows to graphic elements and modify the properties of shadows using the **Shadow Style** button.

■ Give graphic elements a three-dimensional look using the **3-D Style** button.

You can **group** several drawing elements together so that you can treat them as one. In this way, you can create a drawing out of several shapes and then copy and paste the entire drawing, or reduce or enlarge it. If you want to treat the drawing as individual elements again, you can **ungroup** them at any time.

The "frame" in which Office Drawings are created in FrontPage is called the **drawing canvas**. You can have the drawing canvas act as an actual frame by formatting it with visible borders and background colors, but its main purpose is to contain all the elements of the drawing that you create, so that the underlying HTML code for the drawing can be selected and treated as a single unit. The formatting of the drawing canvas also determines the way in which text wraps around the drawing and the position of the drawing in relation to other objects on the page.

The Drawing Canvas toolbar, shown here, opens when you insert a new drawing:

It includes these buttons:

■ Click **Fit Drawing to Contents** to enlarge or shrink the drawing canvas to the same size as the drawing it contains.

■ Click **Expand Drawing** to stretch the drawing to the current size of the canvas.

■ Click **Scale Drawing** to enlarge the drawing to the current size of the canvas, but maintain its original height-to-width ratio.

In this exercise, you first draw a horizontal rule, then you create and insert a drawing that incorporates pre-defined shapes, and finally you insert a shape directly on the Web page.

There is no working folder for this exercise.

Follow these steps:

Create a new normal page

**1** On the Standard toolbar, click the **Create a new normal page** button to create a new page.

**2** On the **Insert** menu, click **Horizontal Line** to draw a rather boring line.

**3** Right-click the line, and then click **Horizontal Line Properties** on the shortcut menu to display this dialog box:

**4** In the **Horizontal Line Properties** dialog box, do the following:

■ Set the **Width** to **80** percent of the window.

■ Set the **Height** to **3** pixels.

■ In the **Color** drop-down box, click **Green**.

■ Click **OK** to close the dialog box and apply your settings.

## Tip

Move the mouse over the colors in the **Color** drop-down box to see each color's name displayed as a ScreenTip.

The page now looks like this:

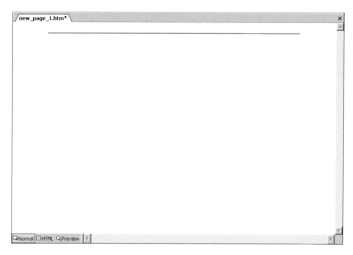

**5**   Now press `Ctrl`+`End` to move the insertion point to the end of the page.

**6**   On the **Insert** menu, point to **Picture**, and then click **New Drawing**.

FrontPage displays an empty drawing canvas, the Drawing Canvas toolbar, and the Drawing toolbar, like this:

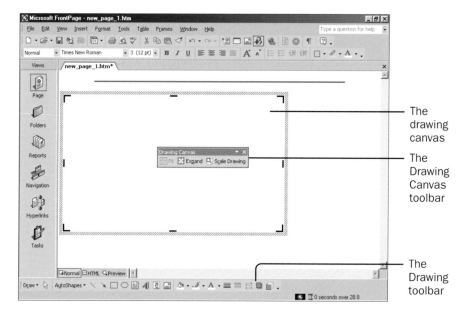

The drawing canvas

The Drawing Canvas toolbar

The Drawing toolbar

## Tip

You can drag the toolbars out of the way while you're working.

7    On the Drawing toolbar, click **AutoShapes** to see the menu of available shapes.

## Tip

When you see a drop-down menu with a "handle" on it (horizontal lines in a shaded stripe), you can drag the menu onto the work area, and it will float there until you click the toolbar's **Close** button. Alternatively, you can drag the menu onto the toolbar or dock it at the left, right, or bottom edge of the window.

8    Point to **Stars and Banners**, and then click the **Explosion 2** symbol, shown here:

## Tip

Move the pointer over a symbol to see the symbol's name displayed as a ScreenTip.

9    Drag down from the top right corner of the drawing canvas to create a small "explosion" shape, like this:

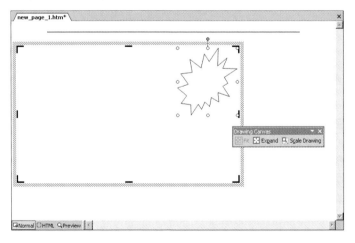

**19** Right-click the sun in your picture, and click **Format AutoShape** on the short-cut menu to display this dialog box:

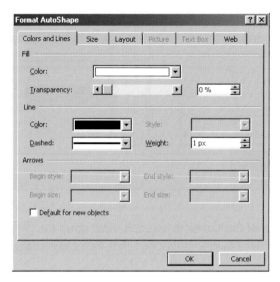

**20** In the **Format AutoShape** dialog box, do the following:

- On the **Colors and Lines** tab, set the **Fill Color** to **Yellow**.
- On the **Layout** tab, set the **Wrapping style** to **None** and the **Positioning style** to **Absolute**.
- Click **OK** to close the dialog box and apply your settings.

**21** Color the flower elements to create a cheerful garden scene like this one:

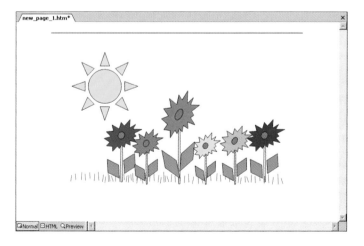

**22** Close the Drawing toolbar when you're finished.

Close

**23** Click the page's **Close** button to close the current file; save your work when prompted if you want to.

# Creating a Photo Gallery

FP2002-4-4
FP2002e-4-1

Photo Gallery

new for
**Office**XP

Companies like The Garden Company often want to include photo galleries on their Web sites—sometimes of products, sometimes of offices or other company buildings, or sometimes of key people whom Web visitors will deal with. To create a photo gallery by hand, you can simply add your pictures to a page, format them as thumbnails, and arrange them the way you want them.

FrontPage offers an even easier method. You can use the **Photo Gallery** Web component to quickly and easily create an attractive display of personal or business photos or images. You can choose from four styles, arranging your pictures either horizontally, vertically, in a tableau-style montage, or in a slideshow. With the **Photo Gallery** Web component, you can add captions and descriptions to your images and update the layout and content in seconds.

# About Web Components

FrontPage 2002 offers many exciting, ready-made Web components that can be dropped onto a Web page to give your site added zing with very little effort.

FrontPage Web components range from decorative to informative to downright useful, and they are one of the most appealing aspects of the program. Web components enable any FrontPage-savvy designer to create a well-programmed, fully functional site without ever having to go "behind the scenes" to do any actual programming.

In this exercise, you will create a photo gallery in a pre-existing Web site using the **Photo Gallery** Web component. The photos used in this exercise are from the Carnivorous Plant Database at *www2.labs.agilent.com/bot/cp_home/* and are used by permission of the database owner.

GardenCo

The working folder for this exercise is *SBS\FrontPage\Pictures\PhotoGallery*. In addition to the GardenCo Web site, you will link to the 12 plant photographs located in the working folder. Because the **Photo Gallery** Web component must be saved as part of a FrontPage-based Web site in order for it to work, you will complete this exercise within the structure of a sample Web site.

Follow the steps on the next page.

**1** On the **File** menu, click **Open Web**. Browse to the working folder, click **GardenCo**, and then click **Open** to open the Web site.

Create a new normal page

**2** On the Standard toolbar, click the **Create a new normal page** button to open a new page.

**3** On the **Insert** menu, click **Web Component**, and then select **Photo Gallery** to see these options:

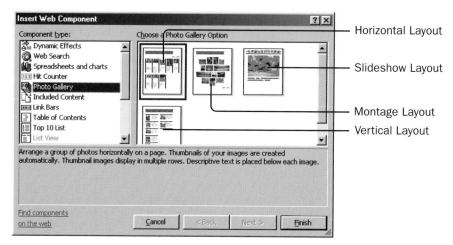

**4** In the **Choose a Photo Gallery Option** box, click each of the four options and read the description that appears in the pane below.

**5** Select the **Montage Layout** option, and click **Finish**.

The **Photo Gallery Properties** dialog box opens so that you can add photos to the photo gallery.

## Tip

If you later change your mind about the layout of your photo gallery, simply right-click the **Photo Gallery** Web component in Page view, and click **Photo Gallery Properties** on the shortcut menu to display the **Photo Gallery Properties** dialog box. On the **Layout** tab, select a different layout option, and click **OK** to reformat your photo gallery.

**6** Click **Add**, and then click **Pictures from Files**.

**7** Browse to the *SBS\FrontPage\Pictures\PhotoGallery* folder, where you'll find 12 photos of carnivorous plants.

**8** Select all the files at once by clicking the first file, holding down the ⌷shift⌷ key, and clicking the last file. Then click **Open**.

FrontPage imports the pictures into the photo gallery and displays them in the **Photo Gallery Properties** dialog box.

**9** Select **plant1.jpg** on the file list.

**10** In the **Caption** box, type **Four Deadly Beauties**.

**11** Click **Override and use custom font formatting**.

**12** Select the text in the **Caption** box.

**13** In the **Font** drop-down list, click **Batang**.

**14** In the **Font Size** drop-down list, click **2 (10 pt)**.

**15** In the **Font Color** drop-down list, click **Purple**.

Bold

**16** Click the **Bold** button.

**17** Select the text in the **Description box**, and repeat steps 14 and 15 to change the font and font size.

The dialog box now looks something like this:

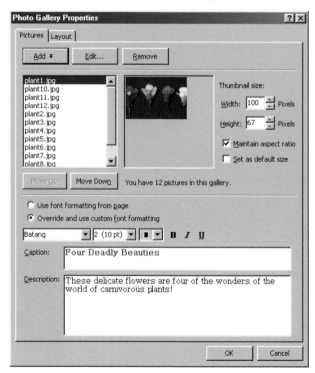

**18** Click **OK** to close the **Photo Gallery Properties** dialog box and generate the photo gallery.

Preview in
Browser

**19** On the Standard toolbar, click the **Preview in Browser** button to preview the file in your default browser and window size. When prompted to do so, save the page file with the name **Gallery.htm** and the embedded graphics with their default names.

Your photo gallery looks something like this:

Pretty impressive for a few minutes' work!

**20** Close the browser to return to FrontPage.

Close

**21** Click the page's **Close** button to close its file; save your work when prompted if you want to.

**22** On the **File** menu, click **Close Web** to close the Web site.

# Adding Fancy Text

FP2002-2-2

**WordArt** objects are text objects with special formatting applied. You can choose from 30 basic formatting options and then make further changes from the WordArt toolbar. This toolbar opens automatically when you insert a WordArt object and contains the following buttons:

■ Click **Insert WordArt** to open the **WordArt Gallery** dialog box so that you can create a new WordArt object.

- Click **Edit Text** to open the **Edit WordArt Text** dialog box, where you can change the text, font, font size, and font formatting of your WordArt object.

- Select from 30 basic formatting styles in the **WordArt Gallery**.

- Change the colors and lines, size, layout, and alternate Web text of your WordArt object through the **Format WordArt** dialog box.

- Click **Edit Shape** to choose from 40 basic shapes, curves, and angles around which your WordArt is built.

- Click **WordArt Same Letter Heights** to make uppercase and lowercase letters the same height.

- Click **WordArt Vertical Text** to change the text from the default horizontal alignment to vertical alignment.

- Use the **WordArt Alignment** button to specify that the WordArt text be aligned to the left, center, or right within the available space, or that it be word-justified or stretched to fill the space.

- Use the **WordArt Character Spacing** button to control the kerning between letters.

If you have already used WordArt to create fancy headings in Word documents, you know how easy it is to work with this tool to create effects that would be very hard, if not impossible, to replicate with regular formatting. For those times when ordinary formatting simply will not do the trick, you can use WordArt in FrontPage to create headings for your Web pages.

In this exercise, you create an eye-catching WordArt page title in a sample page.

There is no working folder for this exercise.

Follow these steps:

Create a new
normal page

**1**   On the Standard toolbar, click the **Create a new normal page** button to create a new page.

The new page opens in the Page view editing window with the insertion point positioned at the top of the page.

**2**   On the **Insert** menu, point to **Picture**, and then click **WordArt**.

**3**   Select your favorite style in the **Word Art Gallery** dialog box shown on the next page.

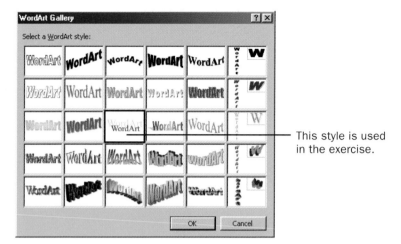

This style is used in the exercise.

**4**   Click **OK** to display this **Edit WordArt Text** dialog box:

**5**   In the **Text** box, type **Carnivorous Plants**.

**6**   In the **Font** drop-down list, click **Verdana**.

**7**   In the **Size** drop-down list, click **24**.

Bold

**8**   Click the **Bold** button.

**9**   Click **OK** to close the dialog box and apply your settings.

FrontPage creates the page title according to your specifications, inserts it in the Web page at the insertion point, and displays the WordArt toolbar.

**10**   Click the WordArt toolbar's **Close** button to close the toolbar.

**11**   Right-click the WordArt object, and click **Paragraph** on the shortcut menu to display the **Paragraph** dialog box.

**12** In the **Alignment** drop-down list, click **Center**, and then click **OK** to close the dialog box and display this result:

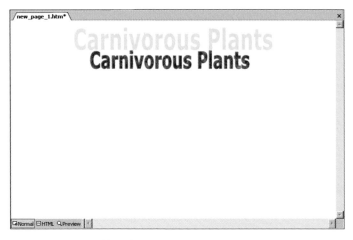

**13** Close the page file without saving your changes.

**14** If you are not continuing on to the next chapter, quit FrontPage.

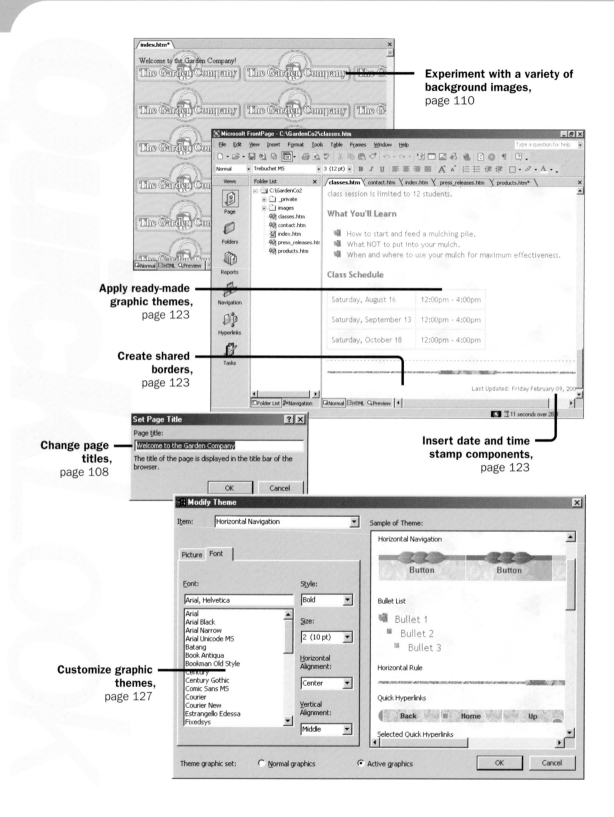

**Experiment with a variety of background images,** page 110

**Apply ready-made graphic themes,** page 123

**Create shared borders,** page 123

**Change page titles,** page 108

**Insert date and time stamp components,** page 123

**Customize graphic themes,** page 127

# Chapter 5
# Creating a Web Site from Scratch

## After completing this chapter, you will be able to:

✔ **Create an empty Web site using a template.**

✔ **Add new pages to a Web site and change their titles.**

✔ **Change the colors, graphics, borders, and shading used on page backgrounds.**

✔ **Create and modify shared borders and banners.**

✔ **Apply and customize graphic themes.**

Microsoft FrontPage provides many useful wizards and templates that you can use to create complex Web sites with very little effort. But what if none of these options fits your needs? It's then that you need to know how to create a Web site from scratch.

Building a custom Web site from the ground up also gives you a better understanding of how Web sites created with templates and wizards work. For example, although you don't need to know the intricacies of a FrontPage-based Web site's navigational structure to use it, a basic understanding of how pages are linked will help you determine how to go about making changes without "breaking" anything. The simplest way to learn how a "canned" Web site is constructed is to build one piece by piece, and that's what this chapter is all about.

You will be working with files that are stored in the following subfolders of the *SBS\FrontPage\FromScratch* folder: *NewPage, PageTitle, Backgrounds, Borders, Banners,* and *Themes.*

## Creating a New Web Site

FP2002-1-1

Suppose you have tried creating a Web site using a wizard but you aren't satisfied with the results. Perhaps the wizard created pages you don't need and didn't create pages you do need. You could modify the existing Web site in various ways, but you are not sure how to go about it and you are nervous about messing things up. You want to try your hand at creating a Web site from scratch so that you can become more familiar with what's involved.

With very little effort, you can create the framework upon which to build a new FrontPage-based Web site. Using the empty Web site as a foundation, you can then add pages and link them in any way you want. But the important thing is to get the basic structure of a FrontPage-based Web site in place first.

In this exercise, you will use the Empty Web template to create the structure required for a FrontPage-based Web site.

There is no working folder for this exercise.

Follow these steps:

**1** If FrontPage is not already open, start it now.

**2** If the **New Page or Web** task pane is not displayed, point to **New** on the **File** menu, and then click **Page or Web** to open it.

**3** In the **New Page or Web** task pane, click **Empty Web**.

The **Web Site Templates** dialog box opens with the **Empty Web** icon selected, like this:

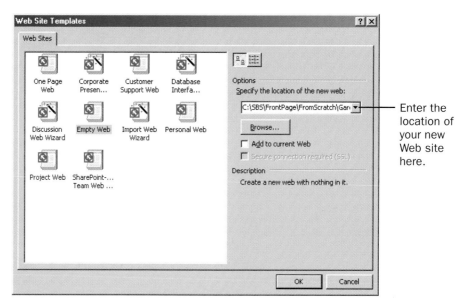

Enter the location of your new Web site here.

You need to specify the location and name of the new Web site. Precede the location with a drive letter for disk-based sites or with **http://** for server-based sites.

**4** Specify the location and name of your new Web site as **C:\SBS\FrontPage \FromScratch\GardenCo**.

**5** Click **OK**.

FrontPage creates a new, empty Web site and saves it with the name and in the location you specified. When the process is finished, you see the supporting structure of the site in the **Folder List**, as shown here:

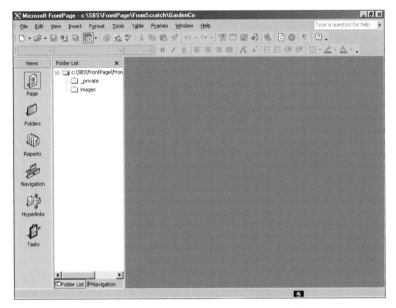

**Tip**

If the **Folder List** is not open, click the **Toggle Pane** button on the Standard toolbar to open it.

In FrontPage, your new Web site appears to consist of two empty folders called _private and images.

**Tip**

The _private and images folders might initially appear with plus signs (signifying that they contain subfolders) next to their names. The plus signs disappear the first time you click them.

**6** Open Windows Explorer, and browse to the new GardenCo Web site in the working folder.

Here is the structure created by FrontPage for this Web site:

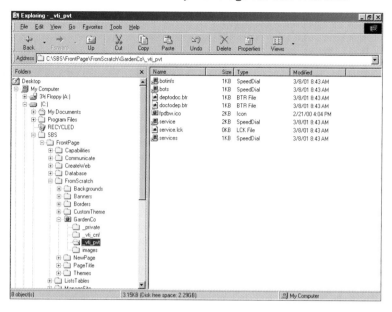

**7** Close Windows Explorer.

**8** On the **File** menu, click **Close Web** to close the Web site.

# Adding a New Web Page

FP2002-1-2

Adding pages to a Web site is very easy. The first (and only) page that is required for any Web site is the home page. This page opens first when a visitor types in the site's URL. The home page file is named either *default.htm* for server-based Web sites or *index.htm* for disk-based Web sites. When you create a FrontPage-based Web site, FrontPage suggests an appropriate file name for your home page depending on which type of site you are creating. If you initially create a disk-based site with a home page file named *index.htm* and then publish the site to a server, FrontPage will rename the home page file during the publishing process.

## Tip

A new page is not actually part of a Web site until you save it as part of the site.

In this exercise, you will create a blank Web page and save it as the home page of the currently empty GardenCo Web site.

GardenCo

The working folder for this exercise is *SBS\FrontPage\FromScratch\NewPage.*

Follow these steps:

**1** Open the **GardenCo** Web site located in the working folder.

Create a new
normal page

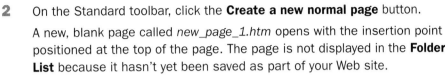

**2** On the Standard toolbar, click the **Create a new normal page** button.

A new, blank page called *new_page_1.htm* opens with the insertion point positioned at the top of the page. The page is not displayed in the **Folder List** because it hasn't yet been saved as part of your Web site.

**3** Type **Welcome to The Garden Company!**

As you begin typing, an asterisk appears next to the file name on the page tab, as shown here:

An asterisk appears on the page tab when the file contains unsaved changes.

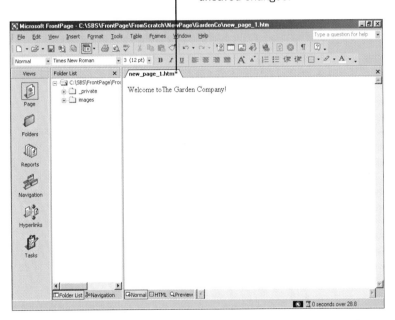

The asterisk indicates that the file has changed since it was last saved (in fact, this particular file has never been saved).

**4** On the **File** menu, click **Save As** to open the **Save As** dialog box, as shown on the next page.

The suggested page title is the first line of the file.

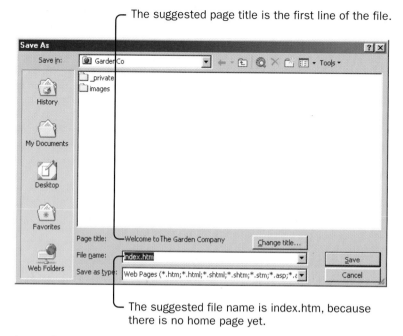

The suggested file name is index.htm, because there is no home page yet.

In the **Save in** drop-down list, the GardenCo Web site is already selected. Because this Web site's folder contains no home page, FrontPage suggests *index.htm* as the page's file name. The suggested page title, *Welcome to The Garden Company*, is appropriate for a home page, so you can leave it as is.

5    Accept the suggested settings by clicking **Save**.

FrontPage saves the file as part of the GardenCo Web site and displays it in the **Folder List**. The file name is preceded by the Home page icon.

Close

6    Click the new home page's **Close** button to close the file.

7    On the **File** menu, click **Close Web** to close the Web site.

## Assigning a Web Page Title

FP2002-1-4
FP2002-1-5
FP2002-5-1

Each page in a Web site is contained in its own file. While you are building a Web site, you will become very familiar with its structure and will have little difficulty identifying pages from their file names. However, visitors to your Web site will expect your pages to have more intuitive names, and that's where page titles come into play.

The **page title** is the text that visitors will see on the status bar when the page is open in their browser. If you use **page banners** on your site, the page title is also the title that visitors will see at the top of the page. The page title does not have to be the same as the file name; it doesn't even have to be similar, although most Web developers use subject-related names that will help them to remember which file is which.

When you save a new page, FrontPage suggests a page title that reflects the first line of text in the page. If this suggestion is not appropriate, changing the page title while you are saving the page for the first time is a simple matter of replacing the suggested title with a different one. If you want to change an existing page title, you can do it in the **Save As** dialog box; in the **Folder List**; or in Page, Navigation, or Hyperlinks view.

In this exercise, you change the name of the home page of the GardenCo Web site using several different methods.

GardenCo

The working folder for this exercise is *SBS\FrontPage\FromScratch\PageTitle*.

Follow these steps:

**1**   Open the **GardenCo** Web site located in the working folder.

**2**   In the **Folder List**, double-click **index.htm** to open it in the Page view editing window.

**3**   On the **File** menu, click **Save As**.

The **Save As** dialog box appears with the current page title, Welcome to The Garden Company, shown.

**4**   Click the **Change title** button.

The **Set Page Title** dialog box appears, displaying the page title:

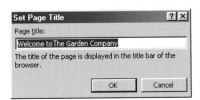

**5**   Replace the page title with The Garden Company, and click **OK** to close the **Set Page Title** dialog box.

**6**   Click **Save** to close the **Save As** dialog box and save your change.

Because a file by this name already exists, you are prompted to overwrite the existing file.

**7**   Click **Yes** to continue.

Folders

**8**   On the **Views** bar, click the **Folders** icon to switch to Folders view.

**9**   Right-click the **index.htm** file in the list of files and folders, and click **Properties** on the shortcut menu.

The **index.htm Properties** dialog box opens with the current page title in the **Title** box on the **General** tab, as shown on the next page.

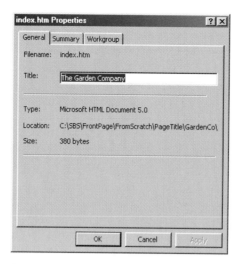

Hyperlinks

**10** Change the title to **Glorious Gardens**, and click **OK** to save the change.

The change is reflected in the **Title** column of the list.

**11** On the **Views** bar, click the **Hyperlinks** icon to switch to Hyperlinks view.

**12** Right-click the **index.htm** file, and click **Properties** on the shortcut menu.

**13** Replace the title in the **Title** box with **Welcome to The Garden Company**, and click **OK** to save your change.

**14** Click the index.htm file's **Close** button to close the file.

**15** On the **File** menu, click **Close Web** to close the Web site.

# Formatting a Web Page Background

FP2002e-1-6

Any newly created blank page looks a little...blank. And although black text on a white background is certainly legible, and legibility is essential if you want to convey information using text, it is not very attractive or exciting.

The simplest way of adding pizzazz to a Web page is to apply a background color. You can add more interest or relate a page more specifically to the subject of the Web site by using a graphic as a background image. For example, you might choose to use your company logo as the background graphic of your business Web site.

Although a background image can give a Web page a more interesting look, remember that, depending on your Web visitor's connection speed and browser, the image might not be displayed as beautifully or as quickly as you would like. When using a background image, it is a good idea to also set the background to a similar color, preferably one from the standard Web palette. That way, when your visitors access your site, they won't be waiting while a series of changes or errors are displayed, and they will still experience the planned color scheme while the graphic is unavailable.

Most background images set a color scheme over which you will want to display text. You must set the font of all the text elements on the page to another color to make it legible. However, that font should not be white. If the background image doesn't load and the text font is white, your Web visitor will not be able to see the text. You can get around this problem by setting the background to one of the colors used in the background image. Then if the background image doesn't load, the text will be visible against the background color.

It's important to select a background color that is light enough so that the text of the page will be legible. You can experiment with various combinations, but dark text on a light background will almost always work best.

In this exercise you experiment with background colors and images, first using The Garden Company's logo as a background image and then switching to a more generic background graphic so that you can compare the effects. You also learn different methods of applying and removing page formatting.

GardenCo
bgimage.gif
tgc_bkgrnd.gif

The working folder for this exercise is *SBS\FrontPage\FromScratch\Backgrounds*.

Follow these steps:

**1** Open the **GardenCo** Web site located in the working folder.

**2** In the **Folder List**, double-click the **index.htm** file to open it in the Page view editing window.

**3** On the **Format** menu, click **Background**.

The **Page Properties** dialog box opens with the **Background** tab on top, as shown here:

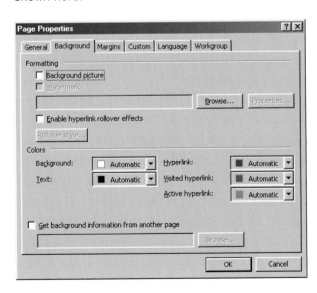

**4** In the **Colors** section, click the down arrow at the right end of the **Background** box to expand the color selection area, like this:

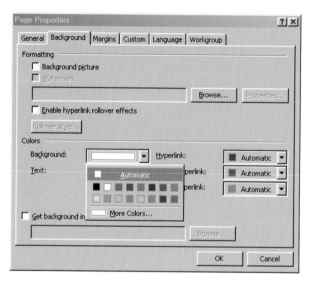

**5** Click **More Colors** to open the **More Colors** dialog box.

**6** Select a pale shade of green that conveys the idea of gardening, yet is still light enough for text to show up well.

FrontPage enters the hexadecimal code of the color in the **Value** box and displays a swatch of the color in the **Background** box, as shown here:

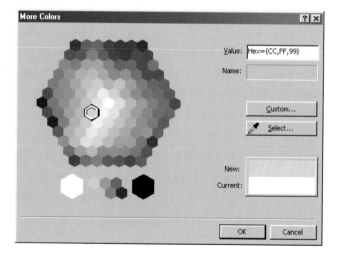

**7** Click **OK** to close the **More Colors** dialog box, and then click **OK** to close the **Page Properties** dialog box and apply the selected background color to the Web page.

As you can see here, your Web page is now a lovely shade of green:

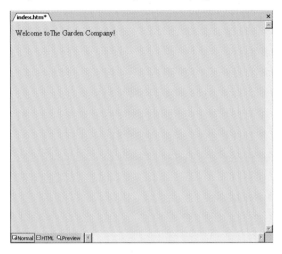

**8** Now try a different approach. On the **Format** menu, click **Background** again.

**9** In the **Formatting** section of the **Page Properties** dialog box, select the **Background picture** check box.

**10** Click the **Browse** button, locate the *SBS\FrontPage\FromScratch \Backgrounds* folder, select **bgimage.gif**, and click **Open**.

The file location is saved in the text box.

**11** Select the **Watermark** check box to keep the background image stationary when the page scrolls, and click then **OK**.

In addition to the background color, your page now features a large, tiled background graphic. The results, shown on the next page, seem somewhat overwhelming.

**12** To make the graphic smaller, right-click the page, and click **Page Properties** on the shortcut menu.

**13** On the **Background** tab, click the **Properties** button to the right of the file name text box.

**14** In the **Picture Properties** dialog box, click **Edit**.

A temporary version of the selected background graphic opens in your default graphics editor.

## Troubleshooting

If you see a warning box prompting you to associate the file type of the graphic with a graphics-editing program, FrontPage is telling you that it does not know which program to use to edit the graphic. On the **Tools** menu, click **Options**, click the **Configure Editors** tab, add an editor association for GIF files, and click **OK**.

**15** Reduce the size of the graphic to about 30 percent of its original size, save it in the working folder as **bgimage_small.gif**, and close the graphics-editing program.

**16**  Back in the **Page Properties** dialog box, change the file name of the background picture to **bgimage_small.gif**, and click **OK**.

These results are perhaps even more overwhelming:

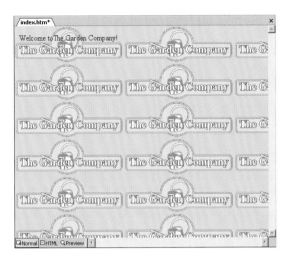

## Troubleshooting

If you make changes to a graphic while it is open in FrontPage, you might have to close and reopen FrontPage to view the effects of your changes in the Normal pane. To view the changes without restarting FrontPage, switch to the Preview pane.

By now it should be obvious that this is a good example of a bad graphic to choose as a background image, but you will see similar backgrounds on many Web sites.

**17**  For a better example of a suitable background image, repeat steps 8 through 11 using the **tgc_bkgrnd.gif** graphic from the *SBS\FrontPage \FromScratch\Backgrounds* folder, which gives the result shown on the next page.

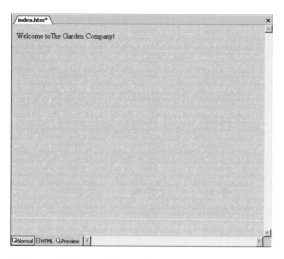

This graphic provides a fairly neutral background with some texture for added interest.

## Tip

To remove background formatting from a Web page, open the **Page Properties** dialog box, clear the check boxes on the **Background** tab, and set the background color to **Automatic**.

Close

**18** Click the index.htm file's **Close** button to close the file, and click **No** when prompted to save your changes.

**19** On the **File** menu, click **Close Web** to close the current Web site.

# Adding Borders and Shading

FP2002e-1-6

Another method of formatting a Web page background is to use **borders** and **shading**. FrontPage gives you a wide variety of page border options—you can control the color, width, and pattern of your border, how much space is left around it, and which borders are affected. The shading options are nearly as varied—you can choose from a nearly limitless number of background and foreground colors or you can choose a background picture and precisely control its placement and movement on the page.

In this exercise you experiment with different methods of making Web pages distinctive by adding borders and shading.

GardenCo

The working folder for this exercise is *SBS\FrontPage\FromScratch\Borders*.

Follow these steps:

**1** Open the **GardenCo** Web site located in the working folder.

**2** In the **Folder List**, double-click the **index.htm** file to open it in the Page view editing window.

**3** Click the line below the heading, and press Enter several times to insert enough new blank paragraphs under the heading to fill the page.

**4** Press Ctrl+A to select the entire page.

**5** On the **Format** menu, click **Borders and Shading**.

The **Borders and Shading** dialog box opens, showing a variety of options similar to those available in Microsoft Word.

**6** On the **Borders** tab, do the following:

- In the **Setting** area, click the illustration to the left of **Custom** to create a custom border.

- Select **outset** from the **Style** list.

- Select **Maroon** from the **Color** drop-down list.

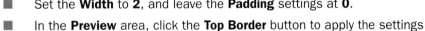

## Tip

Point to the colors in the color selection box to see the name of each color displayed as a ScreenTip.

- Set the **Width** to **2**, and leave the **Padding** settings at **0**.

Top Border

- In the **Preview** area, click the **Top Border** button to apply the settings to this area.

The **Preview** box displays your selections.

Right Border

- Next click the **Right Border** button.

The dialog box now looks as shown on the next page.

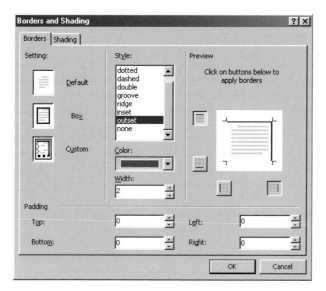

7   On the **Shading** tab, do the following:

- Set **Background color** to pale green and **Foreground color** to maroon.

- In the **Background picture** box, browse to the *SBS\FrontPage\FromScratch\Backgrounds* folder, select **bgimage_small.gif**, and click **Open**.

- In the **Vertical position** drop-down list, click **center**, and then do the same in the **Horizontal position** list.

- In the **Repeat** drop-down list, click **no-repeat**.

- In the **Attachment** drop-down list, click **scroll**.

The dialog box now looks like this:

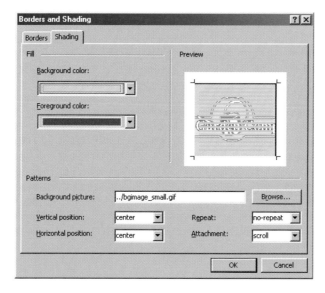

**8** Click **OK** to close the **Borders and Shading** dialog box and apply your settings.

The results look something like this:

Using the borders and shading options, you have told FrontPage to center the logo on the page and to move it with the surrounding text as the page is scrolled.

Close

**9** Click the index.htm file's **Close** button to close the file, and click **No** when prompted to save your changes.

**10** On the **File** menu, click **Close Web** to close the current Web site.

# Using Page Banners and Shared Borders

FP2002-3-3
FP2002e-1-5
FP2002e-8-3

**Page banners** are a quick way to display titles on Web pages. If a **theme** is applied to the current page, the page banner uses the font and graphics of the theme; otherwise the page banner displays only text, which you can format manually. The page banner displays the page title of each page.

Your pages can also have **shared borders**, which are areas at the top, bottom, left, or right of all or some of the pages in a Web site. The advantage of using shared borders is that you can update the information on every page by updating it in only one place. For example, if The Garden Company's corporate logo appears at the top of each page in the GardenCo Web site and a copyright notice appears at the bottom, you can update the logo and copyright notice on one page and have the change instantly reflected on all the other pages. Shared borders ensure that information is presented consistently and correctly throughout the site.

Using a page banner inside a shared border is a way to quickly add or update titles on multiple pages in a Web site. Many developers insert automatically updating date components in bottom shared page borders to indicate the date that the information on the page was last updated. This helps visitors to know that your site is still fresh and that they can count on the information given there.

In this exercise, you start by creating top and bottom shared borders on the pages of the GardenCo Web site. You then insert a page banner in the top shared border, and finish by inserting a date stamp in the bottom shared border.

GardenCo

The working folder for this exercise is *SBS\FrontPage\FromScratch\Banners*.

Follow these steps:

**1** Open the **GardenCo** Web site located in the working folder.

**2** In the **Folder List**, double-click the **index.htm** file and then the **classes.htm** file to open them in the Page view editing window.

**3** On the **Format** menu, click **Shared Borders**.

**4** In the **Shared Borders** dialog box, select the **All pages** option, and select the **Top** and **Bottom** check boxes.

Your selections are reflected in the preview window, as shown here:

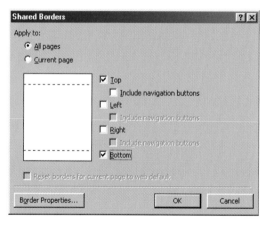

**5** Click the **Border Properties** button to open the **Border Properties** dialog box.

**6** In the **Border** drop-down list, select **Top**.

**7** Select the **Color** check box, and then in the **Color** drop-down list, select pale green.

**8** Repeat steps 6 and 7 to set the color of the bottom shared border to pale green, and then click **OK** to close the **Border Properties** dialog box.

**9** Click **OK** to close the **Shared Borders** dialog box and apply the new border settings.

## Troubleshooting

If your file contains previously formatted content, a message box warns you that changing the settings for the top or left shared borders will overwrite your content. Click **Yes** to continue.

The shared borders appear above and below the rest of the content on each page of the Web site, with a comment identifying each border, as shown here on the classes.htm page:

**10** Click the comment in the top border to select it, and press the [Del] key to delete the comment and leave the empty top border.

**11** On the **Insert** menu, click **Page Banner**.

The **Page Banner Properties** dialog box opens, displaying the current page title, like this:

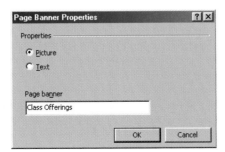

**12** Leave the **Picture** option selected, and click **OK**.

The page banner is inserted. Because there is no graphic theme applied to the Web site, the page banner is currently unformatted and looks just like normal text.

**13** Click the new page banner to select it.

**14** In the **Style** drop-down list, click **Heading 1**.

Center

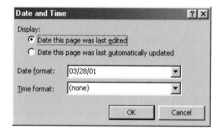

**15** On the Formatting toolbar, click the **Center** button.

**16** Scroll down to the bottom shared border.

**17** Select and delete the comment text.

**18** On the **Insert** menu, click **Horizontal Line** to insert a line that separates the page content from the bottom border.

**19** Under the line, type **Last Updated:** and a space.

**20** On the **Insert** menu, click **Date and Time**.

This **Date and Time** dialog box appears:

**21** In the **Display** area of the **Date and Time** dialog box, leave **Date this page was last edited** selected.

**22** In the **Date format** drop-down list, select the format that expresses the date as *Weekday Month Day, Year*—for example, Wednesday March 28, 2001.

**23** In the **Time format** drop-down list, select the format that expresses the time as *HH:MM AM/PM*—for example, 12:00 PM.

**24** Click **OK** to close the dialog box and apply your settings.

The results look like this:

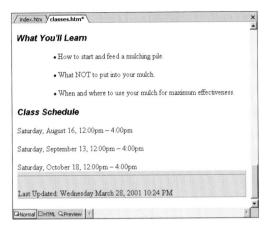

**25** Click the page tab to switch to the index.htm file.

**26** Click the **Preview** button at the bottom of the Page view editing window to view the page in the Preview pane.

The shared borders have been added to this page, with the date in the bottom border.

**27** Close the open files without saving your changes.

**28** On the **File** menu, click **Close Web** to close the current Web site.

# Formatting an Entire Web Site

FP2002-3-5
FP2002-5-1

Formatting pages one at a time is fine if you have a very small Web site, but it would obviously be tedious and inefficient to have to apply page formatting to every page of a Web site of 20, 50, or 100 pages. With FrontPage, you can format entire sites in one fell swoop—backgrounds, headings, fonts, colors, and all—by applying **themes** to them.

Themes are predefined packages of colors, graphics, fonts, and styles that you can apply to a single page or an entire site. FrontPage comes with 23 standard themes, and 44 additional themes can be installed from the Microsoft Office XP CD-ROM. You can use these themes as they are, modify them to suit your personal preferences, or create your own.

In this exercise, you work with a version of The Garden Company's corporate Web site consisting of a home page and four second-level pages: Products, Class Offerings, Press Releases, and Contact Us. The site has top and bottom shared borders and only minimal formatting. The top shared border contains a page banner. The bottom shared border contains a horizontal line and text.

You begin by opening and exploring the Web site to see what you are working with. You then apply a garden-appropriate graphic theme, first to one page of the site and then to the entire site.

GardenCo

The working folder for this exercise is *SBS\FrontPage\FromScratch\Themes*.

Follow these steps:

**1**    Open the **GardenCo** Web site located in the working folder.

**2**    In the **Folder List**, click **classes.htm**, then press ⇧Shift and click **products.htm** to select the five pages of the site. Press ⏎Enter to open them all in the Page view editing window.

The open Products page looks like this:

Click the page tabs to switch between pages.

**3**    Familiarize yourself with the Web site as a whole by looking at the Folders, Reports, and Navigation views.

**4**    Familiarize yourself with the individual Web pages by looking at them in Page view and Hyperlinks view.

You will notice that there are currently no navigational links between the pages.

Page

**5**    On the **Views** bar, click the **Page** icon to switch to Page view.

**6**    In the Page view editing window, click the **classes.htm** page tab to switch to that file.

**7** On the **Format** menu, click **Theme** to open the **Themes** dialog box.

**8** In the **Apply Theme to:** area, click **Selected page(s)**.

**9** Scroll through the list of available themes and preview them in the **Sample of Theme** box.

Each theme has a descriptive name. This example shows the options after the additional themes have been installed:

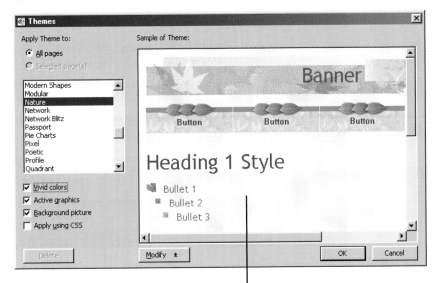

Elements of the selected theme are displayed here.

**10** Select the **Nature** theme.

**11** Select the **Vivid colors** check box to display a bright color scheme.

**12** Select the **Active graphics** check box to display a livelier set of banners, buttons, bullets, and other graphic elements.

**13** Select the **Background picture** check box to display the background image shown in the **Sample of Theme** box.

## Tip

Clearing the **Background picture** check box provides a solid-color background (usually, but not always, white). Many Web designers prefer to use a solid background to avoid the download delays that can be experienced with background graphics and minimize the time it takes to download the site.

**Important**

To create a custom theme, you have to start from an existing theme; you can't create a theme from scratch.

Custom themes can be created independently of a Web site. Once you have created the theme it is stored on your computer with the other installed themes and is always available to you.

In this exercise, you create an alternate variation of the Nature theme.

There is no working folder for this exercise.

Follow these steps:

**1**    Open a new normal page.

**2**    On the **Format** menu, click **Theme** to open the **Themes** dialog box.

**3**    In the list of themes, click **Nature**.

A preview of the Nature theme is displayed in the **Sample of Theme** box.

**4**    Click the **Modify** button.

A new set of buttons appears, showing the areas that can be modified:

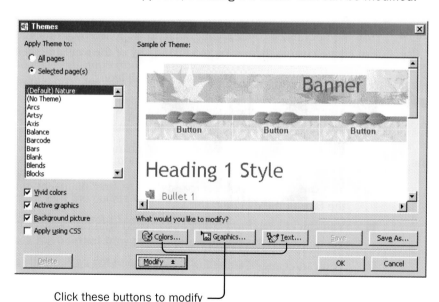

Click these buttons to modify — elements of the current theme.

**5**    Click the **Colors** button.

The **Modify Themes** dialog box opens, displaying the **Color Schemes** tab, which offers these options:

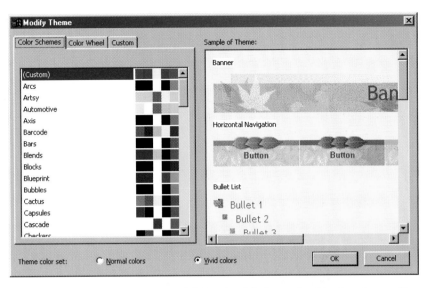

The current color scheme is highlighted, with five color blocks shown. These blocks represent the main colors used for the background, banner text, body, headings, hyperlinks, navigation text, and table borders.

**6** In this case, the current theme is using a custom color scheme. Scroll down through the **Sample of Theme** box to see how each of the colors is applied.

**7** Click the **Color Wheel** tab, and experiment with moving the locator on the color wheel and adjusting the brightness.

Your changes are reflected in the **Sample of Theme** box:

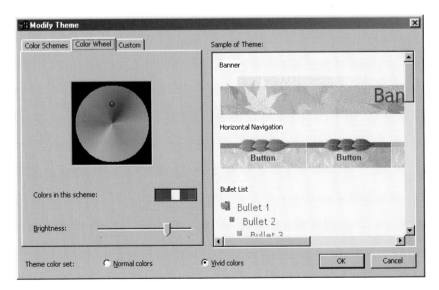

**8** Click the **Custom** tab, which is shown here:

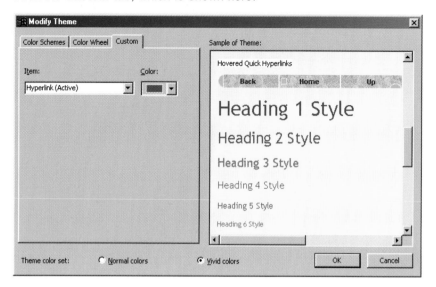

**9** Click the down arrow to expand the **Item** drop-down list.

The list includes each of the elements for which you can specify a color.

**Important**

The background color is applied behind any background graphic that you choose, and it is displayed until the background graphic is loaded. If your visitors' browser settings do not allow background graphics, or if they are using a slow connection, the background color will be displayed instead of the background graphic.

**10** Return to the **Color Schemes** tab.

Notice that the highlighted **Custom** color scheme has been updated to reflect your choices.

**11** Click **OK**, or click **Cancel** to maintain the original color scheme.

**12** Back in the **Themes** dialog box, click the **Graphics** button.

The **Modify Theme** dialog box opens.

**13** Select various elements, and notice the changes that occur on the **Picture** tab and on the **Font** tab, which is shown here:

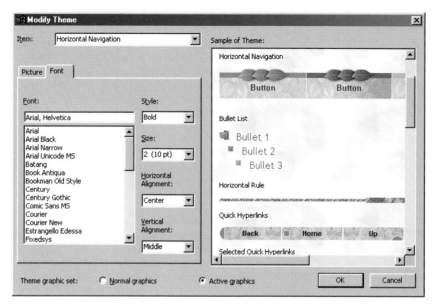

**14** Experiment with making changes in the **Modify Theme** dialog box. When you are done, click **OK** to confirm your choices, or click **Cancel** to stick to the original graphic theme.

**15** Back in the **Themes** dialog box, click the **Text** button.

The **Modify Theme** dialog box opens again, this time offering these options:

Multiple fonts can be called out in order of preference.

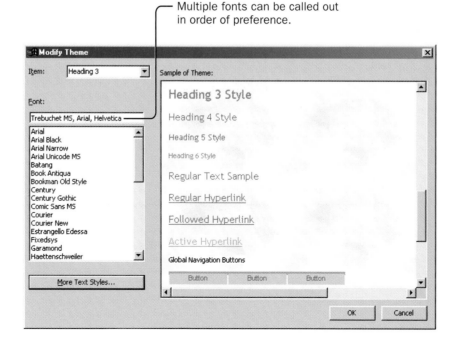

## Tip

To call out multiple fonts for an element, select the element from the **Item** drop-down list. In the **Font** list, select your first choice for the selected element. Position the insertion point at the end of the element's name in the **Font** box, and type the names of the backup fonts, separating all the font names with commas.

**16** Experiment with making changes. When you are done, click **OK** to confirm your choices.

**17** Return to the **Themes** dialog box, and click the **Save As** button in the modification area to display this **Save Theme** dialog box:

**18** Type **Customized Nature Theme** as the name of your new theme, and then click **OK**.

The customized theme is now available from the **Theme** list in the **Themes** dialog box, and it can be previewed in the **Sample of Theme** area, where it looks as shown here:

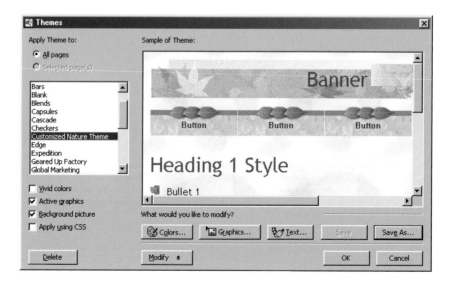

**19** Close the **Themes** dialog box.

**20** Close the current file.

**21** If you are not continuing on to the next chapter, quit FrontPage.

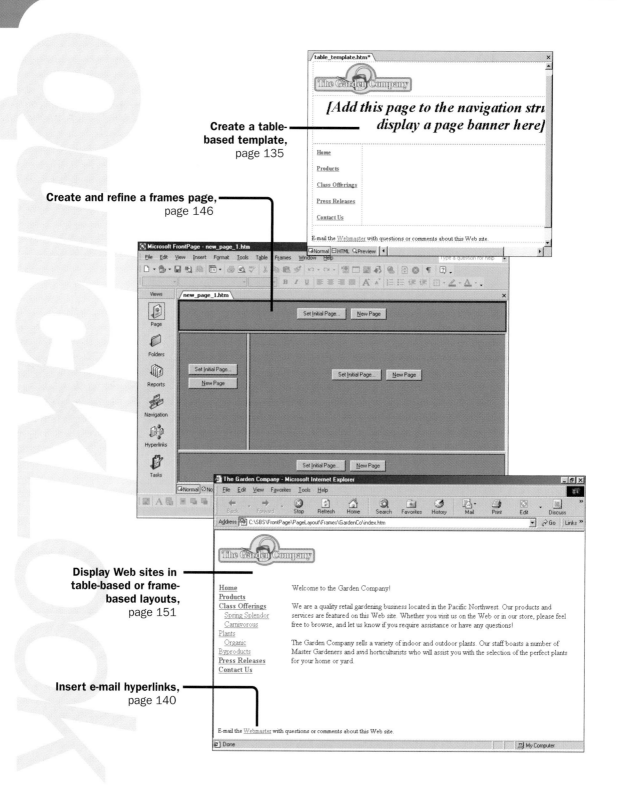

**Create a table-based template,** page 135

**Create and refine a frames page,** page 146

**Display Web sites in table-based or frame-based layouts,** page 151

**Insert e-mail hyperlinks,** page 140

# Chapter 6
# Changing Web Page Layout

## After completing this chapter, you will be able to:

✔ Create a table-based page template.

✔ Apply a template to existing pages.

✔ Create a frame-based page template.

✔ Convert a static site to a frame-based site.

Microsoft FrontPage includes a variety of templates and wizards that produce Web sites of varying complexity and sophistication. When you are anxious to quickly establish a Web presence for yourself, your business, or your group or organization, you can use these ready-made sites to launch a site that will do a creditable job.

If the layout of a predefined site does not quite meet your needs, you can customize it in a few simple ways to make it appropriate. However, without a more in-depth knowledge of how the site is put together, you risk "breaking" the site if you attempt more fundamental structural changes. To allow you to create sophisticated-looking sites with apparent ease, FrontPage shields you from a lot of the complex underpinnings that make the site work correctly. Making a structural change without understanding its implications might cause unexpected results.

To give you a better understanding of the way many professional Web sites are put together, in this chapter you will look at a couple of the more sophisticated techniques used for laying out pages. First you will work with tables to provide page structure, and then you will explore the use of frames.

In this chapter, you will be working with files that are stored in the following subfolders of the *SBS\FrontPage\PageLayout* folder: *Tables*, *Elements*, *ApplyTemp*, *Frames*, and *LayOutFrame*.

## Laying Out Web Pages with Tables

FP2002-3-4
FP2002e-1-1
FP2002e-3-4

The use of **tables** in Web design is quite different from the use of tables in other areas of document design. Web site tables are still made up of **rows** and **columns** just like other tables, and they can still be used to convey specific information just like other tables. But the real purpose of tables in Web design is to break the page up into specific boxes, measured either in terms of absolute number of **pixels** or in terms of the relative percentage of the available **screen real estate**. When you design a Web page using a table, you can control the layout much more precisely. And you can create interesting, magazine-type layouts by filling some **cells** with content and leaving other cells empty. To make things even more interesting, you can **nest** tables inside of other tables to gain tighter control over some areas of the page.

Generally, you should use only one page layout throughout the entire site, although some sites use a different layout for the home page. When planning Web page layout, you need to consider in advance the various elements that will be important for each page so that you can come up with an overall design that meets the needs of all the pages. You should then create and test one template page first. When you have all the elements the way you want them, you can then create your content within the framework, or move existing content into the framework. When you plan your Web site this way, you avoid having to replicate changes across several pages every time you discover something you missed or something new you'd like to add.

In this exercise, you will create a basic page layout **template** with areas for a logo, page title, table of contents, and site information, as well as an area for specific page contents. You will begin by creating a single-cell table to hold the contents of the page, and then you'll nest other tables inside this shell to hold the various page elements.

tgclogo_sm.gif

The working folder for this exercise is *SBS\FrontPage\PageLayout\Tables*.

Follow these steps:

**1** If FrontPage is not already open, start it now.

Create a new normal page

**2** Click the **Create a new normal page** button to create a new page.

A new file called *new_page_1.htm* opens. The file is not shown on the **Folder List** because it hasn't yet been saved to the Web site.

## Tip

To display more precise **ScreenTips** and keyboard shortcuts for toolbar buttons, click **Customize** on the **Tools** menu and select the **Show Shortcut Keys In ScreenTips** check box.

Save

**3** Click the **Save** button.

The **Save As** dialog box opens.

**4** In the **File name** box, type **table_template.htm**.

**5** Click the **Change title** button to open the **Set Page Title** dialog box.

**6** In the **Page title** box, type **Table Layout Template**, like this:

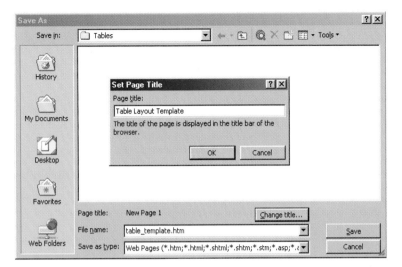

**7**  Click **OK** to close the **Set Page Title** dialog box, and then click **Save** to close the **Save As** dialog box and save your file.

**8**  On the **Table** menu, point to **Insert**, and then click **Table** to display the **Insert Table** dialog box:

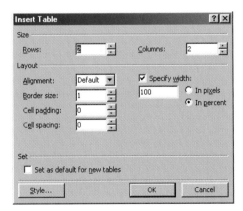

**9**  In the **Size** area, set **Rows** and **Columns** to **1**.

**10**  In the **Layout** area, do the following:

- In the **Alignment** drop-down list, click **Center**.

- Set **Border size** to **0**.

- Select the **Specify width** check box, type **640** in the box, and click **In pixels**.

- Click **OK** to apply your settings and close the dialog box.

FrontPage creates a single-cell table with the insertion point located inside. The Tables toolbar opens.

## Tip

When using tables to lay out a Web page, it is normally a good idea to make the borders of each table visible so that you can easily see the results of your work, and then hide the borders when you're done. This is not necessary in FrontPage, because the table and cell borders are indicated by dotted lines.

**11** Close the Tables toolbar to get it out of the way.

**12** On the **Insert** menu, point to **Picture**, and click **From File**. Browse to the *SBS\FrontPage\PageLayout\Tables* folder, select **tgclogo_sm.gif**, and click **Insert**.

The Garden Company's logo is inserted in the table.

**13** Press [Enter] three times to establish a space within which to nest other tables that will define your page.

Insert Table

**14** Click the line inside the table immediately below the inserted logo, then click the **Insert Table** button on the Standard toolbar, and use the grid to create a one-row-by-one-column table.

**15** Right-click the inserted table, and click **Table Properties** on the shortcut menu to display the **Table Properties** dialog box.

**16** In the **Table Properties** dialog box, do the following:

- In the **Layout** section, set the **Cell padding** to **5**.

- In the **Borders** section, set the **Size** to **0**.

- Click **OK** to close the dialog box and apply your changes.

**17** On the **Insert** menu, click **Page Banner**, and then click **OK**.

Because this page has not been added to the navigation structure of the site, a placeholder is inserted rather than the page title.

**18** Select the inserted placeholder, and do the following:

- In the **Style** drop-down list, click **Heading 1**.

Center

- On the Formatting toolbar, click the **Center** button to center the link within the table.

Your page now looks like this:

19  Click below the table containing the page banner.

20  Click the **Insert Table** button, and insert a one-row-by-two-column table.

21  Right-click the new table, and select **Table Properties** from the shortcut menu.

22  Set the cell padding to **10** and the border size to **0**, and then click **OK**. Here are the results:

23  Select both columns of the two-column table. Right-click the selection, and click **Cell Properties** on the shortcut menu.

**24** In the **Layout** section of the **Cell Properties** dialog box, set the **Vertical alignment** to **Top**, and then click **OK**.

The dialog box closes, and your settings are applied with no visible effect as yet.

**25** Position the insertion point in the left column of the two-column table, and type the following words (without the bullets), pressing Enter after each line:

- **Home**
- **Products**
- **Class Offerings**
- **Press Releases**
- **Contact Us**

This table cell will contain the navigation links to each page of your site. This is commonly referred to as a **TOC** because it functions like a table of contents for your Web visitors.

**26** On the **Table** menu, point to **Select**, and then click **Cell** to select the content of the TOC cell.

Decrease Font
Size

**27** On the Formatting toolbar, click the **Decrease Font Size** button.

The font of the TOC items decreases from 12 points to 10 points.

**28** Point to the column separator, and when the pointer changes to a double-headed arrow, double-click to automatically resize the column to the width of the page titles.

## Tip

If resizing the column causes the TOC titles to **wrap** and you prefer that they didn't, drag the column separator to manually adjust the column width.

**29** Close the current file.

# Adding Repeating Elements to a Template

FP2002-3-2

You can think of Web sites as consisting of two kinds of information: the elements that appear on every page in the site, and the elements that are unique to a particular page. When creating a template page, you should include all of the information that is common to every page in the site in the template so that you have to create it only once. You can keep any areas in which information will change on every page separate from the static areas by designating separate cells for the changing information.

In this exercise, you will add site-wide information to a basic table template, and you will also insert hyperlinks and e-mail links that you want to be available from each page of your site.

You will work with a simple version of The Garden Company's Web site that consists of the home page (index.htm) and four second-level pages: Products, Class Offerings, Press Releases, and Contact Us. A rudimentary set of links to the other pages appears at the top of each page, and an e-mail link appears at the bottom.

GardenCo

The working folder for this exercise is *SBS\FrontPage\PageLayout\Elements*.

Follow these steps:

**1**  Open the **GardenCo** Web site located in the working folder.

**2**  In the **Folder List**, double-click the **table_template.htm** file to open it in the Page view editing window.

The template file currently looks like this:

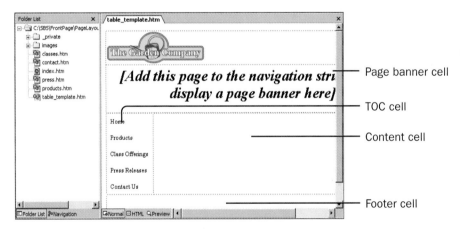

**3**  To insert hyperlinks to each of the pages in the site, start by selecting the **Home** entry in the TOC.

Bold

**4**  On the Formatting toolbar, click the **Bold** button.

**5**  On the Standard toolbar, click the **Insert Hyperlink** button to open the **Insert Hyperlink** dialog box.

Insert Hyperlink

**6**  Click the **Existing File or Web Page** and **Current Folder** buttons to browse for a file in your current folder, as shown on the next page.

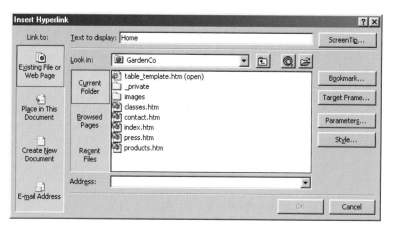

**7** Click **index.htm** and click **OK**.

FrontPage inserts a hyperlink from the word *Home* to the home page of the site and closes the dialog box.

# Linking to Bookmarks

You can insert placeholders called **bookmarks** in your Web pages so that visitors can jump directly to a certain place on the page, rather than just to that particular file. Bookmarks are useful when you have long pages that are divided into logical sections, or when you want to jump from one central list of links to multiple locations on a page. For instance, bookmarks are often used on Frequently Asked Questions pages, in which a list of questions at the top of the page is followed by a list of answers. Clicking each question jumps visitors to the corresponding answer.

In HTML code, a bookmark is a variation on an **anchor tag**, or <a> tag. Creating a bookmark in FrontPage is very easy and does not require that you work with HTML. Simply select the place, word, or phrase that you want to bookmark and click **Bookmark** on the **Insert** menu. You will be prompted to name your bookmark; you can choose a logical name for it (such as naming a link to the word *Plants* as **Plants**), or you might prefer to develop a numeric or alphabetical coding system of your own.

Hyperlinking to a bookmark is also simple. Insert a hyperlink as you normally would. In the **Insert Hyperlink** dialog box, click the page on which the bookmark appears, and then click the **Bookmark** button to show a list of all the available bookmarks on that page. Hyperlinks to bookmarks are expressed as *filename#bookmark*.

8 Repeat steps 3 through 7 for each of the remaining entries in the TOC cell (Products, Class Offerings, Press Releases, and Contact Us), linking each to its corresponding Web page, as follows:

| Page Title | File Name |
| --- | --- |
| Products | products.htm |
| Class Offerings | classes.htm |
| Press Releases | press.htm |
| Contact Us | contact.htm |

Your template page now looks like this:

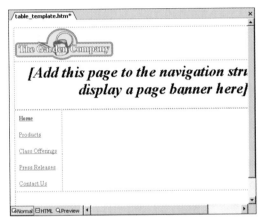

9 Click in the last row of the table, and type **E-mail the Webmaster with questions or comments about this Web site.**

Web visitors expect to see site contact information at the very end of a Web page.

10 Triple-click the sentence to select it, and click the **Decrease Font Size** button to decrease the font from 12 points to 10 points.

11 Double-click the word *Webmaster* to select it, and click the **Insert Hyperlink** button.

12 In the **Insert Hyperlink** dialog box, select **E-mail Address** on the **Link to** bar.

The dialog box changes to look as shown on the next page.

## Tip

The **Paste Options** button enables you to preserve the formatting from the original document, apply the theme or style of the new document, or strip out all of the formatting and just paste in the text.

**10** Scroll down the page, and select the page content, up to but not including the horizontal line that separates the content from the footer information.

Cut

**11** On the Standard toolbar, click the **Cut** button to cut the content to the Office Clipboard.

**12** Click in the content area of the template, and click **Paste** to paste the page content from the Office Clipboard at the insertion point.

**13** Scroll to the bottom of the page, select the horizontal line and redundant e-mail link, and press ⌦ to delete them.

The page is now laid out in the table-based template.

**14** Save and close the file.

**15** Repeat steps 3 through 14 to apply the template to each of the remaining files: classes.htm, contact.htm, press.htm, and products.htm.

**16** Close the Web site.

# Creating a Frames Page

FP2002e-8-1

Instead of using tables to structure a Web page, you can designate that different parts of the page appear in different **frames**. When you lay out a page with frames, the end result looks very similar to a page laid out with tables, but the behind-the-scenes work is much more elaborate.

The concept behind frames is that you create a single shell page, sometimes called a **frameset**, which contains individual frames of information. Each frame can display either static information that has been entered directly in the frame or the content of another file. The beauty of using frames to organize your data is that you can display the information from one file in multiple locations. When you need to make a change that affects every page in your site (for instance, adding a page to the table of contents), you make the change in only one place.

FrontPage makes the process of creating frames pages quite simple by providing several frames-page templates that you can open, save, and complete with very little fuss.

In this exercise, you will create a frames page using a template.

tgclogo_sm.gif

The working folder for this exercise is *SBS\FrontPage\PageLayout\Frames.*

Follow these steps:

**1** On the **File** menu, point to **New** and click **Page or Web** to open the **New Page or Web** task pane.

**2** In the **New from template** section, click **Page Templates** to open the **Page Templates** dialog box.

**3** Click the **Frames Pages** tab.

FrontPage provides these ten simple templates for creating frame-based Web pages:

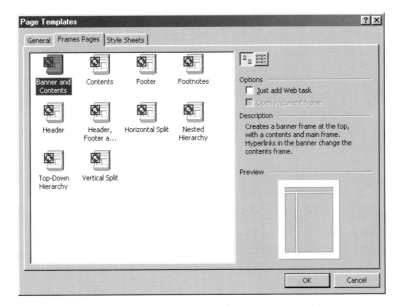

You can click each template to view the corresponding description and preview the page layout.

**4** Click the **Header, Footer and Contents** template, and click **OK** to close the dialog box and create the new page.

FrontPage creates a new page with four delineated frames, each of which displays two buttons, as shown on the next page.

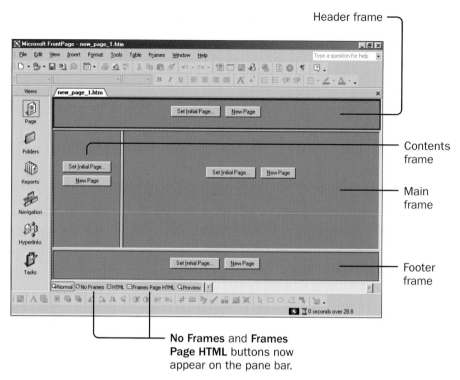

Header frame

Contents frame

Main frame

Footer frame

**No Frames** and **Frames Page HTML** buttons now appear on the pane bar.

You can click the **Set Initial Page** button to link existing content to a frame, or you can click the **New Page** button to create a new content page linked to the frame.

**5** In the top frame, click **New Page**.

A blank page opens within the frame. You have actually created an entirely new file, the contents of which are being displayed in the selected frame.

**6** On the **Insert** menu, point to **Picture**, and then click **From File** to open the **Picture** dialog box.

**7** Now browse to the *SBS\FrontPage\PageLayout\Frames* folder, select the **tgclogo_sm.gif** file, and click **Insert**.

FrontPage inserts The Garden Company's small logo in the frame, but as you can see here, the logo appears to be larger than the space allotted:

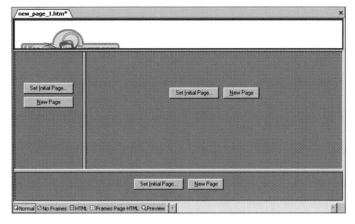

**8** Move the pointer over the bottom border of the top frame. When the pointer changes to a double-headed arrow, drag the border down until the entire logo is visible.

# Splitting and Deleting Frames

You can split a frame into multiple frames or delete extraneous frames from the frames page.

To split one frame into two frames:

**1** Click in the frame you want to split.

**2** On the **Frames** menu, click **Split Frame**.

**3** In the **Split Frame** dialog box, select **Split into columns** or **Split into rows**, and click **OK**.

FrontPage splits the frame horizontally or vertically as directed. The newly created frame contains **Set Initial Page** and **New Page** buttons.

To delete an extraneous frame:

**1** Click in the frame you want to delete to select it.

**2** On the **Frames** menu, click **Delete Frame**.

**9** To save the new file that you've created in the frame, click inside the frame, and then click the **Save** button on the toolbar.

The **Save As** dialog box appears with the selected frame highlighted.

**10** In the **File name** box, type **header.htm**.

**11** Click the **Change title** button to open the **Set Page Title** dialog box.

**12** In the **Page title** box, type **Header Frame**.

**13** Click **OK** to close the **Set Page Title** dialog box, and then click **Save** to close the **Save As** dialog box and apply your changes. Save the embedded logo graphic in the default location when prompted to do so.

To save the frame, you must also save the frameset. FrontPage prompts you to save the frameset page by opening the **Save As** dialog box:

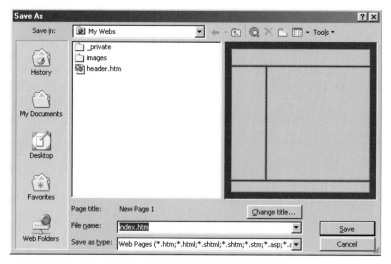

**14** In the **Save In** drop-down list, browse to *SBS\FrontPage\PageLayout\Frames*, and change the **File name** setting to **frames_template.htm**.

**15** Click the **Change title** button, change the page title to **Frames Template**, and click **OK**.

**16** Click **Save** to close the **Save As** dialog box.

**17** Close the open template and the Web site.

# Laying Out Web Pages with Frames

FP2002e-1-1
FP2002e-8-2

When you first start creating Web sites, most of your pages will probably be static. After you have a pretty good understanding of how to build pages, you will begin to explore more complex page layout techniques, and the question then becomes how to convert all the static pages you have already created to take advantage of the new capabilities of your pages.

In this exercise, you will link existing content to a frames page in order to convert existing static pages to a frame-based template.

You will work with a sample Web site consisting of the home page (index.htm) and four second-level pages: Products, Class Offerings, Press Releases, and Contact Us. A rudimentary set of links to the other pages appears at the top of each page, and an e-mail link appears at the bottom. The Table of Contents page contains only the TOC with links to the pages and bookmarks of the site.

GardenCo

The working folder for this exercise is *SBS\FrontPage\PageLayout\LayOutFrame*.

Follow these steps:

**1**   Open the **GardenCo** Web site located in the working folder.

**2**   In the **Folder List**, double-click the **frames_template.htm** file to open it in the Page view editing window.

The template file currently looks like this:

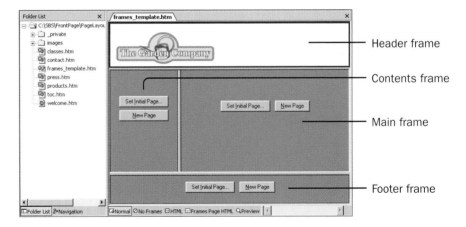

**3**   To link the contents of the toc.htm file to the contents frame, start by clicking **Set Initial Page** in the contents frame.

The **Insert Hyperlinks** dialog box opens with the current folder visible.

**4**   Click **toc.htm**, and then click **OK**.

FrontPage displays the table of contents from toc.htm in the contents frame. The TOC has not actually been inserted in the frame; it is linked to the frame. You can use the vertical scroll bar to see the entire page.

**5**   To define the starting page of the Web site, click **Set Initial Page** in the main frame.

**6**   In the **Insert Hyperlinks** dialog box, click **welcome.htm**, and then click **OK**.

FrontPage displays the home page in the main frame. Again, you can use a vertical scroll bar to see the entire page.

**7**   In the footer frame, click the **New Page** button.

A blank page opens within the frame.

**8**   Type **E-mail the Webmaster with questions or comments about this Web site.**

**9**   Triple-click the sentence to select it, and click the **Decrease Font Size** button on the Formatting toolbar.

Decrease Font Size

**A**

**10**   Select the word *Webmaster*, and click the **Insert Hyperlink** button.

**11**   In the **Insert Hyperlink** dialog box, do the following:

- On the **Link to** bar, select **E-mail Address**.

- In the **E-mail address** box, type **Webmaster@gardenco.msn.com**.

- In the **Subject** box, type **Web site feedback**, to set the subject line of each e-mail message generated from the link so that you can easily identify the source of these messages.

- Click the **ScreenTip** button, and type **E-mail the Webmaster!** in the **ScreenTip text** box.

- Click **OK** to set the ScreenTip text, then click **OK** to insert the e-mail link and close the dialog box.

**12**   Drag the top border of the bottom frame down to resize the bottom frame so that the amount of visible white space is minimized.

**13** Save the new page created in the bottom frame as **footer.htm**, and change the page title to **Footer Frame**.

Your completed page looks like this:

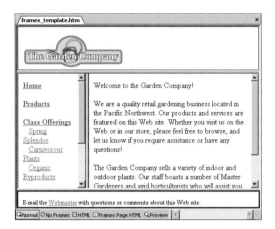

**14** On the **File** menu, click **Save As** to open the **Save As** dialog box.

**15** Ensure that the entire frames template is displayed, and save the file as **index.htm**.

**16** Change the page title to **The Garden Company**.

**17** Now that the layout of the frames page is complete, check how it will look to your visitors. On the **File** menu, click **Preview in Browser**.

**18** In the **Preview in Browser** dialog box, select a browser and window size, and click **Preview**.

The file opens in the browser. Depending on the size of the window, the contents and main frames might display scroll bars. Your results should look something like the one shown on the next page.

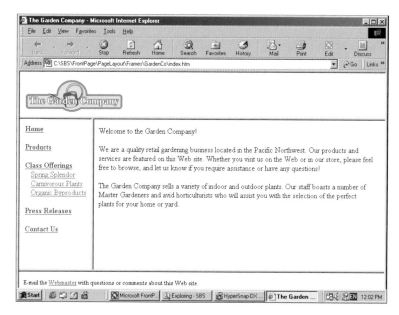

The frame borders are visible, which gives a chunky look to the page.

**19**   Close the browser to return to FrontPage. In the **index.htm** file, right-click the header frame, and click **Frame Properties** on the shortcut menu.

A **Frame Properties** dialog box like this one appears:

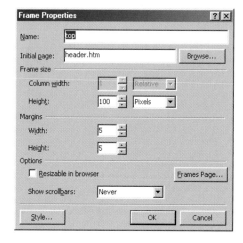

**20** In the **Options** area, click the **Frames Page** button.

The **Page Properties** dialog box opens, with this **Frames** tab visible:

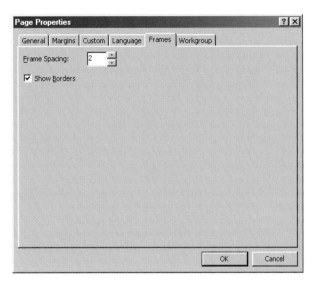

The options set here affect all the frames on the page.

**21** Clear the **Show Borders** check box.

The **Frame Spacing** is reset to 0.

**22** Click **OK** to close the **Page Properties** dialog box, and click **OK** again to close the **Frame Properties** dialog box.

Your page now looks like this:

**23** Right-click the contents frame, and click **Frame Properties** on the shortcut menu to open the **Frame Properties** dialog box.

**24** In the **Show scrollbars** drop-down list, click **Never**, and then click **OK**.

**25** Save your page, and then preview it in the browser to see the results.

This looks much better, but when viewed at a screen area of 640 by 480 pixels, the table of contents extends beyond the bottom of its frame. To make changes to the content of a frames page, you change the content in the source file.

**26** Close the browser and return to FrontPage.

**27** Right-click in the contents frame, and click **Open Page in New Window** to open the toc.htm file in the Page view editing window.

**28** Press [Ctrl]+[A] to select the entire file.

**29** On the **Format** menu, click **Paragraph**.

The **Paragraph** dialog box opens.

**30** In the **Spacing** area, set **Before** and **After** to **0**, and then click **OK**.

**31** Select and delete the extra empty paragraph at the end of the TOC listing.

**32** Save **toc.htm**, and return to the index.htm file.

Notice that the contents frame has already been updated with your changes.

**33** Preview the file in your browser, where it looks like this:

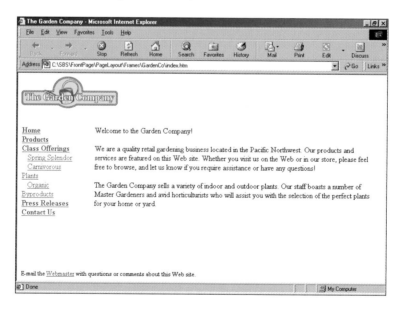

**34** Test the site by clicking the links in the contents frame to verify that the content in the main frame is updated appropriately.

## Tip

You can use your browser's **Back** and **Forward** buttons to move between the pages you have viewed.

**35** Click the **Webmaster** e-mail link.

If you have an e-mail program installed, a new e-mail message opens in your e-mail program with the **To** and **Subject** lines completed, like this:

**36** Close the Web site.

**37** If you are not continuing on to the next chapter, quit FrontPage.

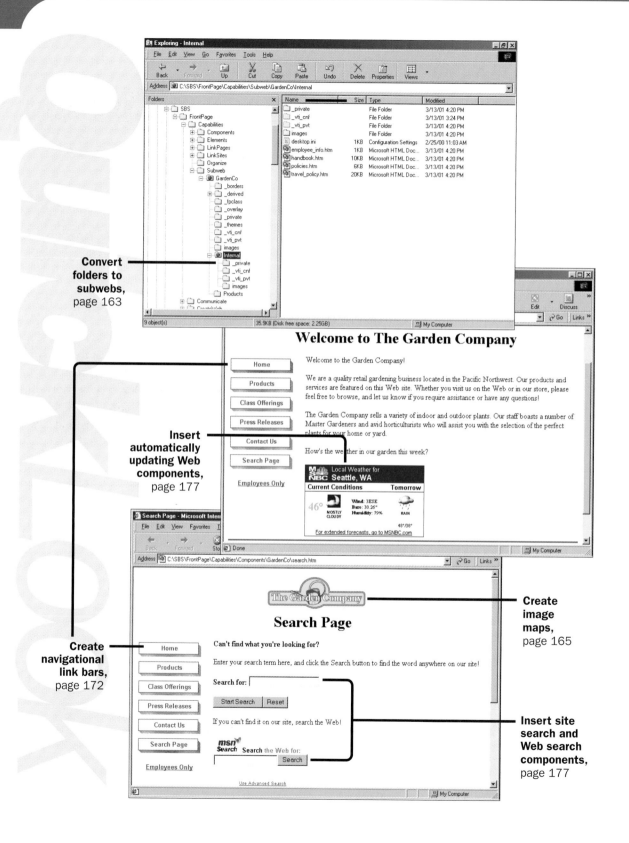

**Convert folders to subwebs,** page 163

**Insert automatically updating Web components,** page 177

**Create navigational link bars,** page 172

**Create image maps,** page 165

**Insert site search and Web search components,** page 177

# Chapter 7
# Enhancing the Capabilities of Your Web Site

**After completing this chapter, you will be able to:**

✔ Organize files and folders efficiently from within FrontPage.

✔ Link between Web pages based on navigational structure or other criteria.

✔ Create a subweb and link to subwebs and external sites.

✔ Add ready-made components and dynamic elements to your site.

In the early days of its existence, the Internet was used primarily as a way of making large volumes of information available to government agencies and universities around the world. This information was static text, and it was of interest only to researchers and people who needed it for their jobs. When the World Wide Web was developed, it added graphics and interactivity, and the ability to jump from one item of information to another. Static pages of text are a thing of the past. These days, to create an effective Web site you have to be able to enhance it with the bells and whistles that distinguish dynamic Web sites from static ones.

There is no point in building a site if your visitors can't easily move among its pages to find the information that interests them. If you have organized your site into a logical system of files and folders, FrontPage can intuit the hierarchy of the site and can add navigational tools so that your Web visitors can easily find their way around using elements such as shared borders and link bars. You can also use graphic elements such as image maps to visually show visitors what's available and how to access it. If your Web site must serve the needs of several different groups of visitors, it might be appropriate to divide your site into a main Web site and one or more linked subwebs so that particular categories of visitors aren't distracted by information they don't need. For example, if The Garden Company wants its Web site to cater to both customers and employees, it might create a subweb that is accessible only to employees with a user name and password and then use the subweb to communicate information of internal interest.

In addition to enhancing the navigational capabilities of your site, you will want to explore the categories of Web components and dynamic elements that come with FrontPage. These ready-made components add a professional touch to your Web site by inserting special-purpose mini-programs that perform such tasks as counting the number of visitors or scrolling banners across the page.

In this chapter, you will organize files and folders within a Web site in a way that makes it easier to enhance the site. You will then refine the navigational structure of the Web site by adding shared borders, link bars, hyperlinks, and image maps. You will also create a subweb and link it to the main Web site. Then you'll take a look at some of the dynamic elements that you can add to a page, including the Web components that come with FrontPage.

You will be working with files that are stored in the following subfolders of the *SBS\FrontPage\Capabilities* folder: *Organize*, *Subweb*, *LinkPages*, *LinkSites*, *Components*, and *Elements*.

# Organizing Files and Folders

FP2002-5-1
FP2002-5-2
FP2002-5-3
FP2002e-7-2

Being able to effectively organize your files into a system of folders is a fundamental computer skill that makes it easier to find things quickly and easily. When it comes to FrontPage, however, this skill is important for another reason. FrontPage can automate some of the processes involved in creating a sophisticated navigation system for your Web site, and organizing the elements of the site into a logical set of folders makes it easier to identify the structure of the site.

In this exercise, you will organize a Web site consisting of many pages and graphics into a useful folder structure.

GardenCo

The working folder for this exercise is *SBS\FrontPage\Capabilities\Organize*.

Follow these steps:

**1** If FrontPage is not already open, start it now.

**2** Open the **GardenCo** Web site located in the working folder.

Portrait/
Landscape

**3** Close the **Folder List**, and switch to Navigation view. If the site doesn't fit onto your screen, click the **Portrait/Landscape** button to change the orientation, like this:

Home page — Second-level pages

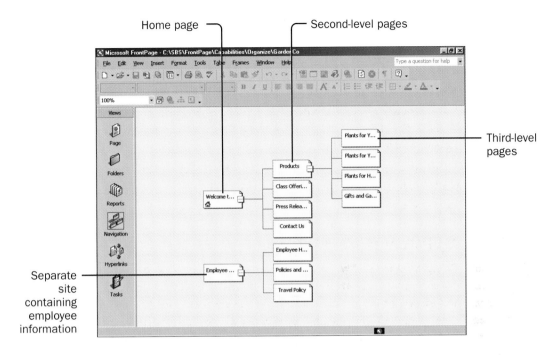

Third-level pages

Separate site containing employee information

In Navigation view, you can see that the site consists of a home page with four second-level pages. The Products page has four third-level pages, and a separate employee site is at the same level as the home page.

**4** Switch to Folders view, and notice the long list of HTML files and graphics files that make up this Web site:

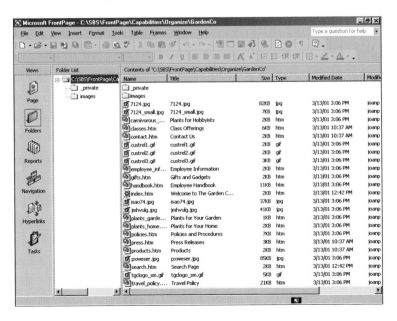

The most obvious way you can impose some organization on this mess is to move the graphic files into the images folder.

**5** Click the **Type** heading to sort the files by type.

**6** Select the GIF images, and drag them into the images folder.

FrontPage moves the graphic files and simultaneously updates the links within the content files to reflect the new location of the graphic files.

**7** Select the JPG images, and drag them into the images folder.

**8** The next step is to organize files into new folders by subject or level. To create a new folder, point to **New** on the **File** menu, and then click **Folder**.

**9** Assign a name to the new folder by typing **Internal** and pressing ⌶Enter⌶.

**10** Drag the following four files into the Internal folder:

- employee_info.htm
- handbook.htm
- policies.htm
- travel_policy.htm

As you saw in Navigation view, these files are part of the separate employee information site. Again, FrontPage moves the files and simultaneously updates the links within all the content files to reflect the new location of the files.

**11** Ideally, the only files that should be located at the root level are the home page and any second-level pages that don't have sub-pages. To achieve this ideal, create another new folder called **Products**, and move the following files into it:

- carnivorous_plants.htm
- gifts.htm
- plants_garden.htm
- plants_home.htm

**12** Click the **Name** heading to sort the folders and files alphabetically.

Your site is now organized like this:

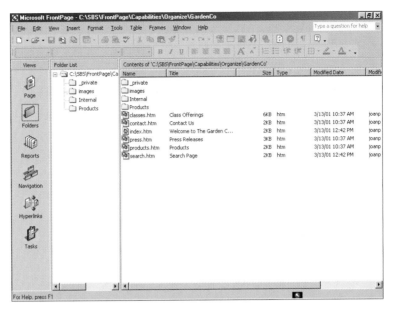

**13** Close the Web site.

# Creating a Subweb

FP2002e-1-2

A **subweb** is a Web site that is nested inside another Web site. A site that contains a subweb is called a **root Web**. If you think of a Web site as a set of folders, a subweb would be a subfolder containing a stand-alone Web site.

Subwebs are commonly used to display restricted information or information that is pertinent to only one group of people. For example, The Garden Company might use a subweb to allow members of a society that the company sponsors to access information about society activities through the company's public Web site.

In this exercise, you will use pages that have already been created and stored in a folder of the GardenCo Web site to create a subweb that is accessible only by employees.

GardenCo

The working folder for this exercise is *SBS\FrontPage\Capabilities\Subweb*.

Follow these steps:

**1** Open the **GardenCo** Web site located in the working folder.

**2** If Folders view is not displayed, switch to that view now.

**3**   Right-click the **Internal** folder, and click **Convert to Web** on the shortcut menu.

This warning appears:

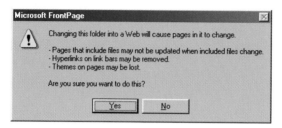

**4**   Click **Yes**.

FrontPage converts the Internal folder to a Web site that is a subweb of the GardenCo site, as indicated in the **Folder List** by the Web site icon on the folder, shown here:

The world icon indicates that this folder is a Web site.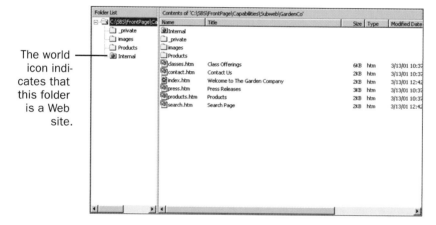

**Important**

If you create a subweb to display information that you don't want all visitors to be able to see, you can assign specific permissions that prevent unauthorized access, or that allow one group of people to view the subweb but only certain people to administer or change it. These permissions are administered through the Web Site Administration page for the subweb.

**5**   Open Windows Explorer, and browse to the *SBS\FrontPage\Capabilities \Subweb\GardenCo\Internal* folder.

FrontPage modified the contents of this folder when you converted it to a subweb. The Internal folder icon has been replaced with a Web site icon here as well, but more importantly, the supporting structure for the new subweb is in place, as you can see here:

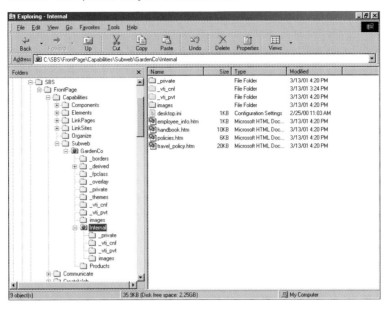

**6** Close Windows Explorer to return to Folders view in FrontPage.

**7** Close the Web site.

# Adding Links Between Web Pages

FP2002-1-2
FP2002-3-2
FP2002-4-2
FP2002-4-3
FP2002e-2-1
FP2002e-2-2
FP2002e-2-3
FP2002e-4-1

When you use a wizard to create a Web site, the site's system of navigation is created for you. You can quickly move from page to page without any real need to understand the underlying mechanisms that make this instant navigation possible. When you create a Web site by hand, however, you need to know how to create a system of navigation from the ground up. And if you ever need to make changes to an existing site—no matter how it was created—you need to understand the basics of navigation in order to avoid breaking things—which is not too hard to do!

You are already familiar with the **hyperlinks** used to move among pages and items of information on a page. You might even have created a few. But with FrontPage, you can create much more sophisticated systems of navigation that add both functionality and visual appeal to your pages.

The primary method of moving around a FrontPage-based Web site is by means of one or more **link bars** that appear in a prominent location on each page. A well-designed link bar on the home page acts as a map to the site's major locations, providing easy access to all the important second-level pages that the site contains.

These second-level pages in turn have link bars that can point back to the home page, to other second-level pages, and to their own third-level pages. (When a page has its own sub-pages, those pages are known as **child pages**.)

Another popular navigation technique is to use **image maps**, which are graphics that contain one or more **hot spots**. A hot spot is a specific region on a graphic that is associated with a hyperlink. When visitors click anywhere in this region, the hyperlink displays the target page or information. Image maps provide an attractive way to link from one central graphic (usually an overview graphic) to multiple individual pages, sites, or graphics. You can even configure a hotspot to generate an e-mail message when clicked.

In this exercise, you will create the navigational system for a Web site whose pages have already been created. You will use a link bar to navigate to the first-level and second-level files, and hyperlinks to navigate to the third-level files. You will also create an image map that links the company logo to the home page.

GardenCo

The working folder for this exercise is *SBS\FrontPage\Capabilities\LinkPages*.

Follow these steps:

**1** Open the **GardenCo** Web site located in the working folder.

Portrait/
Landscape

**2** Switch to Navigation view, and familiarize yourself with the structure of the site, which looks like this (click the **Portrait/Landscape** button to change the orientation if necessary):

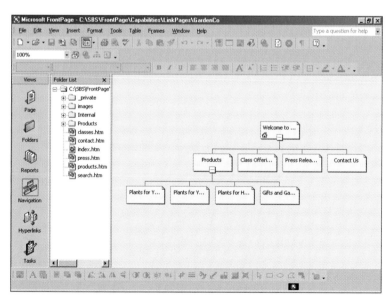

**3** Open **index.htm** in the Page view editing window.

**4** Click the comment in the left shared border to select it, and press <kbd>Del</kbd>.

**5** On the **Insert** menu, click **Navigation**.

The **Insert Web Component** dialog box opens with **Link Bars** selected in the **Component type** list, like this:

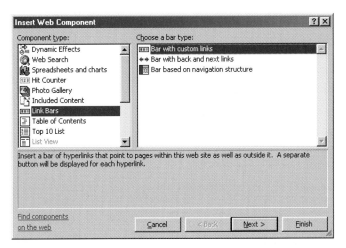

**6** In the **Choose a bar type** box, click **Bar based on navigation structure**, and then click **Next**.

The **Choose a bar style** list includes about 75 choices, ranging from simple to fancy. Many of them correspond to the built-in FrontPage themes.

**7** Scroll to the **Nature** bar style, shown here:

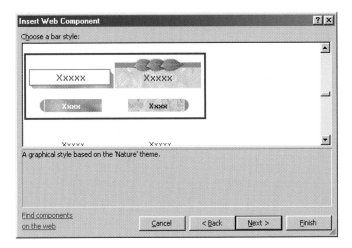

## Tip

You can hover the pointer over any style to display its name in a ScreenTip.

**8** Select the **Nature** bar style, and click **Next**.

**9** In the **Choose an orientation** box, click **Vertical**, as shown here:

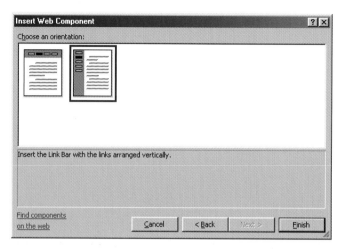

**10** Click **Finish**.

The **Link Bar Properties** dialog box opens so that you can select from these options on the **General** tab:

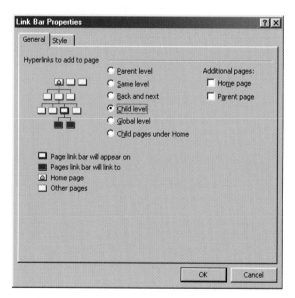

**11** To set the link bar to show the home page and second-level pages, click the **Child pages under Home** option, select the **Home page** check box, and then click **OK**.

The home page now has a link bar, as shown here:

12  Switch to Navigation view, and verify that the Products, Class Offerings, Press Releases, and Contact Us pages shown on the link bar are all child pages of the home page.

13  If the **Folder List** is not already open, click **Folder List** on the **View** menu, and check that all the pages in the **Folder List** are shown in Navigation view.

    One file listed in the **Folder List** is missing.

14  Drag **search.htm** from the **Folder List**, and drop it in the Navigation view window as a second-level page, after Contact Us.

15  Switch to Page view.

    The Search page has been added to the link bar.

16  Open **products.htm** in the Page view editing window.

    The link bar is already present on this page, because it is located in a shared border.

17  In the **Folder List**, click the plus sign next to the **Products** folder to expand the folder.

    There are four files in this folder, corresponding to the four subheadings of the Products page. Because the link bar displays only the first-level and second-level files of this Web site, the product detail pages are not currently accessible by means of the link bar. You need to add another type of navigational device—a simple hyperlink—to enable visitors to find these pages.

18  On the Products page, select the **Plants for your home!** heading.

Insert
Hyperlink

19  On the Standard toolbar, click the **Insert Hyperlink** button. Select **Existing File or Web Page** on the **Views** bar to open the dialog box shown on the next page.

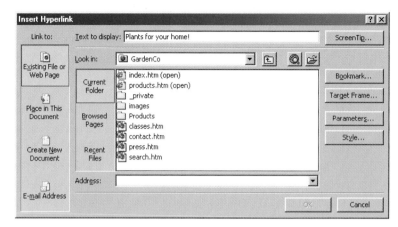

**20**  In the **Look in** box, click **Current Folder**, and then double-click the **Products** folder to open it.

**21**  Click **plants_home.htm**, and click **OK** to insert a hyperlink from the selected heading to the file.

**22**  Repeat steps 18, 19, and 21 for the remaining three headings, mapping them as indicated here:

| Heading | File |
|---|---|
| **Plants for your garden!** | **plants_garden.htm** |
| **Plants for hobbyists!** | **carnivorous_plants.htm** |
| **Gifts and gadgets!** | **gifts.htm** |

**23**  Now you'll turn the company logo into an image map. If the Pictures toolbar is not visible, right-click any toolbar, and select **Pictures** from the shortcut menu.

In FrontPage, image maps can be shaped as rectangles, circles, or polygons, or they can be represented as highlights. The Pictures toolbar provides buttons for generating these four types of hotspots.

**24**  In the top shared border, click the company logo to select it.

Polygonal
Hotspot

**25**  On the Pictures toolbar, click the **Polygonal Hotspot** button.

**26**  Move the pencil pointer to one corner of The Garden Company's logo, and click to start a line. Then follow along the border of the logo, clicking each time you want to change the line's direction.

When you've surrounded the logo, the results look something like this:

**27** Double-click to finish drawing the polygon.

The **Insert Hyperlink** dialog box opens.

**28** Browse to the *SBS\FrontPage\Capabilities\LinkPages* folder, select the **index.htm** file, and then click **OK** to insert a hyperlink from the logo to the home page.

Highlight
Hotspots

**29** On the Pictures toolbar, click the **Highlight Hotspots** button to identify the hotspots on this page.

The outlined area of the logo turns black, like this:

Clicking anywhere in the black area will display the site's home page.

**30** Click **Highlight Hotspots** again to remove the highlight, and then close the Pictures toolbar.

## Tip

To change a hotspot link, right-click the hotspot and select **Picture Hotspot Properties** from the shortcut menu to open the **Edit Hyperlink** dialog box.

**31** On the **File** menu, click **Preview in Browser**.

**32** In the **Preview in Browser** dialog box, select your preferred browser and window size, select the **Automatically save page** check box to save your changes, and then click **Preview**.

When displayed in Microsoft Internet Explorer, your site looks as shown on the next page.

**33**  Browse through the pages using the link bar and the hotspot.

**34**  When you've finished, close the browser and the Web site.

# Adding Links Between Web Sites

FP2002-1-2
FP2002-3-2

You will often want to have links from your Web site to other Web sites, usually to point visitors to external information and resources. For example, the GardenCo Web site might contain links to plant society sites or to specific pages of the Web site maintained by the United States Department of Agriculture.

One of the great things about the Web is that it quickly builds communities around special interests. If you know of other compatible, but not competitive, Web sites in your general area of specialty, you can often arrange to put a link to those sites on your Web site in exchange for a similar link on their sites to yours. This is a great way to build traffic to your site and to get the word out about your products and services.

The most common method of linking to another Web site is to insert a hyperlink from the site name or description to the URL of the site's home page or a particular page file.

**Important**

Other people's Web sites are beyond your control. Nothing makes your site look old and poorly maintained as much as inactive hyperlinks do. So be sure to test any external links regularly to check that their target sites are still active and that they still display the information you think they do.

In this exercise, you will insert hyperlinks to a subweb and to an external Web site. You will then look at how FrontPage automatically recalculates links from your site to ensure that they are all working.

GardenCo

The working folder for this exercise is *SBS\FrontPage\Capabilities\LinkSites*.

Follow these steps:

**1**   Open the **GardenCo** Web site located in the working folder.

Portrait/
Landscape

**2**   Switch to Navigation view. If the entire site doesn't show in the window, click the **Portrait/Landscape** button to change to Portrait mode.

Notice that the GardenCo Web site includes an Internal subweb, which is indicated in the **Folder List** by the Web site icon and in Navigation view by its gray color.

Toggle Pane

**3**   If the **Folder List** is not already open, click the **Toggle Pane** button on the Standard toolbar to open it.

**4**   Double-click **index.htm** in the **Folder List** to open that page in the Page view editing window.

**5**   In the left shared border, click the link bar to select it, and then press ⌨End⌨ and ⌨Enter⌨ to insert a new line after the link bar.

Center

**6**   Type **Employees Only**, and click the **Center** button to center the text within the shared border.

**7**   Highlight the text, and select **Arial** from the **Font** drop-down list on the Formatting toolbar.

Bold

**8**   Click the **Bold** button, and then click the **Decrease Font Size** button to match the new text to the buttons above it.

Decrease Font
Size

**9**   On the **Format** menu, click **Paragraph**. Then in the **Spacing** area of the **Paragraph** dialog box, type **6** in the **Before** box and **3** in the **After** box, and click **OK**.

The text now looks as shown on the next page.

10  With **Employees Only** selected, click **Insert Hyperlink**.

11  Browse to the **employee_info.htm** file in the **Internal** subweb, and click **OK** to insert a link from Employees Only to the home page of the subweb.

Preview in
Browser

12  On the Standard toolbar, click the **Preview in Browser** button. When the Web site opens in your browser, click the **Employees Only** link to test it.

    The home page of the Internal subweb appears in your browser.

13  Close the browser to return to FrontPage.

14  In the **Products** folder, double-click **carnivorous_plants.htm** to open it in the Page view editing window.

    Under Other Resources, two resources are listed along with their URLs.

Copy

15  Select **http://www2.labs.agilent.com/bot/cp_home/** (the URL for the Carnivorous Plant Database), and click the **Copy** button on the Standard toolbar to copy it to the Office Clipboard.

16  Select **Carnivorous Plant Database**, and click **Insert Hyperlink**.

Paste

17  In the **Insert Hyperlink** dialog box, click the **Paste** button on the Standard toolbar to paste the copied URL into the **Address** box.

18  Click **Target Frame** to open the **Target Frame** dialog box, shown here:

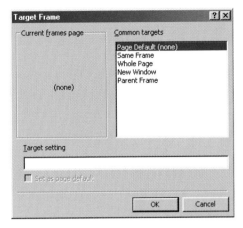

**19** In the **Common targets** box, click **New Window**.

You are telling FrontPage to configure the hyperlink to open the target page in a new window instead of replacing the content of the current window with the new content. The main reason for doing this is so that visitors don't lose track of your site while they go off on this side trip.

## Tip

When you select **New Window**, the **Target setting** box is automatically filled in with the name _blank. The **Target setting** name is primarily used with frame-based sites, where each frame has a name, but you can also use this box to assign a name to a target browser window.

**20** Select the **Set as page default** check box to indicate that any hyperlinks opened from this page should open in a new window.

**21** Click **OK** to close the **Target Frame** dialog box, and then click **OK** to close the **Insert Hyperlink** dialog box and insert the hyperlink.

**22** Select **http://www.carnivorousplants.org** (the URL for the International Carnivorous Plant Society), and copy it to the Clipboard.

**23** Select the words **International Carnivorous Plant Society**, and click **Insert Hyperlink**.

**24** Paste the URL into the **Address** box, and click **Target Frame**.

In the **Common targets** box, the **Page Default** option has changed from **(none)** to **(New Window)**, which is what you want.

**25** Click **Cancel** to close the **Target Frame** dialog box without making changes.

**26** Click **OK** to close the **Insert Hyperlink** dialog box and insert the hyperlink.

Save

**27** Click **Save** to save the page, and then click the **Preview in Browser** button to open the page in your browser.

**28** In the browser, click the **Carnivorous Plant Database** link.

The Carnivorous Plant Database Web site opens in a new window.

**29** Switch back to your site, and click the **International Carnivorous Plant Society** link.

The International Carnivorous Plant Society Web site opens in a separate browser window.

**30** Close the browser to return to FrontPage.

**31** Switch to Hyperlinks view.

The active file, carnivorous_plants.htm, is shown at the center with all hyperlinks to and from the page radiating from it, like this:

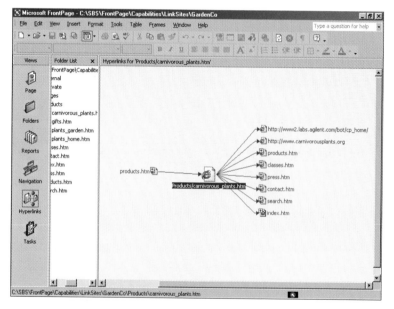

**32** On the **Tools** menu, click **Recalculate Hyperlinks**.

**33** When FrontPage shows you this dialog box, click **Yes** to continue:

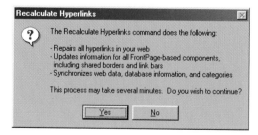

FrontPage checks all the internal and external links in your site and refreshes the Hyperlinks view.

**34** When you have finished checking everything out, close the Web site.

# Adding Ready-Made Components to a Web Page

FP2002-1-2
FP2002-4-3
FP2002e-4-1
FP2002e-4-2
FP2002e-5-2

In the old days, if you wanted to add fancy effects such as scrolling banners or functional elements such as hit counters to your Web site, you needed to be a programmer. These days, many of these types of elements are available as ready-made **Web components**. FrontPage provides the following Web components that you can simply drop into your Web pages to give your site a professional look and feel:

| Component Type | Effect |
|---|---|
| Dynamic Effects | Hover Button |
| | Marquee |
| | Banner Ad Manager |
| Web Search | Current Web |
| Spreadsheets and Charts | Office Spreadsheet |
| | Office Chart |
| | Office PivotTable |
| Hit Counter | Various styles |
| Photo Gallery | Horizontal Layout |
| | Montage Layout |
| | Slideshow Layout |
| | Vertical Layout |
| Included Content | Substitution |
| | Page |
| | Page Based On Schedule |
| | Picture Based On Schedule |
| | Page Banner |
| Link Bars | Bar with custom links |
| | Bar with back and next links |
| | Bar based on navigation structure |
| Table of Contents | For This Web Site |
| | Based on Page Category |
| Top 10 List | Visited Pages |
| | Referring Domains |
| | Referring URLs |
| | Search Strings |
| | Visiting Users |
| | Operating Systems |
| | Browser |

*(continued)*

*(continued)*

| Component Type | Effect |
| --- | --- |
| List View | (only available for SharePoint team Web sites) |
| Document Library View | (only available for SharePoint team Web sites) |
| BCentral Web Components | bCentral Banner Ad<br>bCentral Commerce Manager Add-In<br>FastCounter<br>Revenue Avenue affiliate link |
| Expedia Components | Link to a map<br>Static map |
| MSN Components | Search the Web with MSN<br>Stock quote |
| MSNBC Components | Business Headlines<br>Living and Travel Headlines<br>News Headlines<br>Sports Headlines<br>Technology Headlines<br>Weather Forecast |
| Additional Components | Visual InterDev Navigation Bar |
| Advanced Controls | HTML<br>Java Applet<br>Plug-In<br>Confirmation Field<br>ActiveX Control<br>Design-Time Control |

**Important**

Most of the Web components available with FrontPage are simple to insert and use. However, some work only in SharePoint team Web sites, and others require that special controls be installed on your system before they can be used. The bCentral components require that you have an account with bCentral in order to use them.

Several of the Web components are new to FrontPage 2002:

Top 10 lists
new for
**Office**XP

Top 10 lists generate an automatically refreshed list of the top 10 pages on your site in order of **page hits**, **unique users**, referral source, search strings, or many other factors. Top 10 lists can be used on Internet or intranet sites.

Automatically updated Web content
**new for OfficeXP**

■ The Microsoft Expedia, MSN, and MSNBC Web components are automatically updated over the Web and require an Internet connection in order to function. You can use the Expedia Web components to add links to static and dynamic maps and driving directions. The MSN Web components provide search capabilities and up-to-the-minute stock market information. The MSNBC Web components enable you to add news, business, technology, and sports headlines to your Web pages; you can also display a current weather forecast for a specific area.

In this exercise, you will insert two of the more common components: a weather forecast and a hit counter. You will also add components that enable people to search both your site and the Web.

GardenCo

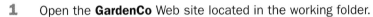

The working folder for this exercise is *SBS\FrontPage\Capabilities\Components*.

Follow these steps:

**1** Open the **GardenCo** Web site located in the working folder.

**2** Open the **index.htm** file in the Page view editing window.

**3** Place the insertion point at the end of the body of the page, and press Enter to create a new line.

**4** Type **How's the weather in our garden this week?** and then press Enter.

Web Component

**5** On the Standard toolbar, click the **Web Component** button to display this dialog box:

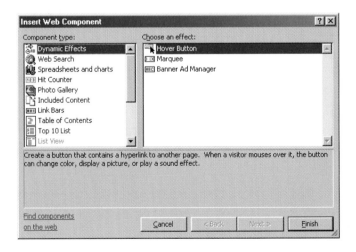

## Tip

Take a few minutes to explore all the Web components that are available in this dialog box, making a note of any that you might want to try out on your own later.

**6** Click **MSNBC Components** in the **Component type** list, click **Weather forecast from MSNBC** in the **Choose a MSNBC component** box, and then click **Finish**.

**7** In the **Weather forecast from MSNBC Properties** dialog box, type Seattle in the **Search for a city by name or U.S. ZIP code** box, and then click **Next**.

Seattle, WA appears below the box as the selected option.

**8** Click **Finish** to close the dialog box and insert the weather component.

A placeholder appears on your page like this:

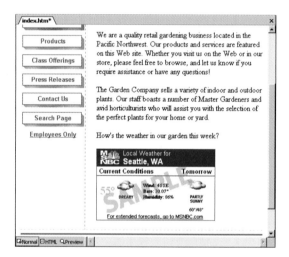

Preview in
Browser

**9** On the Standard toolbar, click the **Preview in Browser** button to test the weather component.

If your Internet connection is active, the weather component connects to the MSNBC Web site, retrieves current weather conditions and tomorrow's forecast, and displays the information on your page, like this:

10  Click the extended forecast link to connect to the MSNBC weather page on the Web.

11  Close the browser to return to FrontPage.

12  Now add a hit counter to the site. Select **Insert hit counter here** in the bottom shared border, and type **Thanks for visiting The Garden Company! You are visitor #**, followed by a space.

## Tip

Hit counters are generally inserted only on the home page of a site, not on every page. In the site used in this exercise, the bottom shared border is shown only on the index.htm page. If this border is shared across all pages, you will want to move the hit counter to the body of the page.

13  On the **Insert** menu, click **Web Component** to display the **Insert Web Component** dialog box.

14  In the **Component type** box, click **Hit Counter**. Then click the last selection in the **Choose a counter style** box, and click **Finish**.

The **Hit Counter Properties** dialog box opens, as shown on the next page.

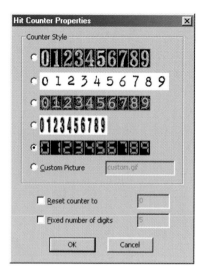

**15** Select the **Reset counter to** check box, and enter **100** in the adjacent box.

For a site that has been up and running for a while, you will want to guess the number of visitors who might already have visited your site and enter that number here.

**16** Select the **Fixed number of digits** check box, and enter **4** in the adjacent box.

When the hit counter nears 1000, you can reset the number of digits to 5. In the meantime, four digits will give the illusion of a larger number (because the number of visitors is preceded by fewer zeros).

**17** Click **OK** to close the dialog box and insert the hit counter.

**18** On the Standard toolbar, click the **Preview in Browser** button to test the hit counter.

**Important**

Hit counters work only on server-based Web sites stored on servers that have FrontPage Server Extensions or SharePoint Team Services installed. Disk-based Web sites don't display the hit counter graphic properly or count the visits, but you can check the placement on a disk-based Web site.

Because this site has not yet been published to the server, your page looks like this:

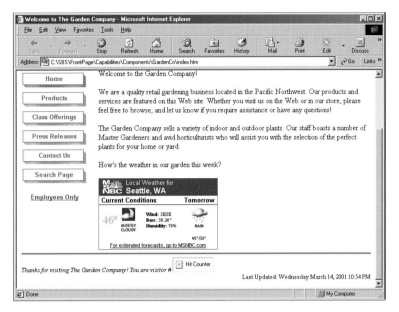

**19** Close the browser to return to FrontPage.

**20** Next, you'll add a search component. Open the **search.htm** file in the Page view editing window.

**21** Select the words **Insert search component here**, and click the **Web Component** button on the Standard toolbar to display the **Insert Web Component** dialog box.

**22** In the **Component type** box, click **Web Search**, and then click **Finish** to accept **Current Web** as the option in the **Choose a type of search** box.

This **Search Form Properties** dialog box opens:

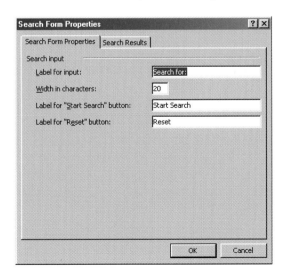

The **Search Form Properties** dialog box specifies the settings for the presentation of the search form and the search results.

**23** View both pages of the dialog box, and then click **OK** to accept the default options.

**24** Press `Enter` to insert the Web Search component on the page.

**25** Type **If you can't find it on our site, search the Web!**, and press `Enter`.

**26** Highlight the new text, and then press `Ctrl`+`Space` to remove the italic formatting.

**27** Click the line below the text, and click the **Web Component** button to display the **Insert Web Component** dialog box.

**28** Click **MSN Components** in the **Component type** box, click **Search the Web with MSN** in the **Choose a MSN component** box, and then click **Finish**.

FrontPage inserts the MSN Search component, and the page now looks like this:

**29** On the Standard toolbar, click the **Preview in Browser** button to test the search components.

**30** When FrontPage displays a message that the page contains elements that need to be saved or published to display correctly, click **OK**.

In the browser, your page is displayed like this:

**31** In the **Search for** box, type **carnivorous**, and click **Start Search** to start the search.

Because this site has not yet been published to the server, you get this result:

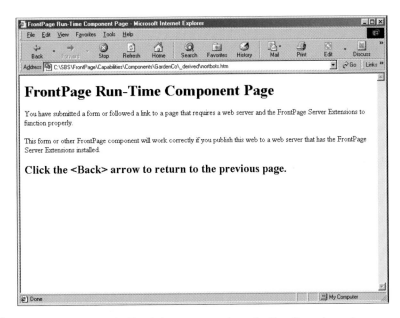

**32** Click the browser's **Back** button to return to the Search page.

**33** Type **carnivorous** in the **MSN Search** box, and click **Search** to start the search.

If your Internet connection is active, you are redirected to the Web Search page of MSN, with the results of your search shown.

**34** Close the browser to return to FrontPage.

**35** Close the Web site.

# Adding Dynamic Elements to a Web Page

FP2002-1-2
FP2002-4-3
FP2002e-4-1

You can add a class of Web components called **dynamic effects** to your pages to create an illusion of movement. Although some components provide information that changes from one visit to your Web site to another, the information itself is static. The dynamic effects components, on the other hand, actually move. With a few simple commands, you can create elements that flash on and off or that scroll across the screen.

In this exercise, you will insert two common dynamic elements: a marquee and a banner ad.

GardenCo
banner1.bmp
banner2.bmp
banner3.bmp

The working folder for this exercise is *SBS\FrontPage\Capabilities\Elements*.

Follow these steps:

**1** Open the **GardenCo** Web site located in the working folder.

**2** Open **classes.htm** in the Page view editing window.

Web
Component

**3** With the insertion point at the beginning of the body of the page, click the **Web Component** button on the Standard toolbar.

The **Insert Web Component** dialog box opens with **Dynamic Effects** selected in the **Component type** box.

**4** In the **Choose an effect** box, click **Marquee**, and then click **Finish**.

The **Marquee Properties** dialog box opens, as shown here:

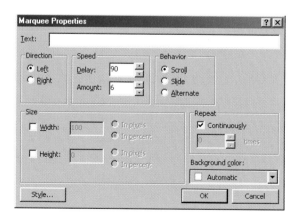

**5** In the **Text** box, type **Register Now for Upcoming Classes!**.

**6** Retain all the default settings, and click **OK**.

In the Normal pane, your marquee has been inserted as a new line of text—not very exciting!

**7** Switch to the Preview pane.

The text scrolls across the top of the content pane from right to left, repeating continuously.

**8** Switch back to the Normal pane.

**9** Right-click the marquee text, and click **Marquee Properties** on the shortcut menu.

Bold

**10** In the **Marquee Properties** dialog box, change the **Behavior** setting to **Alternate** and the **Background** color to **Green**, and then click **OK**.

Italic

**11** With the marquee text still selected in the Normal pane, click the **Bold** and **Italic** buttons on the Formatting toolbar.

Font Color

**12** Click the down arrow to the right of the **Font Color** button, and select **White** from the **Standard Colors** palette.

The marquee text now looks like this:

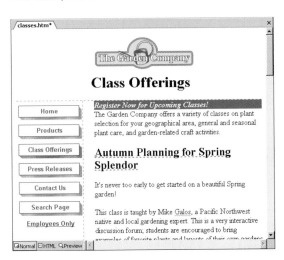

**13** Switch to the Preview pane to see the results of your changes.

**14** Now open **contact.htm** in the Page view editing window.

**15** Place the insertion point at the beginning of the second paragraph of text, which begins with *Please feel free*, and then click [Enter] to create a new line.

**16** With the insertion point on the blank line, click the **Web Component** button on the Standard toolbar to display the **Insert Web Component** dialog box.

**17** With **Dynamic Effects** selected in the **Component type** list, click **Banner Ad Manager** in the **Choose an effect** list, and then click **Finish**.

This **Banner Ad Manager Properties** dialog box opens:

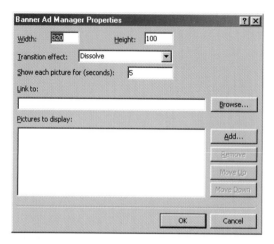

**18** In the **Width** box, type **264**. In the **Height** box, type **72**.

These are the dimensions in pixels of the banner ad that will be inserted.

**19** In the **Transition effect** drop-down list, click **Blinds Horizontal**.

**20** In the **Show each picture for (seconds)** box, type **2**.

**21** Leave the **Link to** box blank.

If you were posting this banner advertisement on another site, you could enter your own URL here to direct visitors to your site.

**22** In the **Pictures to display** area, click **Add**.

**23** In the **Add Picture for Banner Ad** dialog box, browse to *SBS\FrontPage \Capabilities\Elements*, select **banner1.bmp**, and click **OK**.

**24** Repeat step 23 to add **banner2.bmp** and **banner3.bmp** to the **Pictures to display** box, and then click **OK** to insert your banner ad.

Center

**25** With the banner ad selected in the Normal pane, click the **Center** button on the Formatting toolbar to center the ad on the page.

Your page now looks like this:

Preview in
Browser

**26** Click the **Preview in Browser** button, and save the embedded graphic files when prompted to do so.

In the browser, the banner ad cycles between the three graphics according to your specified settings.

**27** Close the browser to return to FrontPage.

**28** Close any open pages, saving them if prompted.

**29** If you are not continuing on to the next chapter, quit FrontPage.

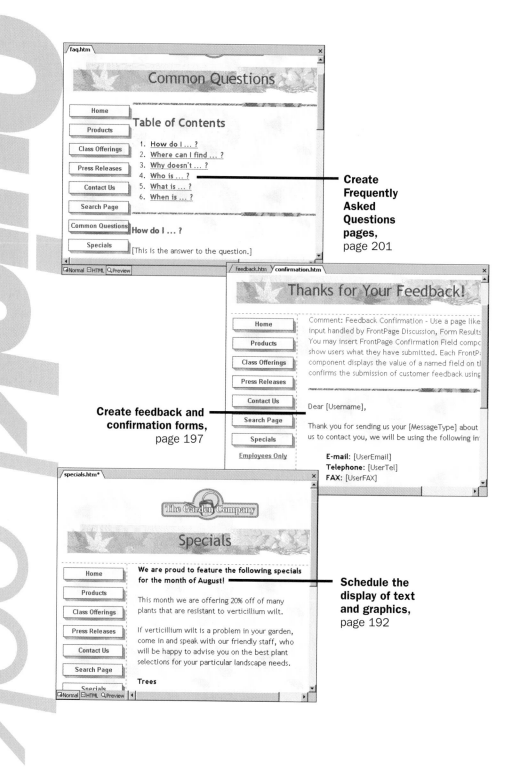

**Create Frequently Asked Questions pages,** page 201

**Create feedback and confirmation forms,** page 197

**Schedule the display of text and graphics,** page 192

# Chapter 8
# Communicating with Your Visitors

**After completing this chapter, you will be able to:**

✔ Keep visitors informed with timely information.

✔ Request information from visitors through feedback forms.

✔ Make information more easily accessible to visitors.

Very few people create a Web site with the expectation that no one will ever see it. Web sites are not like diaries, which are inherently private. They are designed to be published and viewed by other people. The number of visitors, or **hits**, a Web site receives is a common benchmark of its success. In fact, in the late 90's a lot of dot-com companies made money, not by selling products or services, but by selling advertising space based on the number of visitors that passed through their sites. Assuming that you are not interested in just counting numbers but are instead interested in developing a loyal group of visitors who will associate your site positively with your company or organization, you need to spend some time thinking about how you will communicate with those visitors.

Communication is a two-way process: you give your visitors information and, if your Web site meets their needs, they give information back to you. You can attract repeat traffic by ensuring that your information is timely and ensuring that it is easy to find. You can solicit information from your visitors by providing a simple mechanism for giving feedback.

In this chapter, you will first insert information that is to be displayed on a Web page for only one month. Then you will create a feedback form so that visitors can give you information about themselves as well as contact you with suggestions and requests. Finally, you will look at a simple way to enable your visitors to search for information on your site.

 You will be working with files that are stored in the following subfolders of the *SBS\FrontPage\Communicate* folder: *AutoUpdate*, *VisitorInput*, and *FindInfo*.

# Automatically Updating Information

FP2002-1-2
FP2002-4-3
FP2002e-4-1
FP2002e-4-2

FrontPage includes a set of Web components, called **Included Content components**, that you can use to create links to the text or graphics you want to display on a Web page, rather than inserting them directly. Why would you want to do that? Suppose The Garden Company frequently updates the document in which it maintains its calendar of classes and other events. If it also displays the calendar information on its Web site, it has to update not only the document but also the Web page. By displaying the calendar document as included content, the company can maintain the calendar in just one place and know that the Web page always displays the most up-to-date information. Because included content is automatically updated whenever an included page or graphic is updated, a writer or graphic artist can make changes to Web site content without having to open or edit any Web pages. Included content also simplifies the process of reusing content across multiple pages or sites.

FrontPage offers five types of included content:

- The **Substitution component** associates names, called **variables**, with text. In the **Web Settings** dialog box, you can assign a variable to a block of text and then insert the variable on a Web page instead of inserting the text itself. For example, you might assign a variable named *Disclaimer* to a block of text that consists of a 200-word legal disclaimer, and then insert the variable in a Substitution component on every page of your Web site. If you need to change the wording of the disclaimer, you can change it once in the **Web Settings** dialog box, and it is instantly updated on every Web page.

- The **Page component** displays the contents of a file wherever it is inserted.

- The **Page Based On Schedule component** displays the contents of a file for a limited period of time. You can stipulate the beginning and end dates or times of the period during which the file should be displayed. You can also specify alternate content that should be displayed outside of the scheduled time period.

- The **Picture Based On Schedule component** has the same function as the Page Based On Schedule component, except that it works with graphics files.

- The **Page Banner component** is used to create a page title consisting of either text or graphics that appears on every page where the component is inserted. This is the equivalent of inserting a page banner from the **Insert** menu.

In this exercise, you will include a page and a scheduled picture in an existing Web site.

GardenCo

The working folder for this exercise is *SBS\FrontPage\Communicate\AutoUpdate*.

Follow these steps:

**1**   If FrontPage is not already open, start it now.

**2**   Open the **GardenCo** Web site located in the working folder.

**3**   Open **specials.htm** in the Page view editing window.

The page is currently empty.

**4**   On the **Insert** menu, click **Web Component** to open this dialog box:

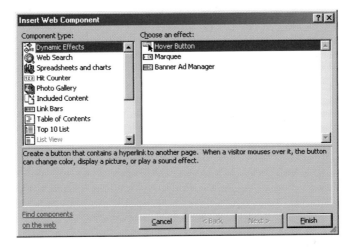

**5**   In the **Component type** list, click **Included Content**.

**6**   In the **Choose a type of content** list, click **Page**, and then click **Finish**.

This **Include Page Properties** dialog box opens:

**7**   Click the **Browse** button.

## Tip

Unlike most **Browse** dialog boxes, this one limits you to browsing the current Web site. However, you can type a file path or URL in the **URL** box.

**8**   Click **monthly_specials.htm**, and then click **OK** to return to the **Include Page Properties** dialog box.

FrontPage enters the file name in the **Page to include** box.

9    Click **OK** to close the **Include Page Properties** dialog box and insert the included component.

The content of the Monthly Specials page is inserted in the Specials page, where it looks like this:

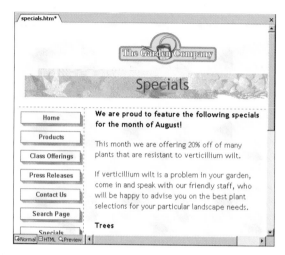

10    Click anywhere on the page.

The included content is selected as a single block and cannot be edited from the Specials page.

11    Click the **HTML** button at the bottom of the Page view editing window to switch to the HTML pane.

Instead of displaying the page content within the <body> tags, you will see this code, which specifies that the contents of the monthly_specials.htm file should be displayed at this location:

```
<!--webbot bot="Include" U-Include="monthly_specials.htm" TAG="BODY" ->
```

Save

12    On the Standard toolbar, click the **Save** button to save your change to the Specials page.

13    Open the **monthly_specials.htm** file in the Page view editing window.

The file itself contains no special formatting. The formatting of the host page is applied to the file content when it is displayed there.

14    Select **August**, and replace it with **September**.

15    On the Standard toolbar, click the **Save** button.

16    Click the **specials.htm** page tab to switch back to that file.

The Specials page reflects the changes you made to the included content.

**17** Open **products.htm** in the Page view editing window.

**18** Press `Ctrl`+`End` to move the insertion point to the end of the page.

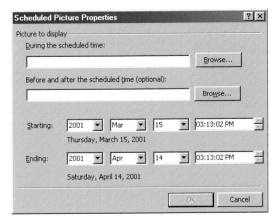

**19** On the Standard toolbar, click the **Web Component** button to display the **Insert Web Component** dialog box.

**20** In the **Component type** list, click **Included Content**.

**21** In the **Choose a type of content** list, click **Picture Based On Schedule**, and then click **Finish**.

The **Scheduled Picture Properties** dialog box opens:

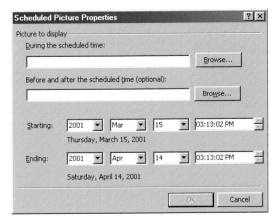

**22** Click the **Browse** button to the right of the **During the scheduled time** box.

Again, browsing is limited to the current FrontPage-based Web site, but you can enter file paths and URLs manually in the **URL** box.

**23** Type **C:\SBS\FrontPage\Communicate\AutoUpdate\September.bmp** in the **URL** box, and click **OK**.

The path you entered in the URL box is changed to a relative path.

This file is a picture that advertises The Garden Company's September Savings deal. The file's path is displayed in relation to your current location.

**24** Type **C:\SBS\FrontPage\Communicate\AutoUpdate\Everyday.bmp** in the **Before and after the scheduled time** box.

## Troubleshooting

If you installed the practice files to a drive other than drive C, use that drive's letter in the **URL** box. Unless you enter a relative path, you must specify a drive letter.

This file is the one you want to display at all times other than during the month of September.

**25** To schedule the September.bmp file to display for the entire month of September, set the **Starting** date and time to **Sep 01** at **12:00:00 AM**, and the **Ending** date and time to **Sep 30** at **11:59:59 PM**.

The dialog box now looks like this:

You can insert an **absolute** or **relative** path to the file.

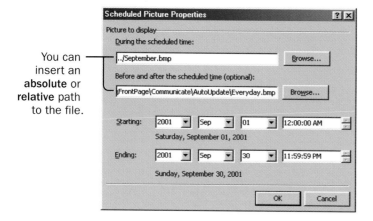

**26** Click **OK** to insert the Web component.

If your system date is currently set to any date in September, you will see the September Savings graphic. Otherwise, you will see a graphic titled *We Love Great Prices!*

Align Right

**27** In the Normal pane, click the Scheduled Picture component to select it, and then click the **Align Right** button on the Standard toolbar.

The graphic aligns with the right edge of the page.

**28** Right-click the component, and click **Scheduled Picture Properties** on the shortcut menu.

**29** Set the **Starting** and **Ending** dates for today's date, leave the times as they are, and click **OK**.

The September Savings advertisement is now visible and will be displayed for the entire day.

**30** On the **File** menu, click **Preview in Browser**.

**31** In the **Preview in Browser** dialog box, select your preferred browser and window size, select the **Automatically save page** check box, and then click **Preview** to preview your file in the selected browser.

**32** Save the embedded graphic file in the images folder when prompted.

Your page now looks something like this:

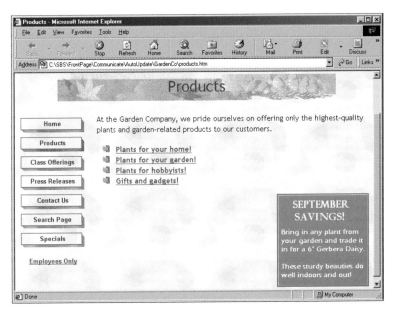

**33** Close the browser to return to FrontPage, and then close the Web site.

# Allowing for Visitor Input

FP2002-1-2
FP2002e-5-1

Providing visitors with information is probably the most common reason for building a Web site. But once you've attracted visitors' attention, you would be missing a prime opportunity if you did not also provide a mechanism for visitors to send information back to you.

The value of the information you receive from your visitors depends to a large extent on the way you present your request. Visitors are unlikely to fill out surveys and provide personal information that might be sold to mailing-list vendors without some significant reward. To get them to take the time and the risk of giving you information, you have to appeal to their best interests. They are more likely to be willing to help you gather information if they have an interest in your specialty area and if your Web site makes an effort to provide them with useful information that goes beyond your money-making endeavors.

Only you can decide how you want to present your request for information to your visitors, and only you can ensure that your Web site offers plenty of value in return. But FrontPage can help by providing ready-made templates for a feedback form and confirmation page that you can use as is or customize to meet your needs.

In this exercise, you will create a feedback form and its accompanying confirmation form for the GardenCo Web site, and you will position them appropriately within the site's navigational structure.

GardenCo

The working folder for this exercise is *SBS\FrontPage\Communicate\VisitorInput.*

Follow these steps:

**1** Open the **GardenCo** Web site located in the working folder.

**2** Familiarize yourself with the site in Navigation view. If the site doesn't fit on your screen, change the **Zoom** level or switch to Portrait mode.

**3** On the **File** menu, point to **New**, and then click **Page or Web**.

The **New Page or Web** task pane opens, as shown here:

**4** In the **New from template** area, click **Page Templates** to open this dialog box:

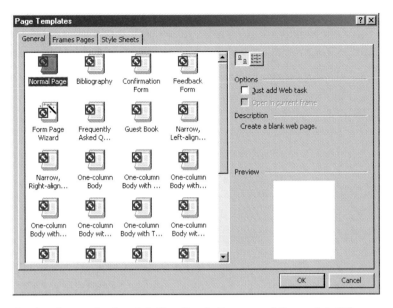

5   On the **General** tab, click **Feedback Form**, and then click **OK**.

FrontPage creates a new page containing a general feedback form.

6   On the Standard toolbar, click **Save** to display the **Save As** dialog box.

7   Type **feedback.htm** in the **File name** box.

8   Click the **Change title** button. In the **Set Page Title** dialog box, change the page title to **Feedback**.

9   Click **OK** to close the **Set Page Title** dialog box, and then click **Save** to close the **Save As** dialog box and save your file.

10  Switch to Navigation view, and drag **feedback.htm** from the **Folder List** to the navigation structure at the same level as the home page, like this:

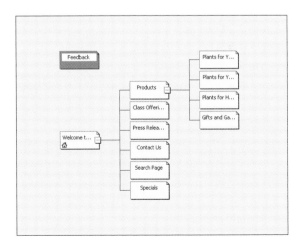

In this position, the feedback form is not a subfile of any other page and will not show up on the current navigation link bars.

**11**  Switch to Page view.

The page title and navigation link bars are now shown correctly on the Feedback page.

**12**  Review the content of the Feedback page, and then double-click the dropdown box that is currently set to **Web Site**.

This **Drop-Down Box Properties** dialog box opens:

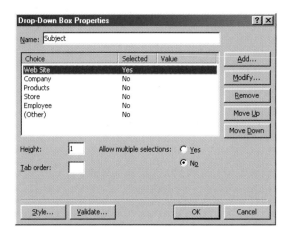

**13**  Click the **Add** button.

The **Add Choice** dialog box opens.

**14**  In the **Add Choice** dialog box, type choose one... in the **Choice** box.

**15**  In the **Initial state** area, click **Selected**, and then click **OK**.

Your new entry is added to the **Choice** list in the **Drop-Down Box Properties** dialog box.

**16**  Click **choose one...** in the list, and then click the **Move Up** button until it is the first choice.

**17**  Use the **Move Up** and **Move Down** buttons to arrange the other items on the list in alphabetical order, with the exception of the **(Other)** choice, which should remain last.

**18**  Click the **Validate** button.

**19**  In the **Drop-Down Box Validation** dialog box, select the **Disallow first choice** check box to indicate that the form cannot be submitted with **choose one...** selected. Then click **OK**.

**20**  Click **OK** again to close the **Drop-Down Box Properties** dialog box, and then switch to the Preview pane.

**21** Click the down arrow to expand the list of choices and view the results of your work.

**22** Switch to Normal view, and save the page.

**23** Open the **New Page or Web** task pane.

**24** In the **New from template** area, click **Page Templates** to open the **Page Templates** dialog box.

**25** Click **Confirmation Form**, and then click **OK**.

FrontPage creates a standard confirmation form. Visitors will see this acknowledgement after submitting their feedback forms. Information such as the name and contact information of the person submitting the feedback is pulled from the feedback form to this page.

**26** Save the page as **confirmation.htm**, with a page title of **Thanks for Your Feedback!**

**27** Switch to Navigation view, and drag the Confirmation page to the navigation structure at the same level as the Feedback page.

**28** Switch to Page view to see these results:

**29** Close the Web site.

# Adding Ways to Find Information

FP2002-1-2
FP2002e-5-2

Visitors will come to your Web site for many reasons, but the most common is to search for information. A good Web site presents pertinent information on each page in a concise, easy-to-read, easy-to-locate format. Most sites follow a basic structure in the presentation of general information, and many include a specific page that addresses the questions that are most often asked by visitors. The information on this page can cover all aspects of a business or organization, and this page is often an opportunity to present information that doesn't quite fit elsewhere.

To simplify the process of finding information on a Web site, especially on a large site consisting of many pages or several levels of pages, it is a good idea to provide a search page through which visitors can locate specific information. FrontPage provides two simple methods of incorporating site search functionality into your Web site: the Current Web Search component and the Search Page template.

In this exercise, you will create freestanding Frequently Asked Questions and Search pages using page templates provided by FrontPage. You will experiment with personalizing the template's text in both the Normal and HTML panes, and you will also replace an existing file within the navigational structure of a FrontPage-based Web site.

GardenCo

The working folder for this exercise is *SBS\FrontPage\Communicate\FindInfo*.

Follow these steps:

Portrait/
Landscape

1    Open the **GardenCo** Web site located in the working folder.

2    Switch to Navigation view, and if the entire site is not visible on your screen, click the **Portrait/Landscape** button to switch to Portrait mode.

3    Open the **New Page or Web** task pane.

4    In the **New from template** area, click **Page Templates** to open the **Page Templates** dialog box.

5    Click **Frequently Asked Questions**, and then click **OK** to generate the new page.

6    On the **File** menu, click **Save As**.

7    In the **Save As** dialog box, type **faq.htm** in the **File name** box.

8    Click **Change title**, and change the page title to **Common Questions**.

9    Click **OK** to close the dialog box, and **Save** to apply your changes.

10    Switch to Navigation view.

11    Drag the Frequently Asked Question page to the navigation structure just below the existing search page, like this:

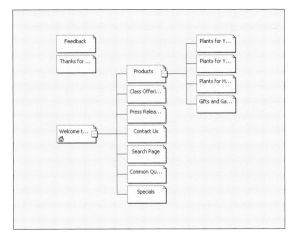

**12** Switch to Page view and the Preview pane to see these results:

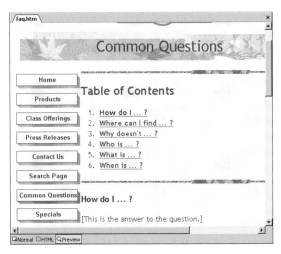

**13** Select the phrase *How do I...?* and then type **What can I do about verticillium wilt?**

You have replaced the first question. Now you need to replace the bookmarked answer. This is one of the few cases in FrontPage where you will want to go behind the scenes and work in the HTML code. There are two reasons for this:

■  First, the questions and answers are linked with bookmarks, and it is almost impossible to replace bookmarked text in the Normal pane without losing the code.

■  Second, the template page was generated with a series of named bookmarks that will not correspond to your new questions.

**14** Click the **HTML** button at the bottom of the Page view editing window to switch to the HTML pane.

**15** Scroll one-third of the way down the page so that you can see both the questions and the answers, like this:

FrontPage-generated questions

FrontPage-generated answers

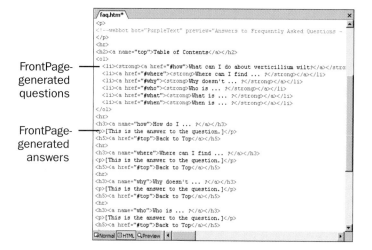

Each question is linked to its answer by an **anchor** tag (<a href>) that jumps to an inserted bookmark tag (<a name>). The question that you just replaced is coded like this:

```
<a href="#how">What can I do about verticillium wilt?</a>
```

The number sign (#) indicates that the anchor tag is linked to a bookmark, rather than a file. The text following the number sign is the bookmark that identifies the corresponding answer. The answer is coded like this:

```
<a name="how">How do I … ?</a>
```

The FrontPage-generated bookmarks reflect the placeholder questions. When you update the questions, the bookmarks no longer reflect the text of the questions, even though they still link the questions to their answers.

# Tip

You can leave the bookmarks as they are, update the bookmarks to reflect the new questions, or use an alternative naming convention, such as numbers, dates, keywords, department codes, author initials, or any other combination of characters (without spaces). Some Web designers are uncomfortable using numbered bookmarks because they feel constrained to present the questions in order. However, the questions and answers do not have to appear in the same order; each question is linked to its matching answer as long as the bookmarks match.

Copy

Paste

**16** Select **What can I do about verticillium wilt?** (the new question), and click **Copy** to copy the phrase to the Office Clipboard.

**17** Select **How do I ... ?** (the linked answer), and click **Paste** to replace it with the new question.

## Tip

To avoid errors, it is always best to cut or copy and paste text such as bookmarks rather than retype them.

**18** In the bookmark for both this question and answer, select **how**, and replace it with **verticillium_wilt**.

The text of the bookmark now corresponds to the question.

**19** Switch to the Normal pane, and select **[This is the answer to the question.]** (the bracketed phrase in the verticillium_wilt answer block).

**20** Type the following to replace the selected text:

**Verticillium wilt is caused by fungi in the soil that may persist for many years. There is no known treatment that will guarantee the safety of wilt-susceptible, deep-rooted trees and shrubs, but thorough fumigation has been found to make the soil safe for the growing of shallow-rooted plants.**

Your page now looks like this:

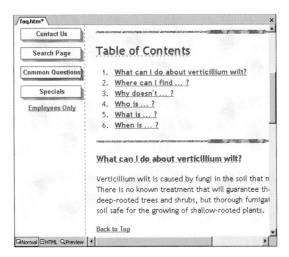

If you want, you can complete this Frequently Asked Questions page by replacing the FrontPage-generated questions, answers, and bookmarks with your own.

## Tip

To include more questions and answers than the six provided in the page template, copy and paste an existing question and answer and customize the copy. To include fewer questions and answers, simply delete the unused items.

**21**  Now open the **New Page or Web** task pane, and in the **New from template** section, click **Page Templates** to open the **Page Templates** dialog box.

**22**  Click **Search Page**, and then click **OK**.

The Search Page template creates a freestanding page from which users can search for keywords across all the documents in a Web site using Boolean queries.

**23**  On the **File** menu, click **Save As** to open the **Save As** dialog box.

# Office Proofing Tools

Common to all the Microsoft Office XP applications are the proofing tools—including spelling and grammar checkers, thesauruses, and AutoCorrect lists—that help you create and edit Office documents. These tools are especially helpful when you are entering large amounts of text. In FrontPage, the **Spelling** and **Thesaurus** commands can be run individually from the **Tools** menu, or you can configure FrontPage to check your spelling automatically by doing the following:

**1**  On the **Tools** menu, click **Page Options**.

**2**  On the **General** tab, select the **Check spelling as you type** check box, and then click **OK**.

When automatic spell checking is turned on, words that don't appear in the Office dictionary are underlined with wavy red lines. Right-clicking a word flagged in this way presents a list of replacement suggestions, as well as the options to ignore the word and add it to the dictionary. Similarly, grammatically incorrect phrases are underlined with a wavy green line, and replacement suggestions are presented on the shortcut menu.

In Page view, the spelling and grammar tools are available only in the Normal pane, and not the HTML or Preview pane.

The different language versions of Office come with the proofing tools that are most likely to be used in those languages. For example, the English version of Office includes proofing tools for the English, Spanish, and French languages. If you require a broader selection of language resources, you can install the Microsoft Office XP Proofing Tools add-in, which contains resources for over 30 languages.

For more information about proofing tools, see the Microsoft Office Web site at *office.microsoft.com*.

**24** Double-click **search.htm**.

A message box warns you that the file already exists.

**25** Click **Yes** to replace the existing page.

**26** Switch to Navigation view.

Because you saved the file by overwriting an existing file, the new page inherited the old file's page title and location in the navigational structure of the Web site.

**27** Switch to Page view, and if the page title and link bar have not been updated, click **Refresh** on the **View** menu to refresh the page.

Your visitors can now search the contents of your Web site.

**28** Close any open pages, saving them if prompted.

**29** Close the Web site.

**30** If you are not continuing on to the next chapter, quit FrontPage.

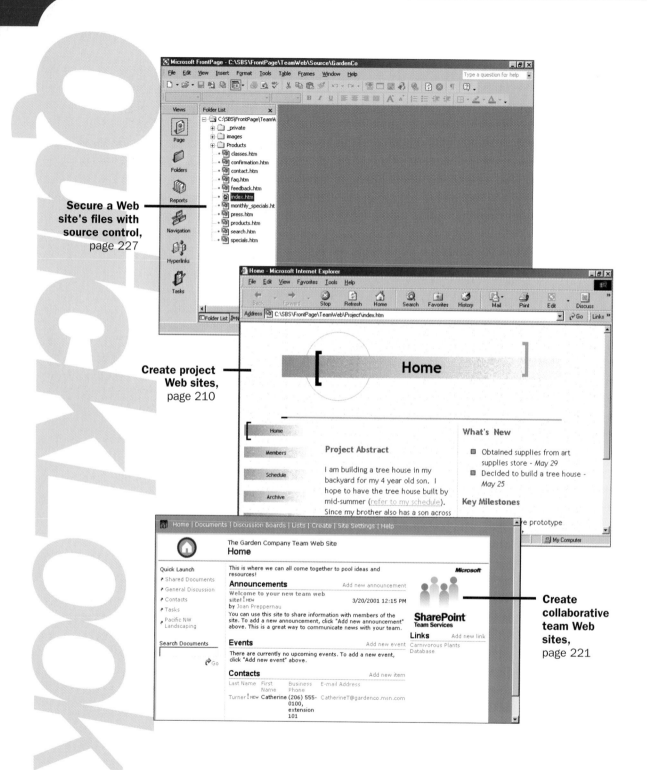

Secure a Web
site's files with
source control,
page 227

Create project
Web sites,
page 210

Create
collaborative
team Web
sites,
page 221

# Chapter 9
# Creating a Web Site to Support Team Projects

**After completing this chapter, you will be able to:**

✔ Track a project using a Web site.

✔ Set up a Web site for discussing a topic.

✔ Create a central Web site for storing team resources.

✔ Protect Web site source files that are worked on by a team.

These days, very few people work in isolation. The ability to work in **teams** and manage teams in such a way that whatever needs to get accomplished is done on time and on budget is a valued skill. To facilitate team **collaboration**, FrontPage provides a number of templates to help you create Web sites that keep everyone informed, that enable people to share information, and that provide a central repository for all the information people need to do their jobs successfully.

**Important**

All of the sites discussed in this chapter are server-based. For them to be accessible to a team of people, they must be hosted on a Web server running Microsoft Windows NT 4 or Microsoft Windows 2000 and the FrontPage Server Extensions or **SharePoint Team Services**. For more information, search for the topic for the specific type of site in FrontPage online Help.

This chapter shows you how to create a Project Web site, a Discussion Web site, and a SharePoint team Web site. It offers insights into how you might use these Web sites to support the work of your company. For those times when the focus of a team is the creation of a Web site, the chapter also shows you how to use FrontPage's **source control** feature to prevent more than one person from working on the same file at the same time. You will be creating new sites and working with files that are stored in the *Productivity* and *Source* subfolders of the *SBS\FrontPage\TeamWeb* folder.

# Using a Web Site to Track a Project

FP2002-1-1
FP2002-1-2

One of the hardest parts of project management is making sure that at any given point in time, everyone knows the project's goals, schedule, and status. It is also important for everyone to be kept informed about known problems and their solutions.

For example, suppose The Garden Company has invested a lot of money to register as an exhibitor at the annual Pacific Northwest Flower and Garden Show. Its exhibit needs to be designed, plants and accessories need to be obtained, and the logistics of shipping soil and plants and keeping the plants alive for the five days of the show all need to be worked out.

The FrontPage Project Web site template can help by enabling you to quickly build a Web site to track such a project. When hosted on an **intranet**, the Web site provides a central location for project management and enables everyone involved to see at a glance where the project stands.

In addition to the home page, where the overall project, recent updates, and key milestones are outlined, a FrontPage project Web site contains six **second-level** pages:

- The Members page lists all the project team members. Members' names are linked to a description area, which can include their photographs, job titles, and contact information.

- The Schedule page lists the full timeline of project milestones and provides space to talk about upcoming tasks.

- The Archive page contains links to archived documents that team members or other interested parties might want to access. Currently, the links aren't hooked up to content; the <a href> tags are merely placeholders.

- The Search page contains a basic site search feature, which FrontPage created by inserting one of its ready-made Web components.

- The Discussions page contains links to any public project discussions that might be available to this project team. These discussions are hosted in specially created discussion Web sites that were created with another of FrontPage's templates.

- The Contact Information page contains contact information for this specific project.

In this exercise, you will use the Project Web site template to create a new project-management Web site that you can customize the sites to fit the needs of The Garden Company.

There is no working folder for this exercise.

Follow these steps:

**1**  If FrontPage is not already open, start it now.

**2**  If the **New Page or Web** task pane is not open, point to **New** on the **File** menu, and then click **Page or Web**.

**3**  In the **New from template** area, click **Web Site Templates** to open this dialog box:

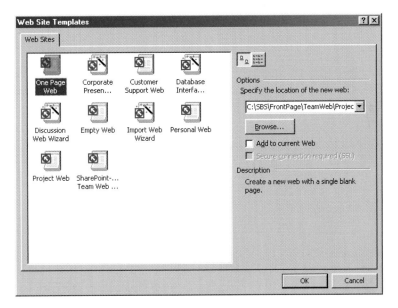

**4**  Click the **Project Web** icon.

**5**  Type **C:\SBS\FrontPage\TeamWeb\Project** in the **Specify the location of the new web** box, and click **OK**.

## Troubleshooting

If you installed the practice files to a drive other than drive C, use that drive's letter in the **URL** box. Unless you enter a relative path, you must specify a drive letter.

**6**  Switch to Folders view to see the extensive list of files that FrontPage creates for this type of Web site, as shown on the next page.

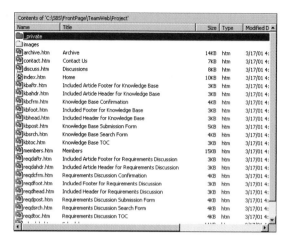

The **Title** column indicates that many of the files are merely headers and footers, and not actual Web pages.

**7** To better see the full extent of the Web site, switch to Navigation view where the Web site looks like this:

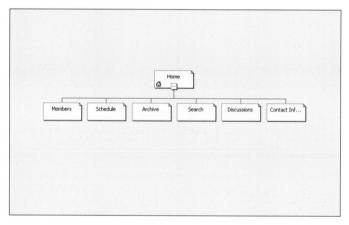

**8** Double-click the **index.htm** file to open it in the Page view editing window.

The best way to experience a site of this size is as visitors to the site will.

**9** On the **File** menu, click **Preview in Browser**.

## Troubleshooting

If you attempt to preview a Web site when no pages are open, you will see the file structure in Windows Explorer rather than the actual site in your Web browser.

**10** In the **Preview in Browser** dialog box, select your preferred browser and window size, and click **Preview**.

The project Web site opens, as shown here in Microsoft Internet Explorer:

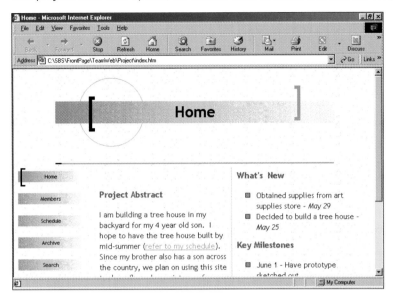

**11** Browse through the site, and notice the pages and text FrontPage has supplied.

**12** Close the browser to return to FrontPage.

**13** To give this site the same look as The Garden Company's main Web site, click **Theme** on the **Format** menu to display the **Themes** dialog box, shown here:

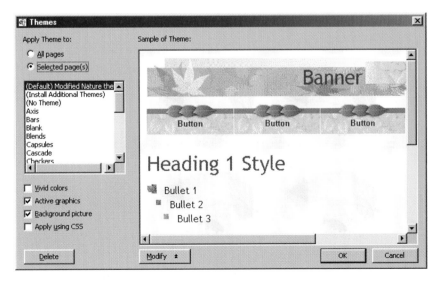

**14** Select **All pages**, and click **Nature** in the list of available themes.

**15** Because this project site is internal and doesn't need the pizzazz of a site that will be viewed by the general public, clear the **Active Graphics** check box to simplify the site presentation, and then click **OK**.

A message box appears, warning you that previous formatting will be over-written.

**16** Click **Yes** to apply the Nature theme to the site.

Save

**17** On the Standard toolbar, click the **Save** button to save your changes.

**18** Close the Web site.

# Using a Web Site to Discuss a Topic

FP2002-1-1
FP2002-6-1
FP2002e-10-3

One of the advantages of the World Wide Web is the fact that it enables people who might otherwise never interact in any way to form a community around a topic of interest. Whether the topic is general enough to be of public interest or specific to a particular project or a particular team, FrontPage can help you create a forum that facilitates communication.

Using the FrontPage Discussion Web template, you can create a Web site where people communicate by submitting, or **posting**, messages, or **articles**. Discussion Web sites include the following features:

■ The Submission form is a required form through which a visitor posts an article consisting of a subject line, author line, and comments.

■ The Table of Contents page lists all the articles submitted to date.

■ The Search form is a standard site search form that searches the articles posted to the current discussion.

■ The Threaded Replies page lists all of the articles by subject.

■ The Confirmation page appears after a visitor submits an article, and prompts them to refresh the main page in order to see their submission.

In this exercise, you will use a FrontPage Web site template to create a new discussion Web site. You will then publish the discussion Web site to a Web server in order to test it.

**Important**

This exercise requires that you have access to a Web server running **SharePoint Team Services**.

There is no working folder for this exercise.

Follow these steps:

**1**  On the **View** menu, click **Task Pane** to open the **New Page or Web** task pane.

**2**  In the **New from template** area, click **Web Site Templates**.

**3**  In the **Web Site Templates** dialog box, click **Discussion Web Wizard**.

   The **Discussion Web Wizard** opens.

**4**  Type **C:\SBS\FrontPage\TeamWeb\Discussion** in the **Specify the location of the new web** box, and then click **OK**.

   A new instance of FrontPage opens, along with the **Discussion Web Wizard's** first page, as shown here:

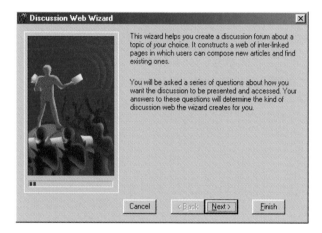

**5**  Click **Next** to display this page:

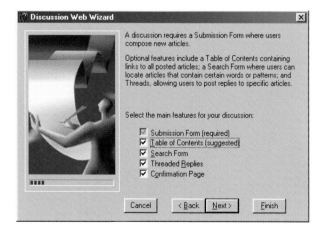

On this page, you specify the features you want to have available in your discussion Web.

**6** Leave all the check boxes selected, and click **Next** to display this page:

You need to supply a title for the discussion and the name of the discussion folder. A discussion can be created for a very specific issue (such as Indigestion Problems of Venus Flytraps) or a very general subject (such as Herbs).

**7** In this instance, type **Soil-Borne Diseases** for the discussion title, type **disc_sbd** for the folder name, and then click **Next**.

## Troubleshooting

Discussion folders whose names begin with an underscore (_) character will be hidden in the **Folder List** and will be visible only when you select the option to show documents in hidden folders in the **Web Settings** dialog box.

On the next page, you choose from these submission form input fields:

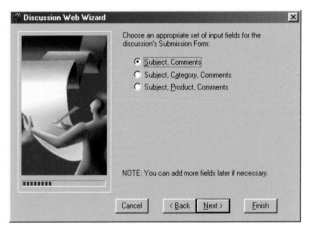

The choices you make here are not permanent; you can update them later.

**8** For now, accept the default selection of **Subject, Comments** by clicking **Next**.

The next page of the wizard appears, giving you the option of allowing access to the discussion Web site only to registered users, as shown here:

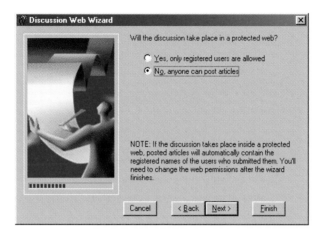

**9** Because this discussion will take place on your public Web site, accept the default selection of **No, anyone can post articles** by clicking **Next**.

On the next page, you are prompted to choose the sort order of articles as they are posted in the table of contents:

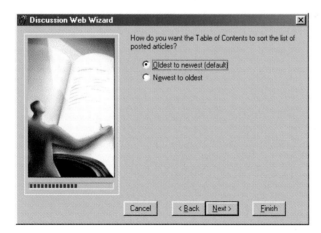

You see this page only if you chose to include a table of contents in this discussion Web site.

**10** To make the most recent information visible to users, select **Newest to oldest**, and then click **Next** to display the page shown on the next page.

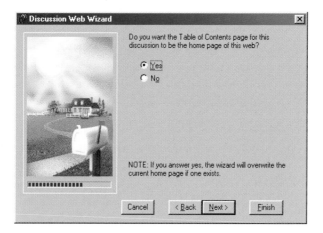

FrontPage can create a welcome page with links to your discussion site, or you can incorporate the table of contents into the welcome page. (Again, you see this page only if you chose to include a table of contents.)

**11** Click **Yes**, and then click **Next**.

**12** On the next page, accept the default selection of **Subject, Size, Date, Score**, and then click **Next**.

**13** Click **Choose Web Theme**, and then click **Next**.

The **Choose Theme** dialog box opens.

**14** Click **All pages**.

**15** In the **Theme** list, click **Nature**.

**16** Because this site will be viewed by the general public, select the **Active graphics** check box to provide more interesting graphics.

**17** Click **OK** to close the dialog box and return to the wizard, and then click **Next**.

The next page of the wizard appears, as shown here:

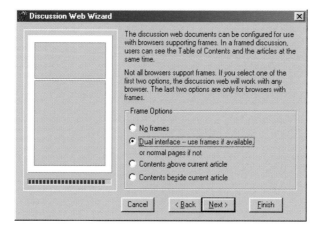

If you know that your visitors will be working in an environment that does not support frames—for example, on a corporate server that uses Netscape Navigator 3.0—you should select the **No frames** option.

**18** Because your discussion group will be Internet-based and open to all users, click **Dual interface – use frames if available**, and then click **Next**.

**19** Click **Finish** in the wizard's final page.

FrontPage generates all the necessary files for the discussion Web site.

**20** On the **File** menu, click **Publish Web** to open this dialog box:

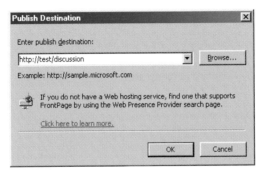

**21** In the **Enter publish destination** box, type **http://**<server>/**Discussion**, substituting the name of your Web server for <server>, and then click **OK**.

**22** Click **OK** when prompted to create a new Web site at the specified location.

The files and folders to be published are listed in the **Publish Web** dialog box, like this:

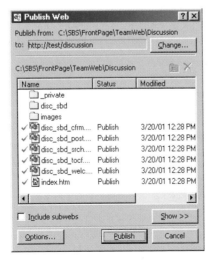

**23** Click the **Publish** button to complete the publication of the site.

When the process is finished, this message appears:

**24** Click the first link to view your published Web site.

The discussion Web site opens in your browser at the specified location.

**25** On the welcome page, click **Post a new article** to open the Submission form.

**26** In the **Subject** box, type **Test message**.

**27** In the **From** box, type your name.

**28** In the **Comments** box, type **This is a message to test the discussion Web site.**

**29** Click the **Post Article** button.

Depending on your Web server's security settings, you might see a warning about sending information to your local intranet.

**30** If you see the warning, click **In the future, do not show this message**, and then click **Yes** to continue.

The Confirmation page is displayed.

**31** Click **Refresh the main page** to see your message.

Your finished discussion Web site looks something like this:

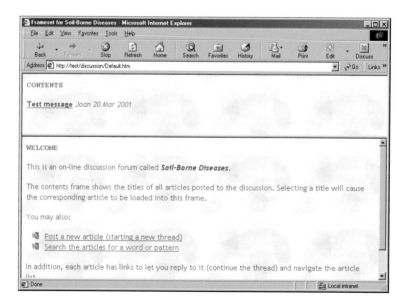

**32**   Close the browser to return to FrontPage.

**33**   Click **Done** to close the message box.

**34**   Close the Web site.

# Using a SharePoint Team Web Site to Enhance Productivity

FP2002-1-1
FP2002e-10-3

SharePoint team Web site
new for **Office**XP

An exciting new feature in FrontPage 2002 is **SharePoint team Web sites**, which are full-scale team **collaboration sites** consisting of the following pages:

- The Home page features Announcements and Events, links to favorite sites, and Quick Launch links to other team Web site elements, as well as a site search component. You can use simple buttons to add new announcements, events, and links to this page.

- The Document Libraries page provides links to existing libraries of shared documents. You can click buttons to make new document libraries and shared documents available to team members.

- The Discussion Boards page provides links to existing discussions and an easy way to add new discussion boards to the team Web site.

- The Lists page provides links to five ready-made lists: Announcements, Contacts, Events, Links, and Tasks. Team members can post messages to each of these pages. Lists can be included on the home page, and their information can be sorted in a variety of ways to find items quickly.

- The Create Page page makes it easy to create new team Web site elements, including custom lists, document libraries, surveys, discussion boards, link lists, announcement lists, contact lists, events lists, and task lists. You can also create new lists based on information that you import from an existing spreadsheet.

- The Site Settings page is where the Web site administrator can set the name and description of the site, change the permissions that control who can use it, edit and view user information, customize the site content, or create new content.

SharePoint team Web sites can only be created as server-based sites on Web servers running SharePoint Team Services. With this set of powerful team collaboration features, you can open up new collaboration possibilities, including those listed on the following page.

Browser-based
editing of Web
sites
**new** for
**Office**XP

■ You can edit SharePoint team Web site content, upload documents, and participate in threaded discussions directly from your Internet browser. Multiple users can contribute to and interact with your team Web site, and receive automatic notifications when pages or discussions are modified.

Customization
and
integration
**new** for
**Office**XP

■ You can use FrontPage 2002 to customize SharePoint team Web sites; create and apply custom themes; insert graphics, link bars, and automatic live content; and insert lists such as Announcements, Events, Contacts, Surveys, and Links on the Web site for the entire team to view.

Document
libraries
**new** for
**Office**XP

■ You can also add a document library to your team Web site so that documents can be stored centrally for general or restricted access.

The FrontPage online Help provides extensive information and instructions for creating and using SharePoint team Web sites.

**Important**

This exercise requires that you have access to a Web server running SharePoint Team Services.

Landscape1.doc

In this exercise, you will use a wizard to create a SharePoint team Web site, and you will work with some of the available options to customize the site. The working folder for this exercise is *SBS\FrontPage\TeamWeb\Productivity*.

Follow these steps:

Create a new
normal page

**1** On the Standard toolbar, click the **Create a new normal page** button's down arrow to expand the list of elements that can be created.

**2** Click **Web** to open the **Web Site Templates** dialog box.

**3** Click the **SharePoint-based Team Web Site** icon.

**4** Type **http://**<server>**/TeamSite**, where <server> is the name of your Web server in the **Specify the location of the new web** box. Then click **OK**.

FrontPage creates a new team Web site at the specified location. This process takes significantly longer than the creation of other FrontPage-based Web sites.

**5** When the Web site creation process is complete, expand the folders in the **Folder List** to see all the files, like this:

**6**   Open your Web browser, and in the **Address** box, type **http://**<server> **/TeamSite**, where <server> is the name of your Web server.

Your SharePoint team Web site opens, looking like this:

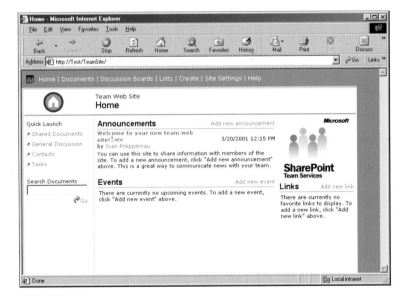

# Tip

You can apply a theme to your team Web site in the normal manner. However, be aware that most distinguishing theme elements (such as buttons and icons) are not used in the team Web site. At best, the theme will update the background and font of the site.

**7** Browse through the site, clicking each of the navigation links across the top: **Documents**, **Discussion Boards**, **Lists**, **Create**, **Site Settings**, and **Help**.

It is simple to update this powerful and useful site to fit your specific needs.

**8** To add a document library to the site, start by clicking **New Document Library** on the **Document Libraries** page.

The **New Document Library** page opens.

**9** In the **Name** box, type Pacific NW Landscaping.

**10** In the **Description** box, type General landscaping information for the Pacific Northwest.

**11** In the **Template Type** drop-down list, click **Blank Microsoft FrontPage Document** to indicate that the default document type is a Web page.

**12** In the **Navigation** section, click **Yes** to display the new document library on the site's Quick Launch bar.

**13** Click the **Create** button to create the new document library.

Your new page looks like this:

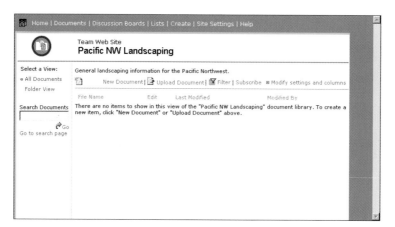

**14** On the Pacific NW Landscaping menu, click **Upload Document**.

**15** In the **File Name** box, browse to the *SBS\FrontPage\TeamWeb\Productivity* folder, and click **Landscape1.doc**.

**16** Click **Save and Close** to return to the Pacific NW Landscaping page, which now features the new addition.

Notice that you can sort documents listed on this page by **File Name**, **Last Modified** date, and **Modified By**.

**17** On the Lists page, click **Contacts**.

**18** On the Contacts page, click **New Item**.

**19** On the Contacts: New Item page, create a new item for this person, as follows:

| In this box | Enter this |
|---|---|
| **Name** | Catherine Turner |
| **E-mail Address** | Catherinet@gardenco.msn.com |
| **Company** | The Garden Company |
| **Job Title** | Owner |
| **Business Phone** | (206) 555-0100, extension 101 |
| **Fax Number** | (206) 555-0101 |
| **Address** | 1234 Oak Street, Seattle, WA 10101 |
| **Web Page** | www.gardenco.msn.com |

**20** Click **Save and Close** to save the new contact in your contact list.

The Contacts page now looks like this:

The new contact is shown here.

**21** On the Lists page, click **Links**.

**22** On the Links page, click **New Item**.

**23** In the **URL** box, type **www2.labs.agilent.com/bot/cp_home/**.

**24** In the description box, type **Carnivorous Plants Database**.

**25** Click **Save and Close** to save the new link to your Links list.

**26** On the Site Settings page, click **Change site name and description**.

**27** In the **Web Site Name** box, type The Garden Company Team Web Site.

**28** In the **Description** box, type **This is where we can all come together to pool ideas and resources!**

**29** Click **OK** to return to the Site Settings page.

**30** Click **Customize home page layout**.

**31** Drag the Contacts list from the gray left column to the center column, and drop it below the Events list, like this:

These lists are currently unused.

These lists appear in the center column of the home page.

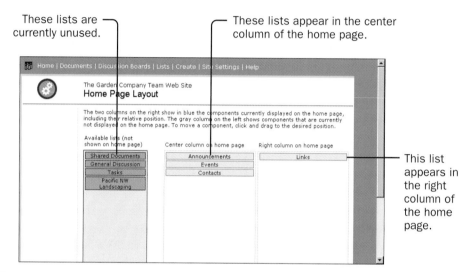

This list appears in the right column of the home page.

**32** Click **Save**.

You return to the home page, where you can see these results of your work:

The page title has been added.

The new document library is available in the Quick Launch area.

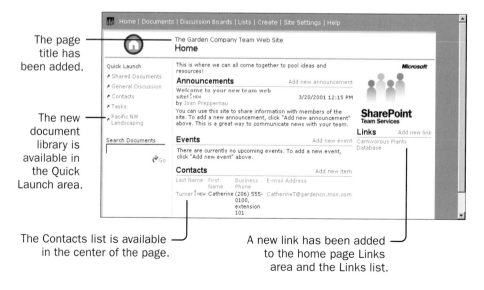

The Contacts list is available in the center of the page.

A new link has been added to the home page Links area and the Links list.

**33** Close the browser to return to FrontPage.

**34** Close the Web site.

# Maintaining the Security of Web Site Files

FP2002e-7-1

Most small business or personal Web sites have only one developer working on them at any given time, in which case there is no need to worry about who is working on which files. In some cases, however, especially with larger corporate sites, multiple developers need to work on a single site at the same time. In such situations, you can use FrontPage's **source control** feature to protect the integrity of your Web site's files. The source control feature ensures that only one person at a time can edit a particular file. This avoids the frustration and anguish of having your changes overwritten by someone else.

FrontPage's source control works like a library that has only one copy of everything. You can check a file out, work with it, and then check it back in. While you have the file, no one else can check it out. They can open the file as **read-only** and look at it, but any changes they make to the file will be lost unless they save the file with a different name.

## Tip

FrontPage's source control feature is adequate for small projects, but if you need really rigorous source control, you might want to use Microsoft Visual SourceSafe (VSS). You can integrate a VSS project with a FrontPage project and have FrontPage act as a front end to the VSS project.

Source control options are disabled in the default installation of FrontPage 2002. Unless you need source control, you will probably be happier leaving this feature disabled. It will be simpler to open and edit files, and you will not run the risk of losing changes made to a read-only file.

In this exercise, you will turn on source control and then check a file in and out.

GardenCo

The working folder for this exercise is *SBS\FrontPage\TeamWeb\Source*.

Follow these steps:

**1** Open the **GardenCo** Web site located in the working folder, and display the **Folder List**.

**2** On the **Tools** menu, click **Web Settings** to open the **Web Settings** dialog box shown on the next page.

**3** On the **General** tab, select the **Use document check-in and check-out** check box, and then click **OK**.

A message box appears, warning you that there will be a delay while FrontPage recalculates the Web site.

**4** Click **Yes** to proceed.

When the site calculation is complete, each file shown in the **Folder List** or in Folders view is preceded by a green dot to indicate that it is available to be checked out, as shown here:

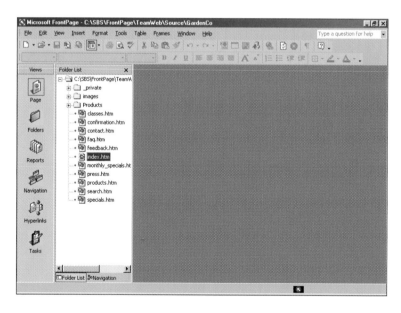

## Troubleshooting

Source control must be enabled for each individual Web site; the setting does not apply across sites.

**5**   Right-click any file name in the **Folder List**, and click **Check Out** on the short-cut menu.

The green dot changes to a red check mark to indicate that the file is checked out to you. You can now open the file in the Page view editing window, but no one else can.

**6**   Change a word or two on the page, save the page, and close it.

**7**   In the **Folder List**, right-click the file name, and click **Check In** on the short-cut menu to check the file back in with your changes.

You can click **Undo Check Out** to discard the changes you made since you last checked out the file.

## Troubleshooting

If you attempt to open a file in the Page view editing window without checking it out, a message box warns you that the file is under source control, and is read-only unless you check it out. You can either check out the file or open it in read-only mode. Be cautious; read-only file status is not indicated on the file name tab!

**8**   Close the Web site.

**9**   If you are not continuing on to the next chapter, quit FrontPage.

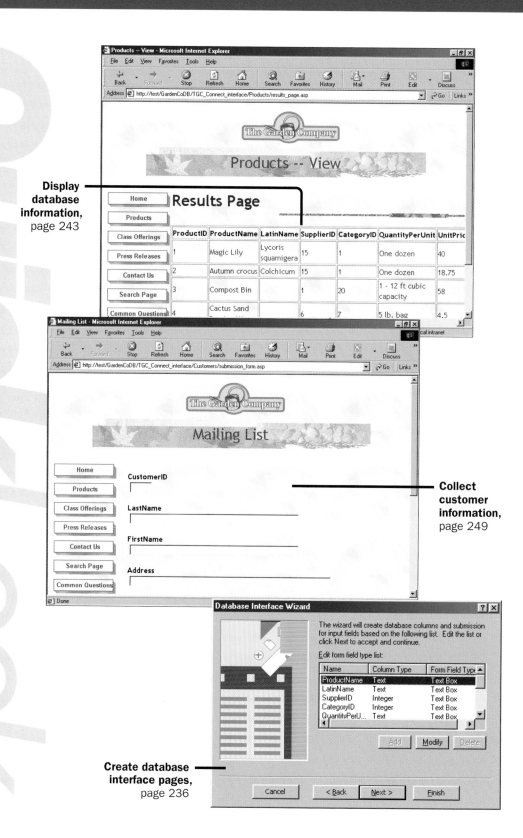

Display database information, page 243

Collect customer information, page 249

Create database interface pages, page 236

# Chapter 10
# Connecting Your
# Web Site to a Database

**After completing this chapter, you will be able to:**

✔ **Connect a database to a Web site.**

✔ **Create Web pages through which visitors can access a database.**

✔ **Enable visitors to search a database over the Web.**

✔ **Collect information from visitors and store it in a database.**

Web site developers often use the terms **static pages** and **dynamic pages** to refer to the source of the information that is displayed on a Web page. Static pages contain **hard-coded** information; that is, the information is embedded in the HTML code that makes up the page. Dynamic pages are shells that host changing information; that is, the information comes from an external source. When the external source is a database, the Web site is said to be **database driven**.

You can link your Microsoft FrontPage-based Web site to databases created in a variety of formats, including Microsoft Access, Microsoft Excel, and Microsoft SQL Server. The database can be stored on the Web server, on a separate file server, or on a separate database server. Because of this flexibility, it is simple to move information from one location to another without your Web site's visitors being aware that anything has changed.

FrontPage simplifies most database-related Web site tasks with the **Database Interface Wizard**, which you use to create database-driven forms. Although the database information comes from an external source, you can format the database information displayed in these forms to maintain the look and feel of your site.

The two main reasons to connect your Web site to a database are so that your visitors can access information directly from your database, and so that you can collect information from your visitors and add it to your database. This chapter briefly discusses how to set up your Web site for either purpose. You will learn how to connect a Web site to a database, how to publish a Web site to a server, how to display database information on a Web page, and how to extract information entered on a Web page into a database.

For the first two exercises of this chapter, you will be working with the GardenCo Web sites that are stored in the *ConnectDB* and *Publish* subfolders of the *SBS\FrontPage\Database* folder. For the remaining exercises, you will be working with a Web site that you have published to your Web server.

## Important

The second exercise in this chapter shows you how to publish a Web site to a Web server. Unlike the exercises in other chapters, those in this chapter build on each other. You cannot do the third and subsequent exercises without having done the second. For this reason it is important to follow along sequentially rather than completing the exercises out of order.

## Setting Up a Database Connection

FP2002e-6-1

You've got a Web site, and you've got a database. Now you want to be able to connect the two, so that after the Web site is published to a Web server, the database's information will be accessible over the Web.

If you'll be hosting the database on your Web server, you might want to move the database file into your Web site's folder. Then when the Web site is published to the Web server, the database will be published along with all the other files, and your Web visitors will be able to access the database through the server. Wherever the database is located, you will need to connect it to the Web site so that it can be accessed through one or more of the site's pages. Once the database is made accessible, you can create the page or pages that either display information from the connected database or request information from visitors so that it can be stored in the connected database.

Obviously, for this process to work seamlessly, you need to think through how to structure your database and how to secure its data so that no one can inadvertently or intentionally gain access to information they are not supposed to see. This type of discussion is beyond the scope of this book, but for information about how to set up a Microsoft Access database to meet this type of need, you might want to check out *Microsoft Access Version 2002 Step By Step* (Microsoft Press, 2001).

In this exercise, you will connect a disk-based Web site to a database in preparation for creating a database interface. An Access database called GardenCo.mdb has been supplied in the Database folder of the GardenCo sample Web site for this purpose.

GardenCo
GardenCo.mdb

The working folder for this exercise is *SBS\FrontPage\Database\ConnectDB*.

Follow these steps:

**1** If FrontPage is not already open, start it now.

**2** Open the **GardenCo** Web site that is located in the working folder.

**3** On the **Tools** menu, click **Web Settings** to open the **Web Settings** dialog box.

**4**  In the **Web Settings** dialog box, click the **Database** tab, which is currently blank, indicating that no databases are connected to the open Web site.

**5**  Click **Add** to display this **New Database Connection** dialog box:

**6**  In the **Name** box, type **TGC_Connect**. You can use any name that will uniquely identify the database.

**7**  In the **Type of connection** area, click **File or folder in current Web**, and then click **Browse** to open the **Database Files in Current Web** dialog box.

**8**  Double-click the **Database** folder to open it.

**9**  Click **GardenCo.mdb**, and then click **OK** to return to the **New Database Connection** dialog box.

The path to the database is now entered in the connection box.

**10**  Click **OK** to return to the **Web Settings** dialog box.

The **TGC_Connect** database connection now appears in the **Connection** list, with a question mark in the **Status** column.

**11**  Click **Verify**.

FrontPage verifies the existence of the database and changes the question mark to a check mark, like this:

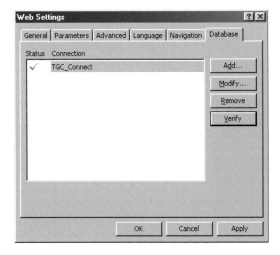

If FrontPage could not verify the database connection, it would change the question mark to a broken link.

**12**  Click **OK** to close the **Web Settings** dialog box.

**13**  Close the Web site.

## Publishing a Web Site for Use with a Database

FP2002-6-1
FP2002e-10-3

Publishing a Web site that is connected to a database is no different from publishing any other Web site. In this section, we briefly walk you through the steps in preparation for the remaining exercises in this chapter. Please note that you cannot complete those exercises without having access to a **server-based Web site** (one that is stored on a Web server); a **disk-based Web site** (one that is stored on your computer) will not work for this purpose.

To be able to publish a Web site to a server, either you must have access via a **local area network (LAN)** or via an Internet connection to a computer designated as a Web server (this may be a server maintained by a Web site hosting company). In either case, to display database information, the Web server must support **Active Server Pages (ASP)** and **ActiveX Data Objects (ADO)**.

In this exercise, you will publish a disk-based Web site to a Web server so that you can use it to interact with a database.

GardenCo

The working folder for this exercise is *SBS\FrontPage\Database\Publish*.

Follow these steps:

**1**  Open the **GardenCo** Web site located in the working folder.

**2**  On the **File** menu, click **Publish Web**.

This **Publish Destination** dialog box opens:

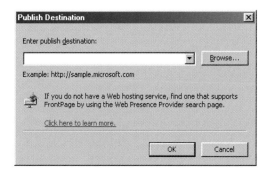

**3**  In the **Enter publish destination** box, type **http://**<server>**/GardenCoDB**, substituting the name of your Web server for <server>, and then click **OK**.

You have specified that you want The Garden Company's Web site to be published on the Web server with the name *GardenCoDB*.

**4**    Click **OK** when you are prompted to create a new Web site at the specified location.

FrontPage displays this **Publish Web** dialog box, which lists the folders and files to be published:

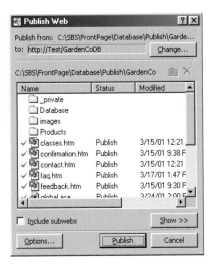

**5**    Click **Publish** to publish the entire Web site to the Web server. When the publishing process finishes, you see this message:

**6**    Click **Click here to view your published web site** to open the site in your default browser and window size.

**7**    Browse around the site to familiarize yourself with it, and then close the browser to return to FrontPage.

## Tip

Because this is the first time the site has been opened since it was published to the Web, the hit counter at the bottom of the home page shows that you are visitor #0001. If you close the browser and then reopen the site, you will then be visitor #0002.

**8**    Click **Done** to close the message box.

**9**    Close the Web site.

# Adding Database Search Capabilities

FP2002-3-1
FP2002-3-2
FP2002-3-5
FP2002-5-1

One of the primary reasons why you might want your database to be publicly available via the Web is so that people can look up specific information. For example, suppose someone learns from one of the many Web search engines that The Garden Company is one of only a very few garden stores that specialize in carnivorous plants. Having found the company's Web site, the visitor wants to know what plants the store carries. You could hard-code the information on a Web page, but the information is already maintained in a Products table in the store's database. Not only does hard-coding a Web page create redundant information, it also introduces the possibility of error. To update information about the carnivorous plant varieties that the store carries, you would then have to type the updates in two places: once in the database and again on the corresponding Web page.

A database-driven Web page is ideal for displaying a catalog of the information that already exists in a database. Each time a product specification, its availability, or its price changes, the information is updated in the database so that it is available to The Garden Company employees who need it, and without any extra effort, the updated information is also available to Web site visitors through the Web page.

You can make this type of information available to your visitors by using the **Database Interface Wizard** to create **Active Server Pages (ASP)**. These pages are stored on the server and generate different views of the data in response to choices visitors make on a Web page. The pages can be viewed with any modern browser, but the server where the pages are stored must be running Microsoft Windows NT 4 or Microsoft Windows 2000.

In this exercise, you will use the **Database Interface Wizard** to create a searchable product database in a Web site that has been published to a Web server, so that visitors can locate products based on product categories.

There is no working folder on your computer for this exercise, but you must have access to the GardenCoDB Web site that you published to your Web server in the previous exercise.

Follow these steps:

Open

**1** On the Standard toolbar, click the **Open** button's down arrow, and click **Open Web** in the drop-down list of options.

The **Open Web** dialog box opens.

Web Folders

**2** At the left side of the dialog box, click **Web Folders**.

You now see any Web sites stored on servers that are available to you.

**3** Click **GardenCoDB on** <server>, where <server> is the name of your Web server, and then click **Open**.

The server-based Web site named *GardenCoDB* opens in FrontPage.

**4** Open the **New Page or Web** task pane by pointing to **New** on the **File** menu and clicking **Page or Web**.

**5** In the **New from template** area, click **Web Site Templates**.

The **Web Site Templates** dialog box opens.

**6** In the **Web Site Templates** dialog box, click the **Database Interface Wizard** icon.

**7** In the **Options** area, select the **Add to current Web** check box to indicate that you want to add a database interface page to the open Web site.

The location of the current Web site is automatically entered in the location box, but it is grayed out so that it can't be changed.

**8** Click **OK**.

The **Database Interface Wizard** opens, like this:

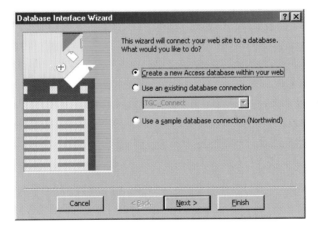

## Tip

The Northwind database mentioned on the first page of the **Database Interface Wizard** is a sample database that ships with Microsoft Office XP and is available from all Office applications.

## Troubleshooting

If you do not have any databases connected to this Web site, the second option will be dimmed and unavailable.

**9** Click **Use an existing database connection**, ensure that the **TGC_Connect** connection is selected in the drop-down list, and then click **Next** to display the wizard's next page.

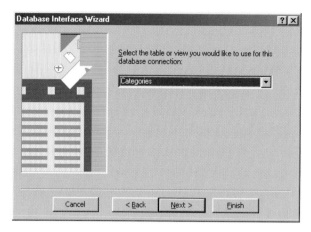

**10** Click the down arrow to expand the drop-down list.

The listed entries—Categories, Customers, Employees, Order Details, Orders, Products, Shippers, Suppliers, and Switchboard Items—correspond with the **tables** in the GardenCo database that is connected to this Web site through the TGC_Connect connection.

**11** To use data from the Products table to create a catalog, click **Products**, and then click **Next** to display the wizard's next page:

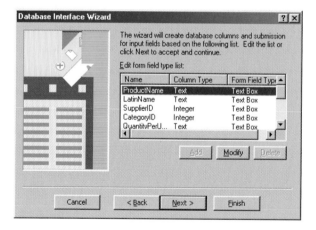

The available database fields are listed, along with the column type and form field type. If you want to change the form field input type, you can click **Modify**.

**12** No changes are necessary, so click **Next**.

The next page of the wizard appears with the Results Page and Submission Form options selected by default:

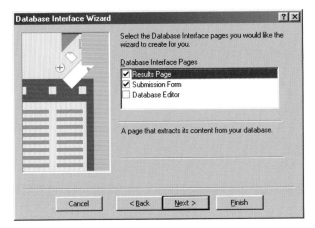

**13** Select only the **Results Page** check box by clearing the other check boxes, and then click **Next**.

The last page of the wizard appears, advising you of the location of the page that will be created:

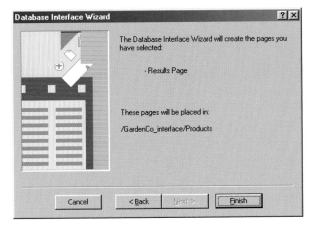

## Tip

The **Database Interface Wizard** creates a new folder named with the database connection name followed by an underscore and the word *interface*.

**14** Click **Finish** to create the results page, which looks like this:

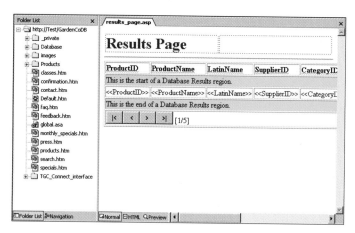

The TGC_Connect_interface folder was created by the **Database Interface Wizard**. This folder is named for the database connection and contains a subfolder named *Products* that is named for the table you specified in the **Database Interface Wizard**. The wizard has stored a results page called *results_page.asp* in this folder.

## Tip

Unlike other types of new pages created in FrontPage, the results ASP page has already been saved as part of your existing Web site. You don't have to do anything to save the page.

New pages you create using the **Database Interface Wizard** do not share the theme and navigation style of the surrounding Web site as they would if you had simply created a new normal page within the site. You will have to apply the theme and shared border settings of the Web site to the new page manually.

**15** On the **Format** menu, click **Theme**.

**16** In the **Themes** dialog box, click **Selected pages(s)**, and then select the default theme, like this:

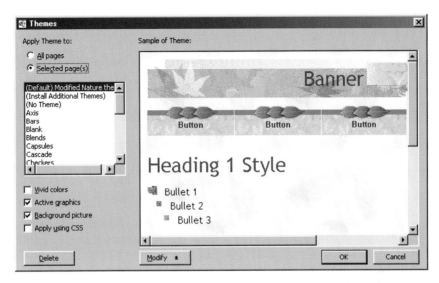

**17** Click **OK** to apply the theme to the page.

The result is an immediate improvement.

**18** Click anywhere in the new page, and click **Shared Borders** on the **Format** menu.

**19** In the **Shared Borders** dialog box, click **Current page**, and then select the **Reset borders for current page to web default** check box to bring the current page in line with the Web site default, like this:

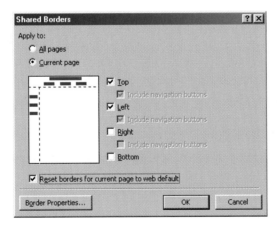

# Tip

The default shared border settings are illustrated in the preview pane of the **Shared Borders** dialog box.

**20** Click **OK** to apply the default border settings.

The look and feel of the page now matches the rest of the site. The page title and link bar are not yet displayed because the page has not been added to the navigation structure.

**Save**

**21** On the Standard toolbar, click **Save** to save the changes you have just made to the results_page.asp file.

**Navigation**

**22** On the **Views** bar, click the **Navigation** icon to switch to Navigation view.

In the **Folder List**, the TGC_Connect_interface folder is automatically expanded so that you can see the current file, results_page.asp.

## Tip

If the **Folder List** is no longer open, click **Folder List** on the **View** menu to open it.

**Portrait/ Landscape**

**23** To fit the entire Web site into the screen, click the **Portrait/Landscape** button on the Navigation toolbar to change the page orientation.

**24** Drag **results_page.asp** from the **Folder List**, and drop it in Navigation view as the last file under the Products page, like this:

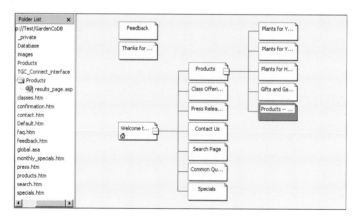

The database page is now a part of the navigation structure of the Web site. This means that the page banner will now show the page title, and the link bar will show the appropriate navigation links.

**25** In Navigation view, double-click the **Products** page to open the products.htm file in the Page view editing window.

**26** Click at the end of the last bulleted list item, and press [Enter] to insert a new line.

Bullets

**27** On the Formatting toolbar, click the selected **Bullets** button to change the new line from a bulleted list item to a normal paragraph, and then click the selected **Bold** button to change the font to regular text.

Bold

**28** Type **Click here to see our Product Catalog!**

**29** Hold down the ⟨Shift⟩ key and press ⟨Home⟩ to select the sentence, and then click **Hyperlink** on the **Insert** menu.

**30** In the **Insert Hyperlink** dialog box, click **Existing File or Web Page** and **Current Folder** to display the files and folders in the current Web site.

**31** Double-click the **TGC_Connect_interface** folder and then the **Products** subfolder to open them. Click **results_page.asp**, and then click **OK** to insert a hyperlink from the selected text to the file.

**32** Close the **products.htm** file, saving the file and the embedded graphic when prompted.

**33** Close the Web site.

## Testing and Refining a Database Interface Page

FP2002-1-2
FP2002e-6-3

When you use the **Database Interface Wizard** to produce an **ASP page** that will display the results of a database search on a Web page, the resulting ASP page is functional, but it might not meet your needs or your design standards. A few manipulations can make all the difference in the page's appearance and therefore in the impression it makes on your visitors.

In this exercise, you will open a Web site that is stored on a Web server, and you will refine an ASP page that retrieves database information so that the results it produces are more useful.

There is no working folder on your computer for this exercise, but you must have access to the GardenCoDB Web site that you published to your Web server in the previous exercise.

Follow these steps:

Open Web

**1** On the Standard toolbar, click the **Open Web** button.

**2** In the **Open Web** dialog box, click **Web Folders**. Then click **GardenCoDB on** *<server>*, where *<server>* is the name of your Web server, and click **Open**.

**3** Start your browser, and enter **http://**<server>**/GardenCoDB**, where *<server>* is the name of your Web server, in the **Address** box.

The GardenCoDB version of The Garden Company's Web site opens.

**4** On the navigation bar, click **Products**.

**5** On the Products page, click the **Click here to see our Product Catalog!** link.

The Results page opens, like this:

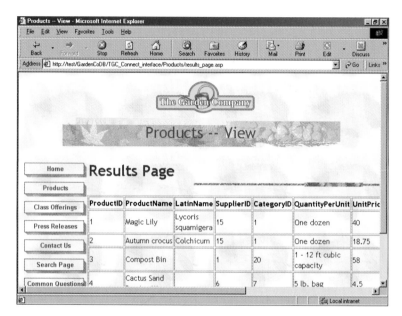

Several of the displayed fields are unlikely to be of interest to your visitors. In addition, the Results Page heading and horizontal rule are superfluous to the page.

**6** Close the browser to return to FrontPage.

**7** Expand the **TGC_Connect_interface** folder and the **Products** subfolder, and then double-click **results_page.asp** to open it in the Page view editing window.

In the results_page.asp file, you can see from the dotted outline that the Results Page heading is part of a table.

**8** Click in the table, point to **Select** on the **Table** menu, and then click **Table**.

The table is selected.

**9** Right-click the selection, and click **Delete Cells** on the shortcut menu.

The table is deleted.

**10** Click the horizontal rule to select it, and then press ⌈Del⌉.

**11** Right-click anywhere in the Database Results region bordered by the two yellow rows, and on the shortcut menu, click **Database Results Properties**.

This first page of the **Database Results Wizard** opens:

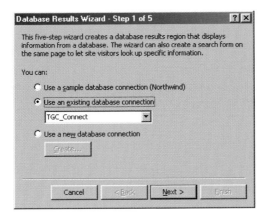

You use this wizard to change the display of the selected database.

**12** Accept the current settings by clicking **Next** to display this page:

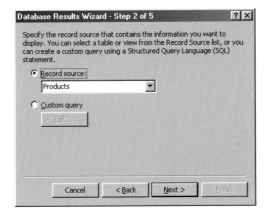

**13** You want to continue pulling information from the Products table, so click **Next** to display this page:

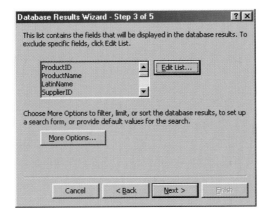

**14** Click the **Edit List** button to open the **Displayed Fields** dialog box.

**15** In the **Displayed fields** list, double-click each of the following field names: **ProductID**, **SupplierID**, **CategoryID**, **UnitsInStock**, **UnitsOnOrder**, **Reorder-Level**, and **Discontinued**.

Double-clicking moves the names to the **Available fields** list. The **Displayed Fields** dialog box now looks like this:

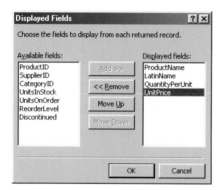

**16** Click **OK** to close the dialog box and return to the wizard.

**17** Click **More Options**, and in the **More Options** dialog box, click **Criteria**.

The **Criteria** dialog box opens, with no criteria currently specified.

**18** In the **Criteria** dialog box, click **Add** to open this **Add Criteria** dialog box:

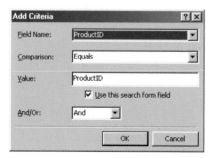

**19** In the **Field Name** drop-down list, click **CategoryID** to indicate that you want Web visitors to be able to filter the product information based on the category number. Leave the other settings alone, and click **OK** to close the **Add Criteria** dialog box.

**20** Click **OK** to close the **Criteria** dialog box.

**21** Back in the **More Options** dialog box, click **Ordering** to open the **Ordering** dialog box. In the **Available fields** list, double-click **ProductName** to move it to the **Sort order** list, like this:

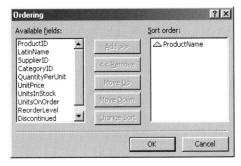

## Tip

The up arrow indicates that the resulting data display will be in ascending alphabetical order by product name. If you want to reverse the order, double-click the up arrow, which then becomes a down arrow.

**22** Click **OK** to close the **Ordering** dialog box.

**23** Back in the **More Options** dialog box, click **Defaults** to open the **Defaults** dialog box.

**24** With **CategoryID** selected in the **Input Parameters** list, click **Edit**, type **1** in the **Value** box, and click **OK** to set the initial catalog display to all records that have a category number of 1.

**25** Click **OK** to close the **Defaults** dialog box.

**26** Back in the **More Options** dialog box, clear the **Limit number of returned records to** check box to indicate that all records matching the criteria should be displayed.

**27** Click **OK** to close the **More Options** dialog box, and then click **Next**.

The next page of the wizard appears:

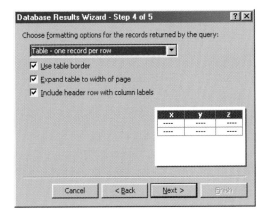

**28** Accept the current settings by clicking **Next**, which displays this page:

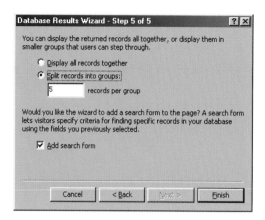

The **Add search form** check box is selected because of your earlier **Criteria** selection. If you had not selected any filter criteria, this option would be dimmed and unavailable.

**29** Click **Display all records together**, and then click **Finish**. If FrontPage asks whether it should regenerate the Database Results region, click **Yes**.

The representative database is regenerated, showing your new filter query at the top and displaying only the selected fields, like this:

**30** Position the insertion point at the top of the page body, and type the following:

**Which product category would you like to see? 1=Bulbs, 2=Cacti, 3=Ground Covers, 4=Grasses, 5=Flowers, 6=Wetland Plants, 7=Soils/ Sand, 8=Fertilizers, 13=Trees, 14=Herbs, 15=Bonsai Supplies, 16=Roses, 17=Rhododendrons, 18=Pest Control, 19=Carnivorous, 20=Tools, 21=Berry Bushes, 22=Shrubs/Hedges.**

**31** Click **Save** to save the file.

**32** Open your browser, and type **http://**<server>**/GardenCoDB**, where <server> is the name of your Web server, in the **Address** box. Then press ⌨Enter.

**33** Open the **Products** page, and click the link to see the Product Catalog.

The Products -- View page opens with only the items in category 1 (bulbs) displayed.

**34** Type **3** in the **CategoryID** box, and click **Submit Query**.

The table is updated to display all items in category 3 (ground covers), like this:

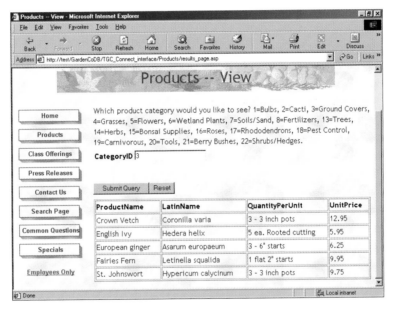

**35** Close the browser to return to FrontPage.

**36** Close the Web site.

# Adding Data Collection Capabilities

FP2002-3-2
FP2002-3-5
FP2002e-5-1
FP2002e-6-2

Nobody likes junk mail, and nobody likes junk e-mail. However, suppose you have a compelling product or service, or you provide something that none of your competitors provides. If you can establish yourself as a source of reliable, interesting, necessary, or timely information, chances are that at least a few people are going to be willing to provide you with their e-mail addresses in return for the convenience of having you send information to them.

To collect information from your visitors, you can use the **Database Interface Wizard** to set up an ASP page that acts as a submission form. The form receives the information from the visitor and channels it into an underlying database table.

In this exercise, you will create a mailing list registration form in a database-driven Web site so that visitor information is added to the Customers table of the GardenCo database.

There is no working folder on your computer for this exercise, but you must have access to the GardenCoDB Web site that you published to your Web server in the previous exercise.

Follow these steps:

1   On the Standard toolbar, click **Open Web**.

2   In the **Open Web** dialog box, click **Web Folders**. Then click **GardenCoDB on** <*server*>, where <*server*> is the name of your Web server, and click **Open**.

3   Click the **New Page** down-arrow, and click **Web** in the drop-down list to open the **Web Site Templates** dialog box.

4   Click the **Database Interface Wizard** icon to select it.

5   In the **Options** area, select the **Add to current Web** check box, and click **OK**. The **Database Interface Wizard** opens.

6   Click **Use an existing database connection**, ensure that **TGC_Connect** is selected in the drop-down list, and then click **Next**.

7   On the next page of the wizard, display the list of tables in the GardenCo database, click **Customers**, and then click **Next**.

8   Accept the default settings on the next page by clicking **Next**.

9   For the mailing-list registration database, select only the **Submission Form** check box by clearing the other check boxes, and then click **Next**.

The last page of the wizard appears, advising you of the location of the page that will be created.

10   Click **Finish** to create the submission form in your Web site.

The **Database Interface Wizard** creates a Customers subfolder, which is named for the database table being accessed, within the existing TGC_Connect_interface folder. The wizard then creates and saves the submission_form.asp file in this folder.

The results look something like this:

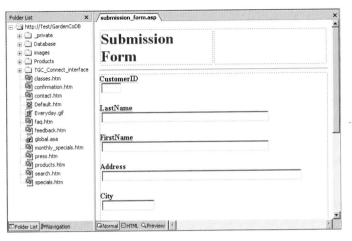

11    To give this page the same look as the rest of the site, click anywhere in the new page, and then click **Theme** on the **Format** menu.

12    In the **Themes** dialog box, click **Selected pages(s)**, select the default theme, and then click **OK** to apply the theme to the page.

13    On the **Format** menu, click **Shared Borders**. In the **Shared Borders** dialog box, click **Current page**, select the **Reset borders for current page to web default** check box, and click **OK** to apply the shared border settings.

The look and feel of the page now matches the rest of the site. The page title and link bar are not yet displayed because the page has not been added to the navigation structure.

14    To delete the superfluous Submission Form heading, click in the table, point to **Select** on the **Table** menu, and then click **Table**.

15    Right-click the selection, and click **Delete Cells** on the shortcut menu to delete the table.

16    Click the horizontal rule to select it, and then press ⌷ to delete the line.

17    Save the submission_form.asp file.

Portrait/
Landscape

18    Switch to Navigation view, and then if necessary click the **Portrait/Landscape** button on the Navigation toolbar to change the page orientation so it fits in the window.

**19** In the **Folder List**, expand the **TGC_Collect_interface** folder until you can see the submission_form.asp page.

## Tip

If the **Folder List** is no longer open, click **Folder List** on the **View** menu to open it.

**20** Drag **submission_form.asp** from the **Folder List**, and drop it in Navigation view at the same level as the home page, like this:

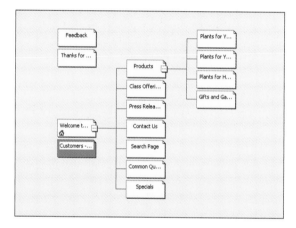

The database page is now a part of the navigation structure of your site.

**21** Right-click the rectangle representing the submission_form.asp file, and click **Rename** on the shortcut menu. Rename the file by overtyping the current file name with **Mailing List** and pressing [Enter].

**22** In the **Folder List**, double-click the **contact.htm** file to open it in the Page view editing window.

**23** Click at the end of the fax number, and press [Enter] to insert a new line.

Center

**24** On the Standard toolbar, click the **Center** button to center the line on the page.

**25** Type **Join our mailing list!**

**26** Hold down the [Shift] key and press [Home] to select the sentence.

Insert
Hyperlink

**27** Click the **Insert Hyperlink** button on the Standard toolbar to open the **Insert Hyperlink** dialog box.

**28** Browse to the **Customers** subfolder of the TGC_Connect_interface folder, click **submission_form.asp**, and click **OK** to insert the link.

**29** Close the **contact.htm** file, saving the file when prompted.

**30** Now test the database page by opening your browser and, in the **Address** box, entering **http://**<server>**/GardenCoDB**, where *<server>* is the name of your Web server.

The GardenCoDB Web site opens.

**31** On the navigation bar, click **Contact Us**.

**32** On the Contact Us page, click the **Join our mailing list!** link.

The Mailing List page opens, like this:

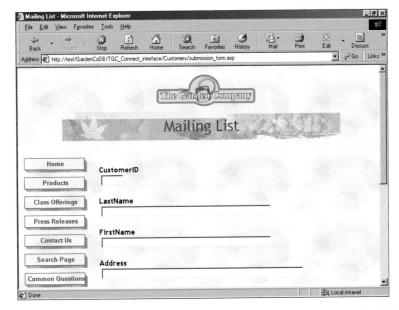

When visitors enter their information on this page and click the **OK** button, the information will be stored in the database.

**33** Close the browser to return to FrontPage.

**34** Close the Web site.

**35** If you are not continuing on to the next chapter, quit FrontPage.

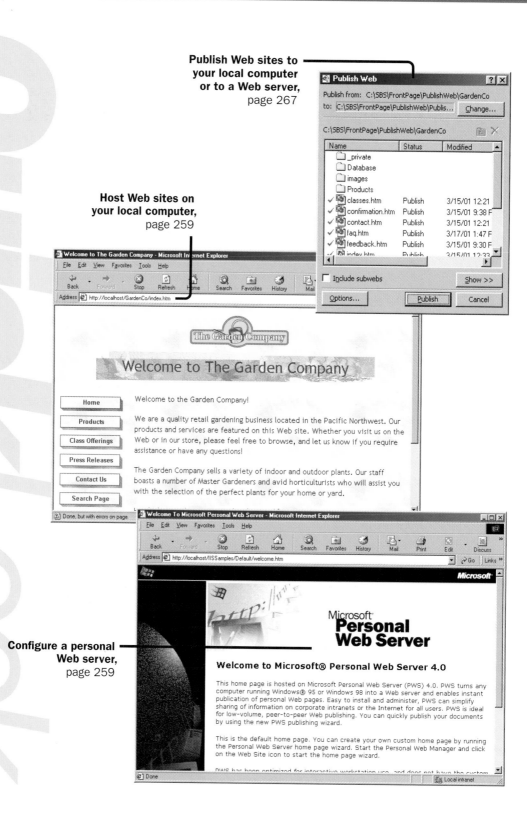

**Publish Web sites to your local computer or to a Web server,** page 267

**Host Web sites on your local computer,** page 259

**Configure a personal Web server,** page 259

# Chapter 11
# Publishing Your Web Site

**After completing this chapter, you will be able to:**

✔ Configure a computer as a personal Web server.

✔ Find a Web hosting company or Internet service provider.

✔ Publish a Web site to a personal Web server.

✔ Publish a Web site to an intranet or Internet server.

There is no point in going to all the trouble of building an attractive, informative, creative Web site if no one is going to look at it. The culmination of all your work is the moment when you make your Web site available to the outside world by publishing it either to an intranet or to the Internet. Publishing a Web site for the first time is also known as **launching** the site.

In Web site terms, **publishing** means copying all of your Web site files to a **Web server**. After the site is published, it is considered "live"; that is, the intended private group of people (in the case of an intranet) or the general public (in the case of the Internet) can view the site in their Web browsers.

You can publish a Web site in three ways:

■ You can use **Hypertext Transfer Protocol (HTTP)** to publish to a Web server that has the FrontPage Server Extensions or SharePoint Team Services from Microsoft installed.

■ You can use **File Transfer Protocol (FTP)** to publish to a Web server that does not have the FrontPage Server Extensions or SharePoint Team Services installed. To use FTP, you need to know the name of the FTP server that will receive your files and have a valid user name and password.

■ You can copy your Web site to a folder on your own computer. With a FrontPage-based Web site, it is advisable to publish the Web folder rather than simply copying the files, to ensure that the structure and integrity of the site is maintained.

This chapter discusses how and where you can publish your FrontPage-based Web site. For the first exercise, you don't need any sample files. For the remaining exercises, you will be working with a sample Web site that is stored in the *SBS \FrontPage\PublishWeb* folder.

**Important**

The second exercise in this chapter shows you how to configure your computer as a personal Web server. In the fourth exercise, you publish a Web site to your personal Web server, so you will need to complete the second exercise before you can complete the fourth.

# Finding a Suitable Host for Your Web Site

Web sites fall into two categories: **disk-based Web sites** and **server-based Web sites**. When you are developing a Web site, it's important to understand the difference.

Disk-based Web sites can be run on any kind of computer, or even from a floppy disk or CD-ROM. They support basic HTML functionality, and that's all. Most of the Web components provided with FrontPage won't work in disk-based sites.

Server-based Web sites are run on a Web server—a computer that is specifically configured to host Web sites. On a small scale, a local computer such as your own might be designated as a Web server, or the server that hosts your company's intranet might serve this function. Personal Web sites are often hosted on the servers of **Internet service providers (ISPs)**. On a larger scale, Web servers that host corporate Web sites are usually located at professional **Web hosting companies**.

A bewildering number of Web hosting companies are available to choose from, each offering different rate plans and different levels of support. As is the case when choosing any kind of a service provider—from cellular phones to hairdressers—it can be difficult to evaluate all the choices and determine which one will best fit your needs.

The Web hosting industry is large and worldwide. Several paper-based and online magazines are dedicated to reviewing and reporting on the field of Web hosting, such as *Web Hosting Magazine*, which you can buy at full-service newsstands and bookstores, and *The Web Host Industry Review*, which you can browse on the Internet at *www.thewhir.com*. Both types of magazines are filled with news, information, and advertising.

The best way to start your search for a Web hosting company is to do a search on the World Wide Web for *Web hosting*. You will find a variety of Web sites representing individual Web hosting companies. You can also find sites that collate and categorize hosting companies. Good resources you might want to check out include TopHosts at *www.tophosts.com*, HostSearch at *www.hostsearch.com*, and Web Host Directory at *www.webhostdir.com*. These sites help you sort through the choices based on different criteria.

Some Web hosting companies offer free or very inexpensive hosting services; be wary of these offers, though, because this is one of those times when you really do get what you pay for. Reliable, high-speed servers and reliable, high-speed technicians are neither free nor inexpensive! Changing Web hosting services can be difficult (although not impossible), so it is a good idea to make an informed decision from the beginning rather than learning from your mistakes.

Geographic location should not be a factor in your choice of Web hosting companies, other than choosing a Web host located in your own country to avoid any potential problems if there is a disagreement over payment. You will never need to physically visit your hosting company's office, and almost all companies have toll-free numbers in the event that you need to telephone them.

One good way to make a decision, or at least to narrow the field to fewer choices, is to talk to people who have established businesses and ISP-hosted corporate Web sites and ask for their positive and negative impressions of any ISPs they have used. Most of the professional ISPs offer very good information on their own Web sites that should also help you to decide.

As the developer of a FrontPage-based Web site, your choices are already limited because if you use any of the special FrontPage functionality, your ISP must support FrontPage Server Extensions. Web hosting companies that support FrontPage Server Extensions will advertise this fact on their Web sites. Many of the previously listed resources will enable you to search specifically for FrontPage-enabled hosting services.

Microsoft also maintains a list of registered Web Presence Providers—ISPs that have agreed to offer full support of FrontPage Server Extensions. A list of Web Presence Providers around the world is available at *www.microsoftwpp.com/wppsearch/*.

## What are FrontPage Server Extensions?

FrontPage Server Extensions are a set of **server-side applications**—programs that are run on the Web server rather than on the Web visitor's own computer—that enable you to do the following:

- Publish content directly to the Web server via the Internet.
- Include forms, discussion Webs, and hit counters on a Web site.
- Provide full-text site search capability.

Because the programs are run on the server, Web designers are spared the need to write the code and scripting that would be necessary to embed the functionality of these types of elements in the Web pages themselves. Instead, the code is "called" from the page and run on the Web server.

The FrontPage Server Extensions are not necessary to host FrontPage-based Web sites; however, they extend what the Web site is capable of doing. For a full list of the features that currently require FrontPage Server Extensions, visit Microsoft's Web site at *www.microsoft.com/frontpage/*.

# Choosing and Registering a Domain Name

Before launching a commercial Web site on the Internet, you will need to choose and register a **domain name**. The domain name is the base of the alphanumeric address, called the **uniform resource locator (URL)**, where visitors locate your Web site on the World Wide Web. For example, *www.microsoft.com* is Microsoft Corporation's URL, and *microsoft.com* is its domain name. Your domain name may be your name, the name of your company, a word or phrase that represents what your company does, or any string of letters and numbers you desire.

When choosing a domain name, it is prudent to look for a name that will be easy for people to remember and easy for people to spell. Domain names that spell common words are good choices. Your domain name might be made up of more than one word, in which case you must decide to run the words together as one string, or to separate them with other characters; underscores are common word separators. Remember, though, that you will need to spell the name out over the phone, so you should look for something short and simple!

Choose a name that means something to your company; if you have a registered trademark, consider using that. Domain names are not case-sensitive. You can use uppercase and lowercase letters in your written material to separate and differentiate between words, but visitors do not need to follow your capitalization to get to your site.

Part of your choice of a domain name is the extension. Depending on the type of Web site you are registering, you might choose an extension of .com, .org, .net, .edu, or one of the new extensions that have recently been made available in order to handle the increasing numbers of new Web site registrations. Each of these extensions has a meaning: *.com* is for companies, *.org* is for non-profit organizations, *.net* is for networks, and *.edu* is for educational institutions.

Some examples of domain names tied to product lines include *QuickCourse.com* and *eclecticClassroom.com*. You can use humor or wit in your choice of a domain name, such as *eFishinSea.com*, which is owned by a witty boat enthusiast. (When you pronounce the name it sounds like "efficiency.")

Obviously, for URLs to work, each domain name must be unique. To avoid duplication, all domain names are registered. You can register a domain name through many Web hosting companies; some of them will even help you with your search for the right name. Network Solutions (*www.networksolutions.com*) is a good one-stop shop for researching and registering domain name/extension combinations. You can also go directly to *www.internic.com*, the United States Department of Commerce's domain registry Web site for more information.

# Configuring Your Own Computer to Host a Web Site

FP2002e-10-2

Most Web sites are initially developed as disk-based sites; that is, the site is developed and tested on a local computer. Only after a site is finished is it published to a Web server that is maintained either by the organization that owns the Web site or by a Web hosting company. And only at that point does it become a server-based site. The drawback to this strategy is that the server-specific components of the site won't work until the site is published to the server; at which time you might find out that they don't work at all.

If you're going to do a significant amount of Web site development, you might consider configuring your own computer as a server for testing purposes. For FrontPage 2002, Microsoft recommends the following configuration for a Web server:

- Windows 2000
- Internet Information Services 5
- FrontPage Server Extensions 2002 or SharePoint Team Services

If your computer does not meet these requirements, or if you do not want to run a full-blown Web server on your computer, you can set up your Windows 98 computer as a personal Web server, using the following configuration:

- Windows 98
- Microsoft Personal Web Server 4.0
- FrontPage 2000 Server Extensions

## Troubleshooting

FrontPage Server Extensions 2002 do not support Windows 9x operating systems. As a workaround, Windows 98 users can install FrontPage 2000 Server Extensions from the Microsoft Web site.

By using a personal Web server, you can develop and run server-based sites locally; that is, on your own computer. You will still need to publish the site to a server that is accessible by its intended audience, but the risk of showing your mistakes to the world will be significantly lower if you thoroughly test your site on your personal Web server first.

## Important

The drawback to configuring your computer as a Web server is that, depending on the computer's configuration, you might find that its overall speed and performance is slightly reduced. You might not want to do this if you have other ways of testing the server-specific components of your Web site.

In this exercise, you will configure a Windows 98 computer as a personal Web server by installing **Personal Web Server (PWS)** and the FrontPage 2000 Server Extensions. (PWS is supplied on the Windows 98 installation CD-ROM; however, by default it is not fully installed with the operating system.) You will then test the installation; first by opening your default home page, and then by opening a Web site.

GardenCo

To work through this exercise, you will need to have available the Windows 98 CD-ROM and an Internet connection.

The working folder for this exercise is *SBS\FrontPage\PublishWeb*.

Follow these steps:

**1**   Close any programs that might be running on your computer.

**2**   At the left end of the taskbar at the bottom of the screen, click **Start**, point to **Settings**, and click **Control Panel**.

The Control Panel window opens.

**3**   Double-click **Add/Remove Programs** to open the **Add/Remove Programs Properties** dialog box.

**4**   Click the **Windows Setup** tab to display these options:

Selections vary based on your computer setup. —

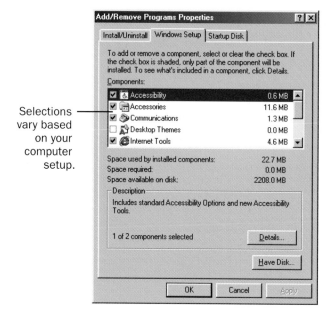

**5**   In the **Components** list, click the words **Internet Tools** (do not click the check box, because you might inadvertently tell Windows to uninstall currently installed components).

## The Windows Internet Tools

Personal Web Server is just one of the tools provided by Windows 98 to help you work with the Internet. Two others are related to FrontPage, and the rest provide miscellaneous Internet-related capabilities, as follows:

■ Microsoft FrontPage Express is a simple HTML page editor.

■ Web Publishing Wizard provides services that enable you to easily upload Web sites to a Web server.

■ Microsoft Virtual Reality Modeling Language (VRML) 2.0 Viewer is a viewer for VRML objects, which are three-dimensional full-color objects with special texture, animation, and lighting effects.

■ Microsoft Wallet provides a secure place to store private information such as credit card details for use while shopping on the Internet.

■ Real Audio Player displays live and on-demand audio, video, and animation.

■ Web-Based Enterprise Management components provide remote problem tracking and system administration capabilities to system administrators and support technicians.

**6** Click **Details** to see the available Internet Tools components.

**7** In the **Components** list, select the **Personal Web Server** check box, and click **OK** to close the **Internet Tools** dialog box.

**8** Click **OK** again to close the **Add/Remove Programs Properties** dialog box and install the Personal Web Server.

You are prompted to insert your Windows 98 CD-ROM.

**9** Insert the Windows 98 CD-ROM in the drive, and click **OK**.

Windows searches for a file called *pws_main.htm*. If it does not find the file in the expected location, you will see a message like this one:

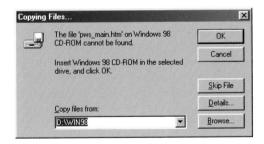

## Troubleshooting

This message might be displayed because Windows is looking on the wrong drive, or because the wrong CD-ROM is in the disk drive. Often the best response to this message is to click the **Browse** button and manually search for the file. More often than not, it will be simple to find. In this case, Windows is looking for a file that can be found inside a Cabinet (CAB) file called *Precopy2.cab*. Browse to this file and then click **OK** to continue.

After locating the file, Windows copies the necessary information to your hard disk and returns you to the Control Panel.

**10**   Close the Control Panel window.

You now need to run the Personal Web Server setup program.

**11**   In Windows Explorer, browse to the *add-ons\pws* folder on the Windows 98 CD-ROM, and double-click **setup.exe**.

The first page of the **Microsoft Personal Web Server Setup Wizard** opens, as shown here:

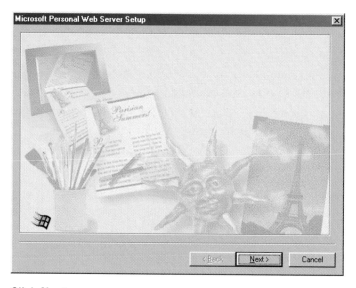

**12**   Click **Next**.

The next page of the wizard appears, offering **Minimum**, **Typical**, and **Custom** installation options:

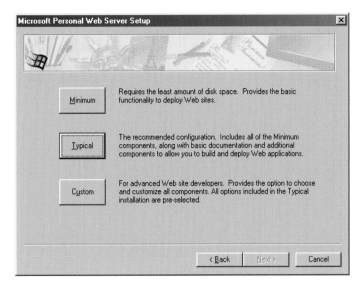

**13** Click **Typical**.

The next page of the wizard appears, with the default Web publishing directory identified as *C:\Inetpub\wwwroot*:

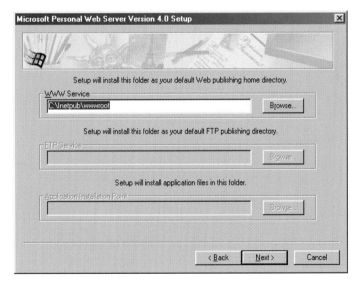

Unless you have a good reason, you should always accept the default installation locations. If you change the default publishing folder, it is important to enter an absolute path that includes a drive letter. The setup program might misinterpret a relative path.

**14** Click **Next**.

The setup program displays a progress bar while it copies the necessary files to your computer and configures a variety of settings. When the setup is complete, this final page of the wizard is displayed:

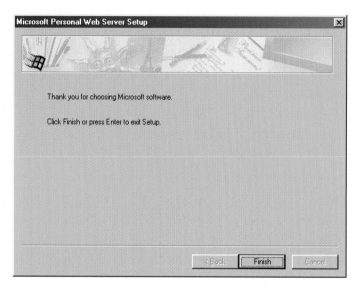

**15** Click **Finish** to close the program.

You are prompted to restart your computer:

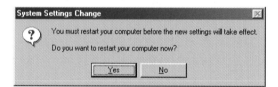

**16** Prepare to restart your computer by doing the following:

- Save and close all open applications.
- Leave the Windows 98 CD-ROM in your CD-ROM drive; it will be accessed again after you restart.
- If there is a floppy disk in the disk drive, eject it.

**17** Click **Yes** in the message box to restart your computer.

When your computer restarts (and after you log on, if necessary), Windows 98 updates its systems settings, and your computer is now configured as a personal Web server.

**18** Remove the Windows 98 CD-ROM from your hard drive, and return it to a safe storage location.

**19**  If necessary, start your Internet connection. Open your Web browser, and in the **Address** box, type http://www.microsoft.com/frontpage.

The Microsoft FrontPage Web site opens in your browser. (This page is updated frequently. Information given here is current as of April 1, 2001.)

**20**  In the Resources area, click **FrontPage Server Extensions**.

You are redirected to the FrontPage section of the MSDN Online Web site.

**21**  Click the **Download the FrontPage Server Extensions for Microsoft Windows-based Servers** link.

The Downloads for Microsoft Windows-Based Servers page opens.

**22**  Scroll down and click the link to the download file for your operating system.

The **File Download** dialog box opens.

**23**  Click **Run this program from its current location**, and then click **OK**.

A progress bar estimating the time left appears while the file is downloaded.

**24**  Select the **Close this dialog box when download completes** check box, if it is not already selected.

When the download is complete, a **Security Warning** dialog box appears.

**25**  Click **Yes** to continue.

The FrontPage Server Extensions installation begins. A setup program walks you through a short registration process and then installs the server extensions on your computer. When the installation is complete, you are prompted to restart your computer.

**26**  Click **Yes** in the message box to restart your computer.

When your computer restarts (and after you log on, if necessary), Windows finishes the configuration of the FrontPage Server Extensions.

**27**  To test whether the installation was successful, start your browser.

**28**  In the **Address** box, type http://localhost and press Enter .

## Tip

When you configure your computer as a personal Web server, a specific Internet Protocol (IP) address is assigned to the PWS root Web site. Localhost is a friendly name for this IP address, meaning that it is easier to remember than the address itself. Entering *http://localhost* in the browser **Address** box displays the root Web site of any configured Web server.

The default PWS home page opens, as shown on the next page.

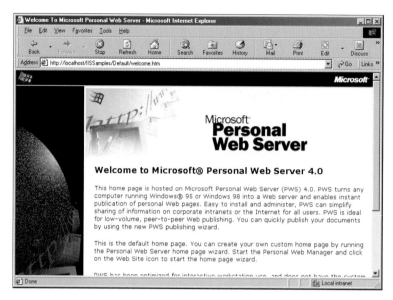

29  Open Windows Explorer, and browse to the C: drive.

Windows created a new folder called *Inetpub* on your C: drive. The Inetpub folder contains four subfolders: iissamples, scripts, webpub, and wwwroot.

30  Copy the **GardenCo** Web site from the *SBS\FrontPage\PublishWeb* folder to the *C:\Inetpub\wwwroot* folder.

31  Start your browser, type **http://localhost/GardenCo/index.htm** in the **Address** box, and press Enter.

The home page of The Garden Company's Web site is displayed, like this:

**32** Test the Web site by displaying various pages and clicking different links and components.

All of the components should be fully functional, including the hit counter and search page.

**33** Close the browser.

## Publishing a Web Site to a Local Folder

FP2002-6-1
FP2002e-10-2
FP2002e-10-3

If you have developed a FrontPage-based Web site on your local machine and you want to move the Web site files to a different location or create a copy of the Web site, it is prudent to publish the site to the new location rather than simply moving or copying the files in Windows Explorer. This guarantees that the underlying structure of the site will be updated as necessary to maintain the integrity of the links.

In this exercise, you will publish a disk-based Web site to a local folder.

GardenCo

The working folder for this exercise is *SBS\FrontPage\PublishWeb*.

Follow these steps:

**1** If FrontPage is not already open, start it now.

**2** On the **File** menu, click **Open Web**.

**3** In the **Open Web** dialog box, browse to the *SBS\FrontPage\PublishWeb* folder, select **GardenCo**, and then click **Open** to open the disk-based Web site.

**4** On the **File** menu, click **Publish Web**.

The **Publish Destination** dialog box opens:

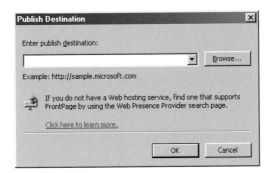

**5** Click the **Browse** button to open the **New Publish Location** dialog box, and browse to *SBS\FrontPage\PublishWeb*.

Create New
Folder

**6** Click the **Create New Folder** button on the dialog box's toolbar to open the **New Folder** dialog box.

**7** In the **Name** box, type **PublishLocal**, and then click **OK** to return to the **New Publish Location** dialog box with your newly created folder selected.

**8** Click **Open** to return to the **Publish Destination** dialog box.

FrontPage has entered the specified name and path in the **Enter publish destination** box.

**9** Click **OK**.

This message appears:

**10** Click **OK** to create the new Web at the specified location.

The **Publish Web** dialog box opens, listing these files to be published:

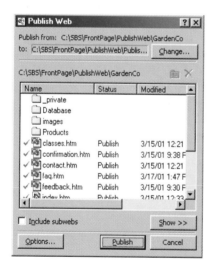

**11** Click the **Options** button.

**12** Review the many settings that you can work with in the **Options** dialog box, and then click **Cancel** to maintain the default settings.

**13** Click **Publish** to publish the Web site to your local drive.

You see this warning:

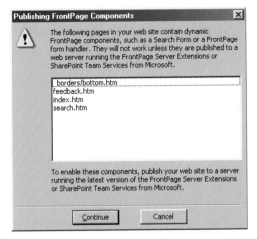

**14** Click **Continue**.

FrontPage displays a progress bar while publishing the selected files, and when the publishing process is finished, this message is displayed:

**15** Click the **Click here to view your publish log file** option.

Because the Publish Log is an HTML file, it opens in your browser. It contains the date and time of each transaction involved in the publishing process.

**16** Scroll through the file and review the publishing process that just finished.

FrontPage first creates the required folder structure, copies each individual file, and then copies the navigation structure. The entire process takes about one minute. (The publishing time depends on the size and complexity of the individual Web site.)

## Tip

You can filter this report to display only certain types of transactions: Publish Starts, Folder Creations, File Copies, File Renames, File Deletions, Confirmations, or Warnings. The default is to display all of the transactions.

**17** Close the browser to return to FrontPage.

**18** Now click the **Click here to view your published web site** option.

The Garden Company's Web site opens in your browser at the default window size.

**19** Browse around the site, testing its functionality.

Notice that FrontPage Web components, such as the hit counter on the home page and the search engine on the search page, do not work properly.

**20** Close the browser.

**21** Click **Done** to close the message box.

Back in FrontPage, the original disk-based Web site is still open, as shown here in the **Folder List**:

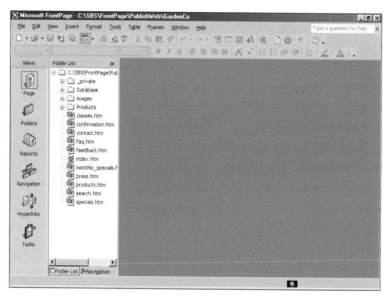

**22** Close the Web site.

## Publishing a Web Site to a Web Server

FP2002-6-1
FP2002e-10-1
FP2002e-10-2
FP2002e-10-3

Developing a Web site is an iterative process. You work on a few pages, and you publish them to see whether they work as intended. Then you make corrections, work on a few more pages, and publish again. Gradually the pages evolve into a full-fledged Web site that you are ready to present to its intended audience.

While you are working on the site, you will want to publish it to a development server, not to one that is accessible to outsiders. Depending on your resources, this development server might be another computer, or it might be a personal Web server hosted on your own computer. When you are finally ready to launch the site, you will need to publish it again, this time to a Web server that is capable of supporting the many visitors you hope will come to take a look.

Single-page publishing
new for
**Office**XP

FrontPage 2002 enables you to publish only the files that you want to rather than the entire Web site. You can even publish a single Web page by right-clicking the file name in the **Folder List** or in Folders view and clicking **Publish Selected Files** on the shortcut menu.

You can also mark specific files for exclusion from the publishing process by right-clicking the file name in the **Folder List** or in Folders view and clicking **Don't Publish** on the shortcut menu.

In this exercise, you will first publish a disk-based Web site to your personal Web server, and you will then publish the site from the personal Web server to a remote Web server.

## Important

To complete this exercise, you must have Personal Web Server and FrontPage 2000 Server Extensions installed on your computer. You must also have access to a Web server on a different computer.

GardenCo

The working folder for this exercise is *SBS\FrontPage\PublishWeb*.

Follow these steps:

1   Open the **GardenCo** Web site located in the working folder.

2   On the **File** menu, click **Publish Web**.

    The **Publish Web** dialog box opens with the previous publish destination shown in the **Publish to** box.

3   Click **Change**.

4   In the **Publish Destination** dialog box, type **http://localhost** in the **Enter publish destination** box, and then click **OK**.

    The **Publish Web** dialog box now shows the location to which the Web site will be published.

5   Click **Publish**.

    The **Publishing FrontPage Components** dialog box opens to let you know which components might not work without the current version of the FrontPage Server Extensions.

## Troubleshooting

If you're running Windows 98, most of the Web site pages are listed here because the program is searching for FrontPage Server Extensions 2002, which are not compatible with Windows 98. Instead, Windows 98 users need to install FrontPage 2000 Server Extensions. Most features usually work when published to a Windows 98 system, in spite of what this dialog box says.

**6** Click **Continue**.

FrontPage displays a progress bar while copying folders and files to your personal Web server, and informs you when the procedure has been successfully completed.

**7** Click the option to view the Web site in your browser.

All of the FrontPage Web components are fully functional.

**8** Next take a look at the Publish Log, shown here:

| | | |
|---|---|---|
| Friday, March 23, 2001 | 11:05:06 AM | Copied "images/custrel3.gif". |
| Friday, March 23, 2001 | 11:05:06 AM | Copied "images/fprotate.class". |
| Friday, March 23, 2001 | 11:05:06 AM | Copied "images/fprotatx.class". |
| Friday, March 23, 2001 | 11:05:06 AM | Copied "images/isao74.jpg". |
| Friday, March 23, 2001 | 11:05:06 AM | Copied "images/jmhvulg.jpg". |
| Friday, March 23, 2001 | 11:05:09 AM | Copied "images/pxweser.jpg". |
| Friday, March 23, 2001 | 11:05:09 AM | Copied "images/September.gif". |
| Friday, March 23, 2001 | 11:05:09 AM | Copied "images/tgclogo_sm.gif". |
| Friday, March 23, 2001 | 11:05:10 AM | Copied "Products/carnivorous_plants.htm". |
| Friday, March 23, 2001 | 11:05:10 AM | Copied "Products/gifts.htm". |
| Friday, March 23, 2001 | 11:05:10 AM | Copied "Products/plants_garden.htm". |
| Friday, March 23, 2001 | 11:05:10 AM | Copied "Products/plants_home.htm". |
| Friday, March 23, 2001 | 11:05:11 AM | Copied home page from "index.htm" to "Default.htm". |
| Friday, March 23, 2001 | 11:05:11 AM | Renamed "index.htm" to "Default.htm". |
| Friday, March 23, 2001 | 11:05:12 AM | Copied navigation structure. |
| Friday, March 23, 2001 11:05:30 AM | | Finished publish from "C:\SBS\FrontPage\PublishWeb\GardenCo" to "http://localhost". |

Notice that the process of publishing the site to the personal Web server included an additional transaction. The index.htm home page file was renamed to *Default.htm* in order to support the expected server-based Web site structure.

**9** Close the browser to return to FrontPage.

**10** Click **Done** to close the message box.

The original Web site is open in FrontPage.

**11** On the **File** menu, click **Open Web**.

**12** Browse to *C:\Inetpub\wwwroot*, and click **Open** to open the site you just published to your personal Web server.

**13** Now publish the personal Web server-based site to a remote Web server (a different computer). Start by clicking **Publish Web** on the **File** menu.

The **Publish Web** dialog box opens with the previous publish destination shown in the **Publish to** box.

**14** Click **Change** to open the **Publish Destination** dialog box.

**15** In the **Enter publish destination** box, type **http://**<server>**/PublishServer**, where <server> is the name of your Web server, and then click **OK**.

**16** When you are prompted to create a new Web site at the specified location, click **OK**.

The **Publish Web** dialog box now displays the new publish location.

**17** Click **Publish**.

FrontPage displays a progress bar while copying files and folders to the Web server, and displays the message box when the procedure has been successfully completed.

**18** View the Web site in your browser, testing its functionality.

All of the FrontPage Web components are fully functional.

**19** Look at the Publish Log to see what transactions were included in the publishing process.

**20** Return to FrontPage, and click **Done** to close the message box.

**21** Close the Web site.

**22** If you are not continuing on to the next chapter, quit FrontPage.

## Publishing a Web Site from a Remote Web Server to a Local Computer

FrontPage enables you to publish any Web site to which you have access to any location. The publishing process goes both ways. In addition to publishing from a local computer to a remote server, you can do the opposite: publish a Web site from the Internet to your computer. In order to publish from the Web to your computer:

- The remote server must have FrontPage Server Extensions installed.

- You must have a valid user name and password for the remote server.

- You must have a working Internet connection.

To publish a FrontPage Web site from a remote server to a local folder or to your personal Web server, follow these steps:

**1** If necessary, start your Internet connection.

**2** On the **File** menu, click **Open Web**. In the **Web name** box, type the URL or IP address of the remote Web site preceding it with *http://* to indicate that it is a server-based site (for example, http://www.microsoft.com/frontpage/ or http://207.46.131.13/frontpage/), and then click **Open**.

**3** If the remote server requires a user name and password, it will prompt you for them. Supply a valid user name and password, and click **OK**.

The remote Web site opens in FrontPage.

**4** On the **File** menu, click **Publish Web**. In the **Publish Destination** box, type the location where you want to publish the Web site, and click **OK**.

**5** In the **Publish Web** dialog box, click **Publish**.

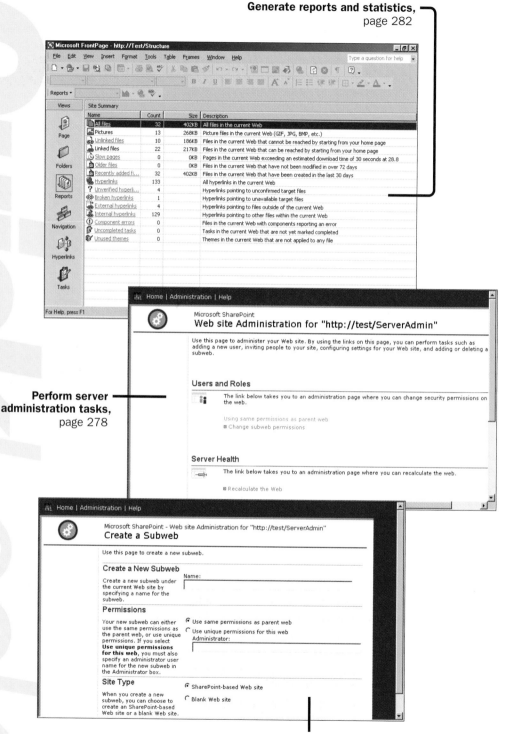

**Generate reports and statistics,** page 282

**Perform server administration tasks,** page 278

**Create and manage a subweb,** page 278

# Chapter 12
# Managing Your Web Site

**After completing this chapter, you will be able to:**

✔ **Control the way you work in FrontPage.**

✔ **Perform basic server administration tasks.**

✔ **Generate reports about a server-based Web site.**

✔ **Generate usage statistics for a server-based root Web site.**

Many of the administrative tasks associated with ongoing site maintenance don't apply to newly published sites, and the administrator of your Web server will handle many of the more difficult site administration tasks. However, as you work your way through this chapter, you will get a broad overview of the administrative tasks you are likely to want to carry out when developing a FrontPage-based Web site, and where to look for the settings needed for a particular task.

Administrative tasks fall into three major categories: working with FrontPage so that future development efforts are efficient; assigning roles and permissions to the people who will have access to your Web site, with the goal of controlling who can do what to the site; and generating reports that tell you whether everything is running correctly and how your site is being used.

This chapter discusses all three categories of administration. The first exercise does not use any sample files. The sample Web site you will be working with in the second exercise of chapter is stored in the *SBS\FrontPage\ManageSite* folder. For the remaining exercises, you will be working with a Web site that you have published to your Web server.

**Important**

In the second exercise in this chapter, you publish a Web site to a Web server. You cannot do the third and subsequent exercises without having done the second. For this reason it is important to follow along sequentially rather than completing the exercises out of order.

## Setting FrontPage Options

Setting up your FrontPage environment is not, strictly speaking, a maintenance task. However, once you have some knowledge of how to create a Web site, you have a better understanding of the development environment's impact on your efficiency and you are more likely to want to customize your FrontPage settings to ensure that future development tasks go as smoothly as possible.

Most of the options you use to set up FrontPage are available on the tabs of the **Options** and **Page Options** dialog boxes. You have several choices available in the **Options** dialog box, including the following:

- You can set startup options that determine what tools are available every time you start FrontPage.

- You can tell FrontPage to alert you when a Web site needs to be updated or when you might inadvertently override a theme.

- You can connect to your browser's **Properties** dialog box.

- You can specify which programs you want to use to edit specific types of files so that double-clicking the file name opens the file in the correct application.

- You can turn the status bar on and off.

- You can define recent files, old files, and slow pages so that your usage reports contain exactly the information you need.

- After you publish a site for the first time, you can specify whether future publications should include the entire site or only changed pages. You can tell FrontPage to determine whether pages have changed by comparing old and new versions of the site or by reading the timestamps of the files.

- You can choose whether to create a Publish Log each time you publish a site, and you can view the most recent log file.

These choices are available in the **Page Options** dialog box:

- You can specify various HTML coding options, set the spelling options, and stipulate whether the **Paste Options** button is shown each time you paste text or graphics into a Web page.

- You can specify the default size, border thickness, and bevel width for thumbnails created using FrontPage's **Auto Thumbnail** command.

- You can specify a different default proportional font and a default fixed-width font for each of the 22 language character sets supported by Microsoft Office XP.

- You can stipulate specific formatting options for various HTML elements. You can also choose to apply these options when you use FrontPage to open HTML files created in other applications.

- When viewing a Web page in the HTML pane, you can stipulate that different types of elements such as HTML tags, attributes, comments, and scripts should be different colors. FrontPage uses a variety of colors by default, but you can adjust these based on your preferences or needs.

■ You can specify the browsers, browser versions, and server applications that you want your FrontPage-based Web site to work with. FrontPage will warn you if you include in your Web site functionality that is not supported by the configurations you selected.

Take the time to explore the **Options** and **Page Options** dialog boxes, both of which are available from the **Tools** menu in FrontPage.

# Publishing a Web Site for Administrative Purposes

FP2002-6-1
FP2002e-10-3

Many server administration tasks can be carried out only on server-based Web sites; that is, Web sites that have been published to a Web server with FrontPage Server Extensions installed. Some of the FrontPage reports will work with a disk-based Web site, but you will require access to a Web server in order to complete most of the exercises in this chapter.

GardenCo

In this exercise, you will publish a disk-based Web site to your Web server so that you have something to work with in the following exercises.

The working folder for this exercise is *SBS\FrontPage\ManageSite*.

Follow these steps:

1   If FrontPage is not already open, start it now.

2   Open the **GardenCo** Web site located in the working folder.

3   On the **File** menu, click **Publish Web** to open the **Publish Destination** dialog box.

4   In the **Enter publish destination** box, type **http://**<server>/**ServerAdmin**, where <*server*> is the name of your FrontPage Server Extension-enabled Web server, and then click **OK**.

5   Click **OK** when prompted to create a new Web site at the specified location.

The **Publish Web** dialog box opens with the files to be copied indicated by green check marks.

6   Click **Publish** to publish the site to your Web server.

7   When a message announces that the publishing process is complete, click **Done** to close the message box.

8   On the **File** menu, click **Close Web**.

The disk-based version of the GardenCo Web site closes.

# Administering Your Web Site

FP2002e-1-2
FP2002e-1-3

If you are creating and publishing full-fledged Web sites, you are most likely using the services of either your own company's Information Technology (IT) department or a professional Web hosting company. In either case, someone else will be taking care of the site's administration.

If you don't have an IT department (or if *you* are the IT department) and you have published a Web site on a local server, you will need to take care of the site's administration yourself. Provided your Web server has the FrontPage Server Extensions installed, you can carry out the following administration tasks on the site's Web Site Administration page:

■ As the Web site's administrator, you can create new **subwebs** within the **root Web** site and specify whether the subweb will be a blank Web site or a Microsoft SharePoint team Web site. For example, The Garden Company might want to set up a For Members Only subweb of the main GardenCo Web site, where members of a special-interest club can meet online.

■ You can allow anyone to have access to your site and assign them to a specific group so you can control what they can see and do. These groups are called **roles**. Members of the general public who view your site are known as **anonymous users**. You can allow specific people to have specific access rights by assigning them to other roles. The default roles are **Administrator**, **Advanced author**, **Author**, **Contributor**, and **Browser**. Each role carries with it particular rights, or **privileges**, enabling or restricting access to view or modify the site. As the Web site's administrator, you can add, modify, and delete roles and privileges.

■ When you create a subweb, you can specify who can access it and, if necessary, designate a different administrator for the subweb. You can stipulate that subwebs should use the same permissions as their root Web site, or that they should have their own unique permissions.

■ You can activate FrontPage's built-in check in/check out system, which requires that anyone who wants to work with the site's files must first check them out. The files then have to be checked back in to have their changes recognized. This system, which is known as **source control**, is recommended only if you have multiple authors working on a single Web site and if work is likely to be lost if more than one person works on the same file at the same time.

■ For a **discussion Web site**, you can turn discussions on and off, allow local or remote discussions, and choose to automatically delete discussion items after a certain number of days. You can view and manage all discussions maintained on the Web server. If your Web server is also configured to send e-mail messages, you can view and manage all Web subscriptions maintained on the Web server.

■ You can track the usage of your site by having FrontPage maintain usage analysis logs. You can set the frequency of recurring usage analysis, delete stored usage data after a certain number of months, process log files for full days only, and (if your Web server has also been configured for e-mail) send e-mail confirmations to specified server or site administrators when the usage analysis processes have been run.

■ You can ensure that your site's links are all working by using a feature called **Server Health** to recalculate the links to and from every page of your Web site, including external links. You can use Server Health features to detect and repair potential server problems on a daily, weekly, or monthly schedule.

In this exercise, you will open a server-based Web site and explore the server administration options offered by FrontPage 2002. Then you will create a subweb and take a look at how you would go about setting its permissions.

There is no working folder on your computer for this exercise, but you must have access to the ServerAdmin Web site that you published to your Web server in the previous exercise.

Follow these steps:

Open

**1** On the Standard toolbar, click the **Open** button's down arrow to reveal a list of options, and then click **Open Web**.

FrontPage opens the **Open Web** dialog box.

Web Folders

**2** On the **Views** bar, click the **Web Folders** icon.

**3** In Web Folders view, click **ServerAdmin on** <server>, where <server> is your Web server, and then click **OK**.

The server-based Web site opens.

**4** On the **Tools** menu, point to **Server**, and then click **Administration Home**.

A Web Site Administration page like the one shown on the next page opens in your browser.

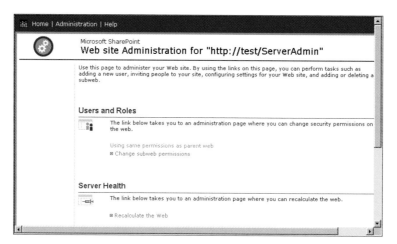

**5** Click **Create a subweb** to open this page in the browser:

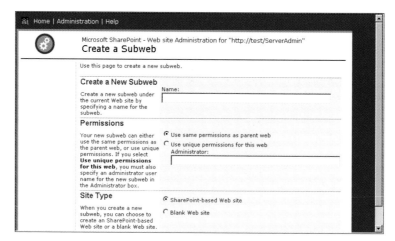

**6** In the **Create a New Subweb** area, type **My Subweb** in the **Name** box.

**7** In the **Permissions** area, select **Use unique permissions for this web**.

**8** In the **Administrator** box, type your own user name.

If you enter a name that FrontPage doesn't recognize, FrontPage will display an error when it tries to create the site.

**9** In the **Site type** area, select **SharePoint-based Web site**.

**10** Click **Submit**.

You will see an animated graphic while FrontPage processes your instructions. When FrontPage has finished creating the subweb, you return to the Web Site Administration page.

**11** Scroll to the bottom of the page, which looks like this:

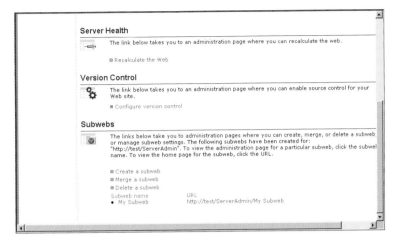

The options listed under **Subwebs** have changed to reflect the addition of your new subweb.

**12** Click the URL link to open your new SharePoint team subweb, which looks like this:

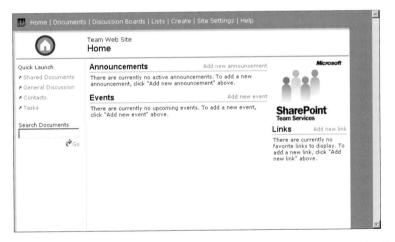

This is a typical SharePoint team Web site that can be customized to your liking.

**13** Close the browser to return to FrontPage.

**14** On the **View** menu, click **Refresh** to refresh the **Folder List** so that it shows My Subweb.

**15** On the **Tools** menu, point to **Server**, and then click **Permissions**.

The Permissions Administration page opens in the browser, as shown on the next page.

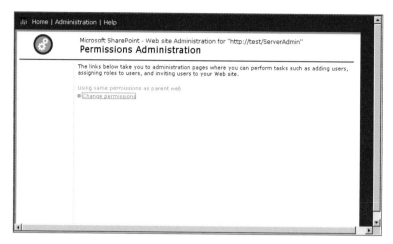

This page contains a link to the Change Subweb Permissions page, where you can set the permissions governing who can do what with this subweb.

## Tip

The Web Site Administration and Permissions Administration pages describe a lot of other useful features. It's worth checking them out to see if they can help you administer your site.

**16** Close the browser to return to FrontPage.

**17** On the **File** menu, click **Close Web** to close the current Web site.

## Generating Reports

FP2002-5-1
FP2002-6-1
FP2002-6-2
FP2002e-9-1
FP2002e-9-3
FP2002e-10-3

You can easily generate a wide variety of **reports** about the condition of a FrontPage-based Web site. The FrontPage 2002 reporting options range from interesting to useful, depending on the size of your Web site and the size of your organization.

After you have published a Web site to a Web server that is running FrontPage Server Extensions, you can generate five types of reports: Site Summary, Files, Problems, Workflow, and Usage. Each of these categories of reports has several options. In this exercise you will look at the first four types of reports, starting with the **Site Summary report**. This report does just what it says it does: it summarizes statistics for the entire site. Many of the statistical groupings are linked to more complete reports, and you can click any hyperlinked group name to see a more specific report.

FrontPage can produce **Files reports** about all the files in the Web site or about these specific groups of files:

- If your Web site has been running well for some time, you might want to see a report that includes only the files you have added recently. By default, any file that was added to the Web site fewer than 30 days ago is considered a recently added file.

■ You can also see a report that includes only files you have recently changed. Again, the timeframe for a file to be considered recently changed is 30 days.

■ FrontPage can identify the older files in the site. By default, any file that is more than 72 days old is considered an older file.

The definitions of *recently added*, *recently changed*, and *older* can be changed on the **Reports View** tab of the **Options** dialog box.

Whether your Web site is having problems or not, you should probably consider running **Problems reports** at regular intervals. FrontPage can report on the following types of problems:

■ You can tell FrontPage to identify unlinked files and broken hyperlinks.

■ You can ask for a report about any pages that are slow to download and that might cause frustration for your visitors. By default, any page that takes at least 30 seconds to download over a 28.8-Kbps connection is considered a slow page. This option can be changed on the **Reports View** tab of the **Options** dialog box.

■ FrontPage can tell you if any of the components inserted in your pages produce errors.

**Workflow reports** give you an idea of the current status of a site that is under development. (Some people think Web sites are *always* under development, and in fact, to stay current and to be appealing to repeat visitors, a Web site should always be changing.) You are able to review the status of files, see whom their development is assigned to, see whether or not files have been published, and see whether files are currently checked out to anyone. (This report is available only when **source control** has been turned on.)

In this exercise, you will open a server-based Web site, generate a series of reports about the Web site, and make changes to the site based on the reported information.

There is no working folder for this exercise, but you must have access to the ServerAdmin Web site that you published to your Web server in an earlier exercise.

Follow these steps:

Open Web

**1** On the Standard toolbar, click **Open Web** to open the **Open Web** dialog box.

**2** On the **Views** bar, click **Web Folders**.

**3** In Web Folders view, click **ServerAdmin on** <server>, where <server> is your Web server, and then click **OK** to open the server-based Web site.

**4** On the **View** menu, point to **Reports**.

**5** Click **Site Summary**.

FrontPage switches to Reports view, displays the Reporting toolbar, and generates this Site Summary report:

The Reporting toolbar

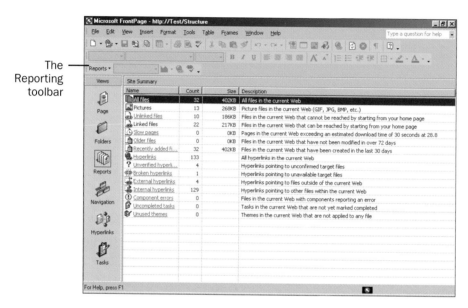

This report contains statistics on the entire site. Using buttons on the Reporting toolbar, you can look at each of the individual report groups that make up the Site Summary report.

**6** On the Reporting toolbar, click **Reports** to display the list of available reports, point to **Files**, and then click **All Files**.

FrontPage generates a report for every file in the site, like this:

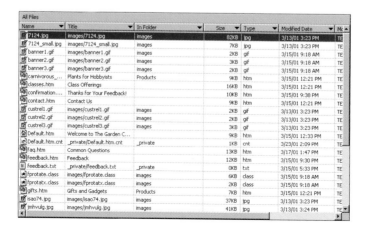

**7**   Click the **Type** column heading to sort the files alphabetically by type.

**8**   Click the **Type** column heading again to reverse the sort order.

**9**   Now click the down arrow at the right end of the **Type** column heading to display a list of the **Type** options, as shown here:

**10**   In the drop-down list, click **htm** to display report information for only the static HTML pages.

**11**   On the Reporting toolbar, click **Reports** to display the list of available reports, point to **Problems**, and click **Unlinked Files**.

FrontPage generates this report of every file contained within the Web site folder that can't be reached by a direct link:

| Unlinked Files | | | | | |
|---|---|---|---|---|---|
| Name | Title | In Folder | Modified By | Type | Modified Date |
| confirmation.... | Thanks for Your Feedback! | | TESTING\JOAN | htm | 3/15/01 9:38 PM |
| custrel1.gif | images/custrel1.gif | images | TESTING\JOAN | gif | 3/13/01 3:23 PM |
| custrel2.gif | images/custrel2.gif | images | TESTING\JOAN | gif | 3/13/01 3:23 PM |
| custrel3.gif | images/custrel3.gif | images | TESTING\JOAN | gif | 3/13/01 3:23 PM |
| Default.htm.cnt | _private/Default.htm.cnt | _private | TESTING\JOAN | cnt | 3/23/01 2:09 PM |
| feedback.htm | Feedback | | TESTING\JOAN | htm | 3/15/01 9:30 PM |
| feedback.txt | _private/feedback.txt | _private | TESTING\JOAN | txt | 3/15/01 5:33 PM |
| isao74.jpg | images/isao74.jpg | images | TESTING\JOAN | jpg | 3/13/01 3:23 PM |
| jmhvulg.jpg | images/jmhvulg.jpg | images | TESTING\JOAN | jpg | 3/13/01 3:24 PM |
| pxweser.jpg | images/pxweser.jpg | images | TESTING\JOAN | jpg | 3/13/01 3:24 PM |

Notice the three *custrel* image files that are not used in the Web site. You don't need them, so you can delete them from within Reports view.

**12**   In the list of unlinked files, click **custrel1.gif**.

**13**   Hold down the Shift key and press the ↓ key twice to select all three *custrel* images.

**14**   On the **Edit** menu, click **Delete**.

The **Confirm Delete** dialog box opens, as shown on the next page.

The three images to be deleted are listed in the **Items to delete** box.

**15** Click **Yes to All** to delete the three unused images.

FrontPage deletes the images and updates the Unlinked Files report.

## Tip

If the view of the report is not automatically updated, or if it is not updated correctly, press the ⌊F5⌋ key to refresh the screen.

**16** Select and delete the three remaining image files listed in the Unlinked Files report, but do not delete the other unlinked files because they are used for specific purposes within the site.

**17** On the Reporting toolbar, click **Reports** to display the list of available reports, point to **Workflow**, and click **Categories** to generate this Categories report:

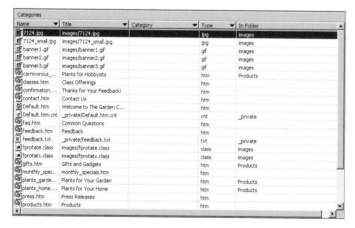

The **Category** column is blank because none of the Web site files are currently assigned to a category.

**18** Right-click the row containing 7124.jpg, and click **Properties** on the shortcut menu to open the file's **Properties** dialog box.

**19** Click the **Workgroup** tab to display these options:

Using categories makes it simple to easily identify a group of files for later use. With Office XP, you can assign categories to all of your documents. A number of categories are set up automatically: Business, Competition, Expense Report, Goals/Objectives, Ideas, In Process, Miscellaneous, Planning, Schedule, Travel, VIP, and Waiting. If you don't like these categories, you can create your own.

**20** Click the **Categories** button to display the **Master Category List** dialog box.

**21** Type **Carnivorous Plants** in the **New category** box, and click **Add**.

Your new category appears in the list, as shown here:

The new category has been added to the list.

**22** Type **Thumbnails** in the **New category** box, and click **Add** to add that category to the list.

**23** Click **OK** to close the **Master Category List** dialog box.

FrontPage has updated the **Available categories** list on the **Workgroup** tab to include the two new categories.

**24** In the **Available categories** list, select the **Carnivorous Plants** check box to assign the 7124.jpg file to that category.

The category appears in the **Item(s) belong to these categories** box.

**25** In the **Assigned to** area of the **Workgroup** tab, click **Names**.

The **Usernames Master List** dialog box opens so that you can designate the person assigned to work on the 7124.jpg file.

**26** In the **New username** box, type Graphic Artist, and then click **Add** to add that name to the list of usernames.

**27** Repeat the previous step to add Web Author to the list.

**28** Click **OK** to close the **Usernames Master List** dialog box.

**29** In the **Assigned to** drop-down list, click **Graphic Artist** to assign that person to work on the 7124.jpg file.

**30** In the **Review status** drop-down list, click **Pending Review**.

You can add additional review status options by clicking the **Statuses** button and adding the options to the **Review Status Master List**.

**31** Click **OK** to close the dialog box and apply your changes.

**32** Now right-click the row containing 7124_small.jpg, and choose **Properties** from the shortcut menu to open the file's **Properties** dialog box.

**33** On the **Workgroup** tab, select the **Carnivorous Plants** and **Thumbnails** check boxes to assign the file to those categories, and then click **OK**.

**34** Click the down arrow on the **Category** title bar to see the filter options, and click **(Custom...)** in the drop-down list to open this **Custom AutoFilter** dialog box:

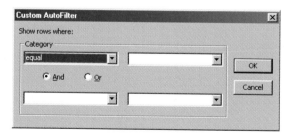

**35** Specify that you want to show only the files that have been assigned to the Thumbnails category by clicking **contains** in the first drop-down list and typing **Thumbnails** in the second drop-down list.

**36** Click **OK** to close the dialog box and apply your selections.

FrontPage regenerates the Categories report and this time shows only the 7124_small.jpg file.

**37** Display the filter list on the **Category** title bar again, and click **(All)** to regenerate the report for all the files.

**38** Close the Web site.

# Monitoring Statistics About Your Web Site

FP2002-5-1
FP2002-6-1
FP2002-6-2
FP2002e-9-2
FP2002e-10-3

Usage
analysis
reports
new for
**Office**XP

After you've published your Web site, it is likely that you will want to know something about the people who come to take a look at it. Armed with information about how your Web visitors use your site, how often they visit it, how they found it, and what operating systems they used, you can make better decisions about the effectiveness of certain elements of your site and how to modify and improve it. With FrontPage, you can have all of this information at your fingertips to analyze, compare, and study.

FrontPage can generate the following types of **Usage reports**:

■ **Usage Summary**, **Monthly Summary**, **Weekly Summary**, and **Daily Summary** reports provide information about the activity on your Web site. These reports summarize all of the other types of reports.

■ **Monthly Page Hits**, **Weekly Page Hits**, and **Daily Page Hits** reports tell you how many times each page of your site was visited during the specified time period. You might decide to eliminate pages that no one seems to be visiting, or you might want to investigate whether they are simply too hard to find.

■ **Visiting Users**, **Operating Systems**, and **Browsers** reports tell you how many different people visited your site during a specific period of time and what operating systems and browsers they used. When you know what kinds of browsers your visitors are using, you can make informed decision about the types of functionality to include on your site. For example, if you find that 95 percent of your visitors are using Microsoft Internet Explorer 4.0 or later, you can safely implement frames on your site without alienating your visitors.

■ **Referring Domains**, **Referring URLs**, and **Search Strings** reports tell you how visitors found your site. For example, if a visitor found you through MSN Search, Dogpile, or Yahoo!, this statistic will be indicated along with the exact search string that was used. You will also know if a visitor clicked a banner ad on another site to link through to your site. These reports help you measure the usefulness of different marketing efforts.

In this exercise, you will open a server-based Web site and investigate the types of visitor information that FrontPage can monitor and report on, including browsers and operating systems. You will also see how to find out where your visitors come from by identifying the referring domains and URLs, and the search strings used by visitors to find your site. Lastly, you will identify the most popular pages of your Web site, based on the number of times visitors come to each page.

There is no working folder on your computer for this exercise, but you must have access to the ServerAdmin Web site that you published to your Web server in an earlier exercise.

## Important

Usage reports are available only for root Web sites (not subwebs) hosted on Web servers running SharePoint Team Services or Microsoft FrontPage Server Extensions 2002. To display the full range of options explored in this exercise, the ServerAdmin Web site must be designated as a root Web site. Ask your Web server's administrator to take care of this task for you.

Follow these steps:

Open

**1** On the Standard toolbar, click the **Open Web** button to display the **Open Web** dialog box.

**2** On the **Views** bar, click **Web Folders**.

**3** In Web Folders view, click **ServerAdmin on <server>**, where <server> is your Web server, and then click **OK**.

The server-based Web site opens.

Reports

**4** If necessary, click the **Reports** icon on the **Views** bar to switch to Reports view.

**5** On the Reporting toolbar, click **Reports** to see the list of available reports, point to **Usage**, and click **Usage Summary**.

FrontPage generates a Usage Summary report like this one:

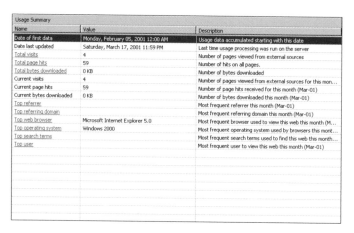

This report contains usage statistics on the entire site. Many of the groupings are linked to more complete reports, which you can see by clicking any hyperlinked group name.

**6** On the Reporting toolbar, click **Reports**, point to **Usage**, and then click **Monthly Page Hits**.

The Monthly Page Hits report looks like this:

**7** Scroll across the page to see the information included in the report.

Each month is tracked in its own column. (You specify the number of months on the **Reports View** tab of the **Options** dialog box.)

**8** On the Reporting toolbar, click **Reports**, point to **Usage**, and then click **Browsers** to see this report:

**9** Browse through the other reporting options.

Because your site is newly published, there won't be much data available to look at right now. But you can see the options offered for the future.

**10** Close the Web site.

**11** Quit FrontPage.

# Quick Reference

**Chapter    2    Creating a Web Site to Promote Yourself or Your Company**

Page       26    To create a Web site using a template

**1**    Select **Web Site Templates** in the **New from template** area of the **New Page or Web** task pane.

**2**    In the **Web Site Templates** dialog box, select the appropriate icon for the type of Web site you want to create.

**3**    Under **Options**, specify what you want to call your Web site and where you want to store it, and then click **OK**.

27    To open the task pane every time you start FrontPage

●    On the **Tools** menu, click **Options**, select the **Startup Task Pane** check box, and then click **OK**.

31    To create a Web site using a wizard

**1**    Click the **New** button's down arrow, and then click **Web**.

**2**    In the **Web Site Templates** dialog box, click the appropriate icon for the type of Web site you want to create, specify the location and name of your Web site, and then click **OK**.

34    To use the tasks list

**1**    With the Web site displayed in Tasks view, double-click the task you want to work on to open a **Task Details** dialog box.

**2**    Change any settings as necessary, and then click the **Start Task** button to open the page in Page view.

35    To insert a comment

●    On the **Insert** menu, click **Comment**.

35    To edit a comment

**1**    Double-click anywhere in the comment's text block to open an editing window.

**2**    Make your changes, and then click **OK**.

37    To insert a symbol

**1**    On the **Insert** menu, click **Symbol** to display the **Symbol** dialog box.

**2**    In the **Font** drop-down list, select the font that contains the symbol you want to use, and then click the symbol to select it.

**3**    Click **Insert**, and then click **Close**.

**39**   **To insert an existing file**

**1**   Click where you want the text to appear, or select the text to be replaced.

**2**   On the **Insert** menu, click **File** to open the **Insert File** dialog box.

**3**   Browse to the folder where the text you want to insert is stored.

**4**   In the **Files of type** drop-down list, select the appropriate option.

**5**   Select the file you want from the list of available files, and then click **Open** to insert the full text of the document in your Web page.

**40**   **To delete a table**

●   Select the table, right-click the selection, and then click ⌧ on the shortcut menu.

**40**   **To customize a page banner**

**1**   Right-click the page banner, and select **Page Banner Properties** from the shortcut menu.

**2**   Change the options you want, and then click **OK**.

**43**   **To increase the font size by one size**

Increase Font Size

●   Select the text you want to change, and on the Formatting toolbar, click the **Increase Font Size** button.

**45**   **To add a border to a paragraph**

**1**   Select the paragraph you want to change.

Borders

**2**   On the Formatting toolbar, click the **Borders** button's down arrow to display the **Borders** toolbar, and then click the desired option.

**45**   **To change paragraph formatting**

**1**   With the paragraph you want to change selected, click **Paragraph** on the **Format** menu.

**2**   Change the options you want, and then click **OK**.

**47**   **To create an embedded cascading style sheet in FrontPage**

**1**   On the **Format** menu, click **Style.**

**2**   Define your styles, and then click **OK**.

**47**   **To create an external cascading style sheet in FrontPage**

●   Select the CSS type from the options available on the **Style Sheets** tab of the **Page Templates** dialog box, and then click **OK**.

**47   To attach a style sheet in FrontPage**

● On the **Format** menu, click **Style Sheet Links**, and browse to the CSS file on your computer or (if you have an Internet connection) anywhere on the Web.

**48   To insert a hyperlink to a file**

**1** Click where you want the hyperlink to appear, and on the **Insert** menu, click **Hyperlink**.

Browse for File

**2** Click the **Browse for File** button, browse to the folder where the file is stored, select the file name, click **OK** to select the file, and then click **OK** again.

**51   To delete a Web site**

**1** On the **File** menu, click **Open Web**.

**2** In the **Open Web** dialog box, browse to the web file you want to delete, and then click **Open** to open the Web site.

**3** In the **Folder List**, right-click the top-level folder of the site, and then click **Delete** on the shortcut menu to open the **Confirm Delete** dialog box.

**4** Select the **Delete this Web entirely** option, and then click **OK** to delete the Web site.

**Chapter   3   Presenting Information in Lists and Tables**

**Page   56   To assign a style to selected text**

Style

Heading 1 ▾

● Select the text to which you want to assign a style, and on the **Style** drop-down list, click the style you want.

**57   To create a list as you type**

**1** Type the text you want to use as the first list item.

Numbering

**2** Click the **Numbering** button or the **Bullets** button on the Formatting toolbar to turn the paragraph into a numbered or bulleted item, and then press ⌷Enter⌷ to create a new line.

**58   To create a table**

Insert Table

**1** Click where you want the table to appear, and on the Standard toolbar, click the **Insert Table** button.

**2** Point to the first cell and hold down the left mouse button. Then, without releasing the button, drag the pointer until the number of rows and columns you want is highlighted (the grid will expand as you drag the mouse to the edge), and then release the mouse button.

58  **To convert existing text to a table**

1   Select the existing text, and on the **Table** menu, point to **Convert** and click **Text to Table**.

2   Select the options you want and click **OK**.

58  **To convert a table to text**

1   Select the table, and on the **Table** menu, point to **Convert** and click **Table to Text**.

2   In the **Convert Table to Text** dialog box, select the character you want to use to separate items, and then click **OK**.

60  **To insert a table with specific formatting settings**

1   Click where you want the table to appear.

2   On the **Table** menu, point to **Insert**, and then click **Table**.

3   Specify the options that you want in the **Size** and **Layout** sections, **and click OK.**

61  **To draw a table**

1   On the **Table** menu, click **Draw Table**.

2   Click where you want to position the top-left corner of the table, and drag the pencil pointer to where you want to position the bottom-right corner.

3   Using the pencil pointer, draw lines to create the table's rows and columns.

65  **To insert a row in a table**

1   Click anywhere in the row that sits above or below where you want the new row to appear.

2   On the **Table** menu, point to **Insert**, and then click **Rows or Columns**.

3   Specify how many rows you want to insert and whether the row(s) should appear above or below the current selection, and then click **OK**.

65  **To delete a column in a table**

1   Click anywhere in the column you want to delete.

2   On the **Table** menu, point to **Select**, and then click **Column**.

3   Right-click the selection, and then click **Delete Cells** on the shortcut menu.

65  **To adjust the size of table columns so that all entries fit on one line**

1   Point to the right border of the column you want to adjust.

2   When the pointer changes to a double-headed arrow, double-click the border to resize the column so that it can hold all its entries on one line.

**65**  **To adjust the size of table columns to the exact width of their contents**

- Click anywhere in the table, and on the **Table** menu, click **AutoFit to Contents**.

**66**  **To change a table's properties**

1. Right-click anywhere in the table, and then click **Table Properties** on the shortcut menu.
2. In the **Table Properties** dialog box, change the options you want, and then click **OK**.

**67**  **To make all columns in a table the same width**

- Select the columns, and on the **Table** menu, click **Distribute Columns Evenly**.

**67**  **To change a cell's background color in a table**

1. Select the cells you want to format, right-click the selection, and then click **Cell Properties** on the shortcut menu.
2. In the **Background** area, click the **Color** box's down arrow.
3. Select the color you want from the palette that is displayed or click **More Colors** to select a custom color, and then click **OK**.

**69**  **To apply an AutoFormat to a table**

1. Click anywhere in the table.
2. On the **Table** menu, click **Table AutoFormat**.
3. Scroll through the **Formats** list and select the format you want, select any options you want in the **Apply special formats** section, and then click **OK**.

**70**  **To merge cells in a table**

- Select the cells you want to merge, and on the **Table** menu, click **Merge Cells**.

**70**  **To split one cell into multiple cells in a table**

1. Right-click the cell and click **Split Cells** on the shortcut menu.
2. In the **Split Cells** dialog box, specify the number of rows or columns you want to split the merged cell into, and then click **OK**.

**70**  **To split a table into multiple tables**

- Click in the row where you want the first table to end, and on the **Table** menu, click **Split Table**.

**To add a caption to a table**

**1** Click anywhere in the table.

**2** On the **Table** menu, point to **Insert** and then click **Caption**.

**3** Type the text you want for the table caption.

**Chapter 4** **Enhancing Your Web Site with Graphics**

**To insert clip art in a page**

**1** Click where you want the clip art to appear.

**2** On the **Insert** menu, point to **Picture**, and then click **Clip Art**.

**3** Make sure that **All media types** is displayed in the **Results should be** box, and then search for the type of clip art you want by typing a keyword in the **Search text** box and clicking **Search**.

**4** Right-click the graphic you want to use, and then click **Insert** on the shortcut menu.

**To convert a graphic to GIF or JPG format**

**1** In Page view, right-click the graphic, and then click **Picture Properties** on the shortcut menu.

**2** In the **Type** area of the **General** tab, click **GIF** or **JPG**, and then click **OK**.

**To insert a picture file on a page**

**1** Click where you want the picture to appear.

**2** On the **Insert** menu, point to **Picture**, and then click **From File** to open the **Picture** dialog box.

**3** In the **Picture** dialog box, browse to the folder that contains the file you want to use, and then click **Insert** to insert the graphic in the Web page at the insertion point.

**To crop a graphic**

Crop

**1** Click the picture to select it, and then click the **Crop** button on the Pictures toolbar.

**2** Drag the handles of the crop box until the box contains the section of the graphic you want to keep.

**3** Click the **Crop** button again to crop the picture to the specified shape and size.

**84**    **To size a graphic**

**1**    Double-click the picture to display a **Picture Properties** dialog box.

**2**    Select the **Specify size** check box, and set the **Width** to the setting you want. Make sure that the **Keep aspect ratio** check box is selected, and then click **OK**.

**85**    **To convert a graphic to black and white**

Color

●    Select the graphic you want to recolor, click **Color** on the Pictures toolbar, and then click **Grayscale** on the **Color** drop-down menu.

**86**    **To create a thumbnail**

Auto Thumbnail

**1**    With the picture selected, click the **Auto Thumbnail** button on the Pictures toolbar.

**2**    Drag the handles surrounding the selected thumbnail to resize it.

**3**    To test the thumbnail link, click the **Preview** button at the bottom of the Page view editing window to switch to the Preview pane, and then click the thumbnail to open the original picture in the Preview pane.

**89**    **To draw a horizontal rule**

**1**    Click where you want the line to appear.

**2**    On the **Insert** menu, click **Horizontal Line**.

**3**    Right-click the line, click **Horizontal Line Properties** on the shortcut menu, and then click **OK**.

**90**    **To insert a drawing with pre-defined shapes**

**1**    On the **Insert** menu, point to **Picture**, and then click **New Drawing**.

**2**    On the Drawing toolbar, click **AutoShapes** to see the menu of available shapes.

**3**    Click the shape you want, and then click the area where you want the shape to appear.

**93**    **To group shapes together**

**1**    Select a shape, hold down the [ shift ] key, and then click any other shapes you want to be included in the group.

**2**    Right-click the selected elements, and on the shortcut menu, point to **Grouping**, and then click **Group**.

**96**    **To create a photo gallery**

**1**    Click where you want the photo gallery to appear.

**2**    On the **Insert** menu, click **Web Component**, and then select **Photo Gallery**.

**3**    In the **Choose a Photo Gallery Option** box, select the option you want, and then click **Finish**.

96    **To change a photo gallery's layout**

**1**    Right-click the **Photo Gallery** Web component in Page view, and then click **Photo Gallery Properties** on the shortcut menu to display the **Photo Gallery Properties** dialog box.

**2**    On the **Layout** tab, select a different layout option, and then click **OK** to reformat your photo gallery.

99    **To add fancy text with WordArt**

**1**    Click where you want to add the fancy text, point to **Picture** on the **Insert** menu, and then click **WordArt**.

**2**    Select the style you want in the **Word Art Gallery** dialog box, and then click **OK** to display the **Edit WordArt Text** dialog box.

**3**    Enter the text, format it as necessary, and then click **OK** to close the dialog box and apply your settings.

**Chapter    5    Creating a Web Site from Scratch**
Page    104    **To create a Web site from scratch**

**1**    If the **New Page or Web** task pane is not displayed, point to **New** on the **File** menu, and then click **Page or Web** to open it.

**2**    In the **New Page or Web** task pane, click **Empty Web**.

**3**    Specify the location and name of your new Web site, and then click **OK**.

107    **To add a blank page to a Web site**

Create a new normal page

**1**    With the Web site open, click the **Create a new normal page** button on the Standard toolbar.

**2**    On the **File** menu, click **Save As** to open the **Save As** dialog box.

**3**    Enter the name you want, and then click **Save**.

109    **To add a Web page title**

**1**    Display the page you want to add a title to in Page view.

**2**    On the **File** menu, click **Save As**, and then click the **Change title** button.

**3**    Replace the page title with the text you want, and then click **OK** to close the **Set Page Title** dialog box.

**111   To change the background of a Web page**

**1**   With the Web page open, click **Background** on the **Format** menu.

**2**   In the **Colors** section, click the down arrow at the right end of the **Background** box to expand the color selection area. Click the color you want or click **More Colors** to open the **More Colors** dialog box and select another color, and then click **OK**.

**113   To add a watermark to the background of a page**

**1**   With the page open, click **Background** on the **Format** menu.

**2**   In the **Formatting** section of the **Page Properties** dialog box, select the **Background picture** check box.

**3**   Click the **Browse** button, locate the folder that contains the file you want to use, select the file name, and then click **Open**.

**4**   Select the **Watermark** check box to keep the background image stationary when the page scrolls, and then click **OK**.

**117   To add a border to a page**

**1**   Press Ctrl+A to select the entire page.

**2**   On the **Format** menu, click **Borders and Shading**.

**3**   On the **Borders** tab, select the options you want, click the buttons in the **Preview** area to apply the settings to the appropriate areas, and then click **OK**.

**118   To add shading to a page**

**1**   Press Ctrl+A to select the entire page.

**2**   On the **Format** menu, click **Borders and Shading**.

**3**   On the **Shading** tab, select the options you want, and then click **OK**.

**120   To create a shared border on a page**

**1**   With the page open, click **Shared Borders** on the **Format** menu.

**2**   In the **Shared Borders** dialog box, select the options you want, and then click **OK**.

**121   To insert a page banner**

**1**   With the page displayed, click **Page Banner** on the **Insert** menu.

**2**   Select the option you want, and then click **OK**.

**122   To insert a date stamp**

**1**   Click where you want the date stamp to appear.

**2**    On the **Insert** menu, click **Date and Time**.

**3**    Select the options you want, and then click **OK**.

125    **To apply a theme to a page**

**1**    With the page displayed in Page view, click **Theme** on the **Format** menu to open the **Themes** dialog box.

**2**    In the **Apply Theme to:** area, click **Selected page(s)**.

**3**    Select the theme, select the color scheme, banners, buttons, bullets, and other graphic elements, and then click **OK**.

127    **To remove a theme from a Web site**

**1**    With the Web site open in Page view, click **Theme** on the **Format** menu.

**2**    Select **No Theme** from the list of themes, and then click **OK**.

128    **To create a custom theme**

**1**    With a new page open, click **Theme** on the **Format** menu to open the **Themes** dialog box.

**2**    Click the theme you want to base your custom theme on, click the **Modify** button, and select the options you want to modify.

**3**    In the **Themes** dialog box, click the **Save As** button in the modification area to display the **Save Theme** dialog box.

**4**    Type the name of your new theme, and then click **OK**.

**Chapter   6**    **Changing Web Page Layout**

Page    136    **To use a table to create a page template**

**1**    In a new page, point to **Insert** on the **Table** menu, and then click **Table**.

**2**    Set the options you want and then click **OK**.

**3**    Insert text and graphics in the table as desired.

Insert Table

**4**    Click the **Insert Table** button, and use the grid to create the table you want.

141    **To insert hyperlinks to each page in a Web site**

**1**    Select the entry in a TOC for one of the pages in your site.

Insert
Hyperlink

**2**    On the Standard toolbar, click the **Insert Hyperlink** button to open the **Insert Hyperlink** dialog box.

**3**    Click the **Existing File or Web Page** and **Current Folder** buttons to browse for a file in your current folder.

**4**    Click the appropriate file name and click **OK**.

142 **To insert a bookmark**

● Select the place, word, or phrase that you want to bookmark and click **Book-mark** on the **Insert** menu.

142 **To create a hyperlink to a bookmark**

1 Insert a hyperlink as usual.

2 In the **Insert Hyperlink** dialog box, click the page on which the bookmark appears, and then click the **Bookmark** button to show a list of all the available bookmarks on that page.

3 Select the bookmark you want and click **OK**.

143 **To insert an e-mail address hyperlink**

1 Select the word or phrase you want to use as the hyperlink, and then click the **Insert Hyperlink** button.

2 In the **Insert Hyperlink** dialog box, select **E-mail Address** on the **Link to** bar.

3 In the **E-mail address** and Subject boxes, type the appropriate information, and then click **OK**.

145 **To apply a template to an existing page**

1 With the template open in Page view, open the home page of the Web site to which you want to apply the template.

2 Click the template's page tab to switch to that page.

3 On the **Edit** menu, click **Select All** to select the entire template.

Copy

4 On the Standard toolbar, click the **Copy** button to copy the template to the Office Clipboard.

5 Click the home page's page tab to switch to that page.

Paste

6 On the Standard toolbar, click the **Paste** button to paste the template into the page.

7 Repeat this procedure to apply the template to each of the remaining files in your Web site.

147 **To create a frames page using a template**

1 On the **File** menu, point to **New** and click **Page or Web** to open the **New Page or Web** task pane.

2 In the **New from template** section, click **Page Templates** to open the **Page Templates** dialog box, and then click the **Frames Pages** tab.

3 Click the template you want, and then click **OK** to close the dialog box and create the new page.

**148** **To insert a new page in a frames page**

**1** Click **New Page** button to create a new content page linked to the frames page.

**2** Click inside the frame, and then click the **Save** button on the toolbar.

**3** In the **File name** box, type the name you want.

**4** Click **Save** to close the **Save As** dialog box.

**5** To save the frameset, browse to the appropriate storage location in the **Save In** drop-down list of the **Save As** dialog box that appears, and then click **OK**.

**149** **To split one frame into two frames:**

**1** Select the frame you want to split, and click **Split Frame** on the **Frames** menu.

**2** In the **Split Frame** dialog box, select **Split into columns** or **Split into rows**, and then click **OK**.

**151** **To add an existing page to a frames page**

**1** Open the frames page, and then click **Set Initial Page** in the appropriate frame.

**2** Click the page you want to add to the frame, and then click **OK**.

**155** **To format a frame's borders**

**1** Right-click the appropriate frame, and then click **Frame Properties** on the shortcut menu.

**2** In the **Options** area, click the **Frames Page** button.

**3** Set the options you want, and then click **OK** twice.

**156** **To change the content of a frames page**

**1** Right-click in the appropriate frame, and then click **Open Page in New Window** to open the file in the Page view editing window.

**2** Make the necessary changes, save the file, and return to the frames page file to check that the page has been updated.

**Chapter 7** **Enhancing the Capabilities of Your Web Site**

Page **163** **To add a subweb to a Web site**

● In the **Folder List**, right-click the folder that contains the pages of the subweb, click **Convert to Web** on the shortcut menu, and click **Yes** in the warning message.

**167  To insert a links bar on a page**

**1**  Click in the shared border where you want the links bar to appear.

**2**  On the **Insert** menu, click **Navigation**, and follow through the wizard's instructions.

**3**  In the **Link Bar Properties** dialog box, select the display options you want, and then click **OK**.

**170  To create an image map**

**1**  With the object selected that you want to convert to an image map, click the **Hotspot** button you want to use on the Pictures toolbar.

**2**  Move the pencil pointer to the object, and drag to create the hotspot.

**3**  Double-click to finish drawing the hotspot.

**4**  In the **Insert Hyperlink** dialog box, browse to the appropriate folder, select the file, and then click **OK** to insert a hyperlink from the object to the selected file.

**171  To identify hotspots on a page**

Highlight
Hotspots

●  On the Pictures toolbar, click the **Highlight Hotspots** button.

**171  To change a hotspot link**

**1**  Right-click the hotspot and select **Picture Hotspot Properties** from the shortcut menu to open the **Edit Hyperlink** dialog box.

**2**  Make the necessary changes and click **OK**.

**173  To insert a hyperlink to a subweb**

**1**  Select the text you want to use as the hyperlink, and then click the **Insert Hyperlink** button.

**2**  Browse to the home page file of the subweb you want to link to, and then click **OK**.

**174  To insert a hyperlink to an external Web site**

**1**  Select the text you want to use as the hyperlink, and then click the **Insert Hyperlink** button.

**2**  In the **Insert Hyperlink** dialog box, type the URL of the Web site you want to link to into the **Address** box.

**3**  Set the page defaults, and click **OK** twice.

**179    To insert a weather forecast on a page**

Web
Component

**1**    Click where you want the weather forecast to appear and then click the **Web Component** button on the Standard toolbar.

**2**    Click **MSNBC Components** in the **Component type** list, click **Weather forecast from MSNBC** in the **Choose a MSNBC component** box, and then click **Finish**.

**3**    In the **Weather forecast from MSNBC Properties** dialog box, type the city you want in the **Search for a city by name or U.S. ZIP code** box, click **Next**. and then click **Finish**.

**181    To add a hit counter to a page**

**1**    Click where you want the hit counter to appear, and then click **Web Component**, on the **Insert** menu.

**2**    In the **Component type** box, click **Hit Counter**. Then click the selection you want in the **Choose a counter style** box, and then click **Finish**.

**3**    Select the **Reset counter to** check box, and enter the number you want in the adjacent box.

**4**    Select the **Fixed number of digits** check box, enter the setting you want in the adjacent box, and then click **OK**.

**183    To add a search component that searches the current Web site**

**1**    Position the insertion point where you want the search component to appear, and then click the **Web Component** button on the Standard toolbar.

**2**    In the **Component type** box, click **Web Search**, click **Finish** to accept **Current Web** as the option in the **Choose a type of search** box, click OK and then press Enter.

**184    To add a search component that searches the Web**

**1**    Position the insertion point where you want the search component to appear, and then click the **Web Component** button on the Standard toolbar.

**2**    Click **MSN Components** in the **Component type** box, click **Search the Web with MSN** in the **Choose a MSN component** box, and then click **Finish**.

**186    To create a marquee**

**1**    Click where you want the marquee to appear, and then click the **Web Component** button on the Standard toolbar.

**2**    With **Dynamic Effects** selected in the **Component type** list, click **Marquee** in the **Choose an effect** box, and then click **Finish**.

**3** In the **Text** box, type the text you want to appear in the marquee, change any other settings as necessary, and then click **OK**.

187 **To format a marquee**

**1** Right-click the marquee text, and then click **Marquee Properties** on the shortcut menu.

**2** In the **Marquee Properties** dialog box, change any settings as necessary, and then click **OK**.

**3** With the marquee text still selected in the Normal pane, use buttons on the Formatting toolbar to format the marquee's text.

187 **To create a banner ad**

**1** Click an insertion point where you want the banner ad to appear, and then click the **Web Component** button on the Standard toolbar.

**2** With **Dynamic Effects** selected in the **Component type** list, click **Banner Ad Manager** in the **Choose an effect** list, and then click **Finish**.

**3** Enter the dimensions of the banner ad and any other options you want.

**4** If you are posting the banner ad on another site, enter your own URL in the **Link to** box to direct visitors to your site.

**Chapter 8 Communicating with Your Visitors**

Page 193 **To insert a page component in a Web site**

**1** With the page open, click **Web Component** on the **Insert** menu, and then click **Included Content** in the Component type list.

**2** In the **Choose a type of content** list, click **Page**, and then click **Finish**.

**3** Click the **Browse** button, click the file name you want, and then click **OK** twice.

195 **To insert a scheduled picture component**

Web Component

**1** Click an insertion point where you want the scheduled picture to appear, and then click the **Web Component** button on the Standard toolbar to display the **Insert Web Component** dialog box.

**2** In the **Component type** list, click **Included Content**.

**3** In the **Choose a type of content** list, click **Picture Based On Schedule**, and then click **Finish**.

**4** Click the **Browse** button, and select the file you want or type its path in the **URL** box, and then click **OK**.

**5** In the **Before and after the scheduled time** box, select another file or type its path.

**6** Set the **Starting** date and time and the **Ending** date and time to the range you want, and then click **OK**.

198 **To insert a feedback form in a Web site**

**1** With the Web site open, point to **New** on the **File** menu, and then click **Page or Web**.

**2** In the **New from template** area, click **Page Templates**.

**3** On the **General** tab, click **Feedback Form**, and then click **OK**.

201 **To add a confirmation page to a Web site**

**1** With the Web site open, point to **New** on the **File** menu, and then click **Page or Web**.

**2** In the **New from template** area, click **Page Templates** to open the **Page Templates** dialog box.

**3** Click **Confirmation Form**, and then click **OK**.

202 **To add a Frequently Asked Questions page using a template**

**1** With the Web site open, point to **New** on the **File** menu, and then click **Page or Web**.

**2** In the **New from template** area, click **Page Templates** to open the **Page Templates** dialog box.

**3** Click **Frequently Asked Questions**, and then click **OK** to generate the new page.

206 **To add a Search page to a Web site**

**1** With the Web site open, point to **New** on the **File** menu, and then click **Page or Web**.

**2** In the **New from template** section, click **Page Templates** to open the **Page Templates** dialog box.

**3** Click **Search Page**, and then click **OK**.

Chapter 9 **Creating a Web Site to Support Team Projects**

Page 211 **To create a project-management Web site using a template**

**1** With FrontPage started, point to **New** on the **File** menu, and then click **Page or Web**.

**309**

**2** In the **New from template** area, click **Web Site Templates**, and then click the **Project Web** icon.

**3** In the **Specify the location of the new web** dialog box, type the path you want, and then click **OK**.

**215 To create a discussion Web site using a template**

**1** With FrontPage started, point to **New** on the **File** menu, and then click **Page or Web**.

**2** In the **New from template** area, click **Web Site Templates**.

**3** In the **Web Site Templates** dialog box, click **Discussion Web Wizard**.

**4** In the **Specify the location of the new web** box, type the path you want, and then click **OK**.

**219 To publish a Web site to a Web server**

**1** With the Web site open, click **Publish Web** on the **File** menu.

**2** In the **Enter publish destination** box, type **http://**<server>/<Web site>, substituting the name of your Web server for <*server*>, and the name of your Web site for <*Web site*> and then click **OK**.

**3** Click **OK** when prompted to create a new Web site at the specified location, and then click the **Publish** button to complete the publication of the site.

**224 To add a document library to a SharePoint team Web site**

**1** With the Web site open, click **New Document Library** on the **Document Libraries** page.

**2** In the **Name** box, type the name you want for the library, and then enter a description of the library in the **Description** box.

**3** In the **Template Type** drop-down list, click **Blank Microsoft FrontPage Document** to indicate that the default document type is a Web page.

**4** In the **Navigation** section, click **Yes** if you want to display the new document library on the site's Quick Launch bar, and then click the **Create** button to create the new document library.

**227 To turn on source control**

**1** With the **Folder List** displayed, click **Web Settings** on the **Tools** menu.

**2** On the **General** tab, select the **Use document check-in and check-out** check box, and then click **OK**.

229  **To check a file in or out of a Web site**

**1**  To check out a file, right-click any file name in the **Folder List**, and then click **Check Out** on the shortcut menu.

**2**  To check a file back in, right-click the file name in the **Folder List**, and then click **Check In** on the shortcut menu.

**Chapter  10**  **Connecting Your Web Site to a Database**

Page  232  **To connect a Web site to a database**

**1**  With the Web site open, click **Web Settings** on the **Tools** menu to open the **Web Settings** dialog box.

**2**  On the **Database** tab, click **Add**, and in the **Name** box, type a name for the database.

**3**  In the **Type of connection** area, click **File or folder in current Web**, and then click **Browse** to open the **Database Files in Current Web** dialog box.

**4**  Move to the appropriate storage folder, click the database file name, and then click **OK** to return to the **New Database Connection** dialog box.

**5**  Click **OK** to return to the **Web Settings** dialog box, click **Verify**, and then click **OK** to close the **Web Settings** dialog box.

236  **To create a searchable database in a published Web site**

Open

**1**  On the Standard toolbar, click the **Open** button's down arrow, and then click **Open Web** in the drop-down list of options.

Web Folders

**2**  In the **Open Web** dialog box, click **Web Folders**, click the Web site you want, and then click **Open**.

**3**  On the **File** menu, point to **New,** and click **Page or Web**.

**4**  In the **New from template** area, click **Web Site Templates**.

**5**  Click the **Database Interface Wizard** icon.

**6**  In the **Options** area, select the **Add to current Web** check box, and click **OK**.

**7**  Click **Use an existing database connection**, check that the database connection you want is selected in the drop-down list, and then click **Next**.

244  **To modify a database results page**

**1**  Display the results page and then right-click anywhere in the Database Results region.

**2**  On the shortcut menu, click **Database Results Properties**.

**3**  Follow the **Database Results Wizard's** instructions, and then click **Finish** on the wizard's last page.

**Chapter 11   Publishing Your Web Site**
Page   260   **To install the Personal Web Server**

**1**   At the left end of the taskbar at the bottom of the screen, click **Start**, point to **Settings**, and then click **Control Panel**.

**2**   Double-click **Add/Remove Programs** to open the **Add/Remove Programs Properties** dialog box, and then click the **Windows Setup** tab.

**3**   In the **Components** list, click the words **Internet Tools** (not the check box), and then click **Details** to see the available Internet Tools components.

**4**   In the **Components** list, select the **Personal Web Server** check box, and then click **OK** to close the **Internet Tools** dialog box.

**5**   Click **OK** again to close the **Add/Remove Programs Properties** dialog box and install the Personal Web Server.

**6**   Insert the Windows 98 CD-ROM in the drive, and then click **OK**.

**7**   If necessary, browse to the file called *pws_main.htm.,* click **OK**, *and then* close the Control Panel window.

**8**   In Windows Explorer, browse to the *add-ons\pws* folder on the Windows 98 CD-ROM, and double-click **setup.exe**.

**9**   Follow the instructions of the **Microsoft Personal Web Server Setup Wizard, and then click Finish** on the wizard's last page to close the program.

**10**   Click **Yes** to restart your computer.

265   **To install the FrontPage Server Extensions**

**1**   If necessary, start your Internet connection. Open your Web browser, and in the **Address** box, type http://www.microsoft.com/frontpage.

**2**   In the Resources area of the Web page, click **FrontPage Server Extensions**, and then click the **Download the FrontPage Server Extensions for Microsoft Windows-based Servers** link.

**3**   Click the link to the download file for your operating system, click **Run this program from its current location**, and then click **OK**.

**4**   Select the **Close this dialog box when download completes** check box, if it is not already selected, and then click **Yes** to continue.

**5**   Work through the dialog boxes of the setup program, and when the installation is complete, click **Yes** in the message box to restart your computer.

267   **To publish a disk-based Web site to a local folder**

**1**   On the **File** menu, click **Open Web**, select the Web site you want to publish, and then click **Open**.

**2** On the **File** menu, click **Publish Web**, and then click the **Browse** button to open the **New Publish Location** dialog box, and browse to the appropriate folder.

Create New
Folder

**3** Click the **Create New Folder** button on the dialog box's toolbar to open the **New Folder** dialog box.

**4** In the **Name** box, type the name you want for the folder, and then click **OK** to return to the **New Publish Location** dialog box with your newly created folder selected.

**5** Click **Open** to return to the **Publish Destination** dialog box, and then click **OK**.

**6** Click **OK** to create the new Web, and then click the **Options** button to change any options as necessary.

**7** Click **Publish** to publish the Web site to your local drive.

271 **To publish a single page of a Web site**

● With the Web site open in FrontPage, right-click the file name in the **Folder List** or in Folders view, and click **Publish Selected Files** on the shortcut menu.

271 **To publish a disk-based Web site to your personal Web server**

**1** With the Web site open, click **Publish Web** on the **File** menu.

**2** To change the publish destination shown in the **Publish to** box, click **Change**.

**3** In the **Publish Destination** dialog box, type **http://localhost** in the **Enter publish destination** box, and then click **OK**.

**4** Click **Publish, click Continue**, and then click the view option you want.

272 **To publish a Web site from a personal Web server to a remote Web server**

**1** With the Web site open in your personal Web server, click **Publish Web** on the **File** menu.

**2** To change the publish destination shown in the **Publish to** box, click **Change**.

**3** In the **Enter publish destination** box, type **http://**<server>**/PublishServer**, where <server> is the name of your Web server, and then click **OK**.

**4** Click **OK** to create a new Web site at the specified location, and then Click **Publish**.

273 **To publish a FrontPage Web site from a remote server to a local folder or to your personal Web server**

**1** On the **File** menu, click **Open Web**.

**2**    In the **Web name** box, type the URL or IP address of the remote Web site preceded by *http://* to indicate that it is a server-based site (for example, **http://www.microsoft.com/frontpage/** or **http://207.46.131.13/frontpage/**), and then click **Open**.

**3**    Supply a valid user name and password if prompted, and then click **OK**.

**4**    On the **File** menu, click **Publish Web**.

**5**    In the **Publish Destination** box, type the disk or server location where you want to publish the Web site, and then click **OK**.

**6**    In the **Publish Web** dialog box, click **Publish**.

**Chapter 12**    **Managing Your Web Site**

Page    279    **To create a subweb and set its permissions**

Open

**1**    On the Standard toolbar, click the **Open** button's down arrow, and then click **Open Web**.

Web Folders

**2**    On the **Views** bar, click the **Web Folders** icon.

**3**    In Web Folders view, click **ServerAdmin on** *<server>*, where *<server>* is your Web server, and then click **OK**.

**4**    On the **Tools** menu, point to **Server**, and then click **Administration Home**.

**5**    Click **Create a subweb**, fill in the options as necessary, and then click **Submit**.

**6**    On the **Tools** menu, point to **Server**, and then click **Permissions**.

**7**    Select the desired option, fill in the options as necessary, and then click **Submit**.

284    **To generate a report about a Web site**

**1**    With the Web site open, point to **Reports** on the **View** menu.

**2**    On the Reporting toolbar, click **Reports** to display the list of available reports, and then click the report you want to run.

286    **To assign a file to a category**

**1**    Right-click the row containing the appropriate file, and then click **Properties** on the shortcut menu to open the file's **Properties** dialog box.

**2**    Click the **Workgroup** tab, and in the **Available categories** list, select the appropriate check box to assign the file to that category, and then click **OK**.

287    **To create a new category for files**

**1**    Right-click the row containing the appropriate file, and then click **Properties** on the shortcut menu to open the file's **Properties** dialog box.

**2** Click the **Workgroup** tab, and then click the **Categories** button to display the **Master Category List** dialog box.

**3** Type the name of the new category in the **New category** box, click **Add**, and then click **OK.**

288 **To assign a file to a person in your workgroup**

**1** Right-click the row containing the appropriate file, and then click **Properties** on the shortcut menu to open the file's **Properties** dialog box.

**2** Click the **Workgroup** tab, and in the **Assigned to** area, click the name you want to assign that person to work on the file, and then click **OK**.

288 **To add a new user name to a workgroup**

**1** Right-click the row containing the appropriate file, and then click **Properties** on the shortcut menu to open the file's **Properties** dialog box.

**2** Click the **Workgroup** tab, and in the **Assigned to** area, click **Names**.

**3** In the **New username** box, type the name you want, click **Add** to add that name to the list of usernames, and then click **OK**.

290 **To generate a usage report on a server-based Web site**

**1** On the Standard toolbar, click **Open Web** to display the **Open Web** dialog box.

**2** On the **Views** bar, click **Web Folders**.

**3** In Web Folders view, click *<Web site>* **on** *<server>*, where *<Web site>* is your Web site and *<server>* is your Web server, and then click **OK**.

Reports

**4** Click the **Reports** icon on the **Views** bar to switch to Reports view.

**5** On the Reporting toolbar, click **Reports** to see the list of available reports, point to **Usage**, and then click **Usage Summary**.

**6** On the Reporting toolbar, click **Reports**, point to **Usage**, and then click the option you want.

# Glossary

**absolute path**   A designation of the location of a file including the root directory and the descending series of subdirectories leading to the end file.

**access violation**   A type of error caused by attempting to access a page or site that is not allowed.

**Active Server Pages (ASP)**   An Internet Information Server (IIS) feature that combines HTML and active scripts or components to create Web pages that are stored on the Web server and generate different views of the data based on input from a Web visitor or from a program.

**ActiveX Data Objects (ADO)**   A collection of programming objects that facilitate the reading and modification of databases with simple computer languages.

**anchor tag**   A tag in an HTML document that defines a bookmark or a link to a bookmark, Web page, Web site, or e-mail address.

**anonymous user**   A member of the general public who views a Web site.

**article**   A message posted to discussion Web sites.

**ASP page**   *See* Active Server Pages.

**bookmark**   An anchor tag that defines a specific location in an HTML document.

**Boolean query**   A True or False query that utilizes logical operators including AND, OR, IF THEN, EXCEPT, and NOT.

**border**   The edge or visible frame surrounding a workspace, window, document, table, cell, or graphic.

**browser sniffer**   A program that detects the Web browser and version used by each Web visitor.

**bulleted list**   An unordered list of concepts, items, or options.

**cascading style sheet**   A file attached to an HTML document that controls the formatting of page elements such as color, font, and spacing.

**cell padding**   The space between the borders of a cell and the text inside it.

**cell**   The intersection of a row and a column in a table or spreadsheet. A cell is displayed as a rectangular space that can hold text, a value, or a formula.

**child page**   A Web page that is subordinate to another Web page, known as the parent page.

**clip art**   Graphics that can be copied and incorporated into other documents.

**collaboration site**   A Web site created, maintained, and used by a group of people rather than by a single person.

**column**   The vertical line of cells in a spreadsheet or table.

**comment**   A note embedded in a Web page that is not visible in the published version of the Web page.

**cropping**   Cutting off parts of a graphic to trim it to a smaller size.

**database driven**   The term that refers to Web pages that host content that is completely or partially generated from a database.

**dimmed**   In reference to menu commands, unavailable and displayed in gray font.

**discussion Web site**   A Web site where people communicate by posting messages or documents.

**disk-based Web site**   A Web site that is located on a floppy disk, CD-ROM, or a computer that is not configured as a Web server.

**docking**   Attaching a toolbar to one edge of the window.

**domain name**   The base of the alphanumeric address, called the uniform resource locator (URL), where Web visitors locate your Web site on the World Wide Web.

**drawing canvas**   The frame in which Office Drawings are created in FrontPage.

**dynamic effect**   A Web component, such as a banner ad or marquee, that adds motion to a Web page.

**dynamic page**   A Web page that is updated with new information from an external source such as a database.

**e-mail link**   A hyperlink that initiates an e-mail message.

**embedded cascading style sheet**   A document embedded within a Web page that defines formats and styles for different page elements.

**external cascading style sheet**   A document outside of a Web page that defines formats and styles for different page elements. External style sheets can be referenced by multiple documents to provide a consistent look across pages and sites.

**file name**   The name of a file.

**File Transfer Protocol (FTP)**   A protocol that allows users to copy files between their local system and any system they can reach on the network.

**Files report**   A report produced by FrontPage with information about the files in the Web site.

**Folder List**   A FrontPage window in which the open Web site's visible folders and files are displayed.

**Folders view**   Displays the visible files and folders that are part of the open Web site.

**frame**   A division of a Web page that contains either content or a link to content from another source.

**frameset**   The single shell page of a frames page that contains individual frames of information drawn together from multiple sources.

**friendly name**   A simple name that translates into a more complex one; friendly names used to identify Web locations are translated by the computer to more complex IP addresses.

**Graphics Interchange Format (GIF)**   A file format for saving pictures that displays well over the Web.

**grouping**   Combining several drawing elements together so that they can be treated as one.

**hard-coded**   Information that has been embedded in the HTML code that makes up a page.

**header column**   The column in a table that contains the title of each row.

**header row**   The row in a table that contains the title of each column.

**hits**   *See* page hits.

**home page**   The starting page for a set of Web pages in a Web site.

**hosting**   The process or service of storing a Web site on a configured Web server and serving it to the intended audience.

**hotspot**   A defined area on an image map that is hyperlinked to a bookmark, Web page, Web site, or e-mail address.

**HTML pane**   The window in which the Hypertext Markup Language (HTML) code behind a FrontPage-based Web page is displayed.

**hyperlink**   The text or graphic that users click to go to a file, a location in a file, an Internet or intranet site, page, or location, and so on. Hyperlinks can also lead to Gopher, telnet, newsgroup, and FTP sites. Hyperlinks usually appear underlined and in color, but sometimes the only indication is that the pointer changes to a hand.

**Hyperlinks view**   The FrontPage windows that display the hyperlinks to and from any selected page in the open Web site.

**Hypertext Markup Language (HTML)**   The system of marking a document so it can be published on the World Wide Web and viewed with a browser.

**Hypertext Transfer Protocol (HTTP)**   A protocol utilizing TCP/IP to transfer hypertext requests and information between servers and browsers.

**image map**   A graphic element containing hotspots.

**Included Content components**   A set of Web components used to create links to the text or graphics to be displayed on a Web page.

**Internet Protocol (IP) address**   The number that uniquely identifies a specific computer on the Internet.

**Internet service provider (ISP)**   A business that provides Internet access to individuals and organizations.

**intranet**   An internal network within a company or organization.

**Joint Photographic Experts Group (JPG)**   A graphics format used for photos and other graphics with more than 256 colors.

**kerning**   The distance between letters in a word.

**launching**   *See* publishing.

**link bar**   A hyperlinked list of Web pages within a Web site, providing access to the specified pages.

**list**   Items of information, either numbered or bulleted, set off from a paragraph.

**local area network (LAN)**   A group of computers connected in such a way that any computer can interact with any other on the network.

**localhost**   The friendly name for the root Web site of a configured Web server.

**media**   Graphics, videos, sound effects, or other material that can be inserted into a Web page.

**menu**   A list of commands a user can select from in order to perform a desired action.

**Microsoft Office XP**   The Microsoft suite of applications for personal and professional use, updated for 2002.

**Navigation view**   A view of all the files that have been added to the navigational structure of the open Web site.

**navigational structure**   A hierarchical map of how Web pages are connected within a Web site and what routes the user can take to get from one page to another.

**nesting**   Embedding one element inside another.

**Normal pane**   The window in which the standard FrontPage development environment is displayed.

**numbered list**   An ordered list of concepts, items, or options.

**Office Drawings**   The specially formatted lines, preformed shapes, WordArt objects, text boxes, and shadowing that can be incorporated into Microsoft Office documents.

**ordered list**   The Hypertext Markup Language (HTML) term for a numbered list.

**Page Banner component**   The component used to create a page title consisting of either text or graphics that appears in the shared border of designated pages of a Web site.

**page banner**   A textual or graphic image that displays the title of a Web page.

**Page Based On Schedule component**   The component that displays the contents of a designated file for a specified period of time.

**Page component**   The component that displays the contents of a designated file.

**page hits**   The number of visits a Web page or site receives. *See also* unique users.

**page title**   The text that is displayed on the page banner of a Web page and in the title bar of a Web browser.

**Page view editing window**   The FrontPage window in which a Web page is edited.

**permissions**   Rules associated with a resource shared on a network, such as a file, directory, or printer; permissions can be granted to groups, global groups, and even individual users. *See also* rights.

**Personal Web Server (PWS)**   An application that transmits information in Hypertext Markup Language (HTML) pages by using the Hypertext Transport Protocol (HTTP). It provides the ability to: publish Web pages on the Internet or over a local area network (LAN) on an intranet.

**Picture Based On Schedule component**   The component that displays the contents of designated graphics files for a specified period of time.

**pixel**   Short for picture element. One pixel is a measurement representing the smallest amount of information displayed graphically on the screen as a single dot.

**point**   A linear unit used to measure font or type size; approximately 1/72 inch.

**posting**   Transferring files or messages to a Web site or server.

**Preview pane**   The FrontPage window in which Web pages can be viewed before they are published.

**privileges**   *See* permissions.

**Problems report**   A FrontPage report that contains information about broken or slow links and errors.

**publishing**   Copying your Web site files to a Web server for the purpose of displaying the site to the intended audience.

**read-only**   A designation of a file that can be opened and looked at but any changes made to it will be lost unless it is saved with a different name.

**relative path**   A designation of the location of a file in relation to the current working directory. *See also* absolute path.

**report**   A presentation of information about a specific topic.

**Reports view**   The FrontPage view that displays the available reports about the open Web site.

**rights**   Rules that allow users to perform certain actions on a system. Rights are associated with a system as a whole, and are granted to local groups, global groups, and users.

**role**   A named set of permissions to which specific users can be assigned.

**root Web**   A Web site that contains a subweb.

**row**   A horizontal line of cells in a spreadsheet or table.

**screen area**   The width and height of your screen, measured in pixels.

**screen real estate**   A term for the amount of space a designer has in which to present the information in a Web page.

**ScreenTip**   The small text box that appears when the cursor passes over a button, telling the user the name of the command.

**server farm**   An area where multiple Web servers are located.

**Server Health**   A FrontPage feature that recalculates the links to and from every page of a Web site, including external links.

**server-based Web site**   A Web site that is located on a computer that is configured as a Web server.

**server-side application**   A program or protocol that is run on the Web server rather than on a Web visitor's own computer.

**shading**   Background and foreground colors or pictures the designer places on the Web page.

**shared border**   The areas at the top, bottom, left, or right of all or some of the pages in a Web site, in which common elements are displayed.

**SharePoint team Web site**   A full-scale team collaboration Web site consisting of a home page, a Document Library, Discussion Boards, a Lists page, a Create Page page, and a Site Settings page.

**site map**   A graphical depiction of the locations of Web pages in a Web site.

**Site Summary report**   A FrontPage report that summarizes statistics for the entire Web site.

**size**   A term referring to the browser-specific font size setting. *See also* point.

**source control**   A feature that ensures that only one person at a time can edit a particular file.

**static page**   A Web page that contains information that is embedded in the Hypertext Markup Language (HTML) code that makes up the page.

**Substitution component**   An Included Content Component that associates variables with text.

**subweb**   A stand-alone Web site that is nested inside another Web site; subwebs can have a unique set of permissions.

**table title**   The overall name of a table that appears either as a separate paragraph above the body of the table or in the table's top row.

**table**   A structured presentation of information consisting of vertical columns and horizontal rows.

**task**   An individual item of work to be performed.

**Tasks view**   The FrontPage window that displays a list of tasks to be completed in the open Web site.

**team**   A group of people working together.

**template**   Predefined layouts and designs for specific types of Web pages and sites.

**theme**   A predefined package of colors, graphics, fonts, and styles that you can apply to a single Web page or an entire Web site.

**thumbnail**   A small versions of a graphic that is hyperlinked to full-size versions.

**TOC**   The group of navigation links to each page of a Web site. Abbreviation of Table of Contents.

**toolbar**   A grouping of commands represented by buttons or icons.

**ungrouping**   Separating a drawing into its individual elements. *See also* grouping.

**uniform resource locator (URL)**   The alphanumeric address where Web visitors locate your Web site on the World Wide Web.

**unique users**   The number of different users (defined on a per-session basis) who view a Web site. *See also* page hits.

**unordered list**   The Hypertext Markup Language (HTML) term for a bulleted list.

**URL**   *See* uniform resource locator.

**Usage reports**   The four kinds of reports FrontPage can generate detailing information about activity on a Web site.

**variable**   A named object that can assume any set of values.

**view**   One of several different ways of focusing in on specific aspects of a FrontPage-based Web site.

**Web browser**   A program used to view Web pages on the World Wide Web.

**Web component**   A ready-made programmatic element that provides capabilities such as link bars and tables of content.

**Web hosting company**   A business that provides Internet access to individuals and organizations.

**Web page**   An individual document that comprises a Web site.

**Web server**   A computer that is specifically configured to host Web sites.

**Web visitor**   An individual who views a Web site.

**wizard**   A program that creates the layout of a Web page or Web site and leads the user through the process of personalizing the content and the appearance of the final product.

**WordArt**   Text objects with special formatting applied.

**Workflow reports**   FrontPage reports that give site administrators an idea of the current status of a site that is under development.

**wrapping**   The breaking of lines of text to fit the width of the cell or text box.

# Index

## Numerics

3-D drawings, 88

## A

access violations, 50
activating source control, 278
active graphics
  previewing, 126
  in themes, 125
adding. *See also* inserting
  bullets, to bulleted lists, 55
  buttons, to toolbars, 21
  contacts, to SharePoint team Web
    sites, 225
  database connections, 233
  database interface pages, 237
  document libraries, to SharePoint
    team Web sites, 224
  drop-down box choices, 200
  to navigation structure, 13
  pages, to Navigation view, 169
  SharePoint team Web site
    contacts, 225
  toolbar buttons, 21
  Web pages, 106
adjusting picture contrast/bright-
  ness, 82
administration, 275, 278
  creating subwebs for, 278
  of discussion Web sites, 278
  privileges, assigning, 278
  publishing Web sites for, 277
  roles, 278
aligning
  background pictures, 118
  cells, 140
  paragraphs, 45
  scheduled pictures, 196
  tables, 66
  WordArt, 99
anchor tags, 142
  bookmarks (*see* bookmarks)
applying
  background color, 118
  background pictures, 113, 118

colors, in shared borders, 120
styles, to link bars, 167
styles, to page banners, 122
table AutoFormat, 69
templates, to existing pages, 144
themes, to database interface
  pages, 241
themes, to discussion Webs, 218
themes, to entire sites, 126
themes, to SharePoint team Web
  sites, 224
themes, to specific pages, 125
watermarks, 113
**arrows, drawing, 88**
**articles, posting to discussion**
  **Webs, 220**
**ASP**
  database interface pages (*see*
    database interface pages)
  and databases, 236
  renaming, 254
**assigning**
  categories, 287
  permissions for subwebs,
    164, 278
  privileges, 278
  roles, 278
  tasks, 34
**associating**
  picture file types, 114
  variables, with text (*see* Substitu-
    tion component)
**AutoFormat, for tables, 67, 69**
**automatically**
  checking spelling, 206
  updating Web sites (*see* included
    content)
**AutoShapes, 88**
  formatting, 94
  positioning style, 94
  wrapping style, 94
**AutoThumbnail.** *See* **thumbnails**

## B

background colors
  applying, 118
  choosing, 111

setting, 118
for themes, 130
**background pictures**
  aligning, 118
  applying, 113, 118
  color schemes, 111
  design considerations, 110
  editing, 114
  positioning, 118
  resizing, 114
  stationary while page scrolls, 113
  for themes, 125
  as watermarks, 113
**backgrounds**
  borders (*see* borders)
  colors (*see* background colors)
  pictures in (*see* background
    pictures)
  shading (*see* shading)
  Web page. (*see* backgrounds, Web
    page)
**backgrounds, Web page**
  formatting, 110
  formatting, removing, 116
  pictures in (*see* background
    pictures)
  watermarks (*see* watermarks)
**banner ads, 188**
**bCentral components, 178**
**beveling pictures, 82, 85**
**black and white pictures, 82**
**blank Web pages, 107**
**bookmarks, 142**
  naming, 142, 204
**borders, 45, 116**
  colors, 117
  customizing, 117
  for frames pages, displaying/
    hiding, 155
  padding, 117
  previewing, 117
  shared (*see* shared borders)
  table (*see* tables, borders)
  width, 117
**boxes, drop-down, 200**
**breaks, line** (*see* line breaks)
**brightness, picture**
  adjusting, 82
**broken hyperlinks, report of, 283**
**browser sniffers, 47**

# Online Training Solutions, Inc. (OTSI)

OTSI is a traditional and electronic publishing company specializing in the creation, production, and delivery of computer software training. OTSI publishes the Quick Course® and Practical Business Skills™ series of computer and business training products. The principals of OTSI and authors of this book are:

**Joyce Cox** has 20 years' experience in writing about and editing technical subjects for non-technical audiences. For 12 of those years she was the principal author for Online Press. She was also the first managing editor of Microsoft Press, an editor for Sybex, and an editor for the University of California.

**Steve Lambert** started playing with computers in the mid-seventies. As computers evolved from wire-wrap and solder to consumer products, he evolved from hardware geek to programmer and writer. He has written 14 books and a wide variety of technical documentation and has produced training tools and help systems.

**Gale Nelson** honed her communication skills as a technical writer for a SQL Server training company. Her attention to detail soon led her into software testing and quality assurance management. She now divides her work time between writing and data conversion projects.

**Joan Preppernau** started working with computers as a PowerPoint slideshow production assistant. As a CD-ROM data-prep manager, she participated in the creation of training products for computer professionals. She now wears a variety of hats including operations manager, Webmaster, writer, and technical editor.

The OTSI team consists of the following outstanding publishing professionals:

**Susie Bayers**

**Jan Bednarczuk**

**RJ Cadranell**

**Liz Clark**

**Nancy Depper**

**Leslie Eliel**

**Jon Kenoyer**

**Marlene Lambert**

**Robin Ludwig**

**Gabrielle Nonast**

For more information about Online Training Solutions, Inc., visit *www.otsiweb.com*.

Get a **Free**
e-mail newsletter, updates,
special offers, links to related books,
and more when you
## *register on line!*

Register your Microsoft Press® title on our Web site and you'll get a FREE subscription to our e-mail newsletter, *Microsoft Press Book Connections.* You'll find out about newly released and upcoming books and learning tools, online events, software downloads, special offers and coupons for Microsoft Press customers, and information about major Microsoft® product releases. You can also read useful additional information about all the titles we publish, such as detailed book descriptions, tables of contents and indexes, sample chapters, links to related books and book series, author biographies, and reviews by other customers.

## Registration is easy. Just visit this Web page and fill in your information:

*http://www.microsoft.com/mspress/register*

**Microsoft**

- - - - - - - - - - - - - - - - - - - - - - - - - - - - - - - - - - - - - - - - -

## Proof of Purchase

Use this page as proof of purchase if participating in a promotion or rebate offer on this title. Proof of purchase must be used in conjunction with other proof(s) of payment such as your dated sales receipt—see offer details.

### *Microsoft® FrontPage® Version 2002 Step by Step*
0-7356-1300-1

_____

**CUSTOMER NAME**

Microsoft Press, PO Box 97017, Redmond, WA  98073-9830

# MICROSOFT LICENSE AGREEMENT
Book Companion CD

**IMPORTANT—READ CAREFULLY:** This Microsoft End-User License Agreement ("EULA") is a legal agreement between you (either an individual or an entity) and Microsoft Corporation for the Microsoft product identified above, which includes computer software and may include associated media, printed materials, and "online" or electronic documentation ("SOFTWARE PRODUCT"). Any component included within the SOFTWARE PRODUCT that is accompanied by a separate End-User License Agreement shall be governed by such agreement and not the terms set forth below. By installing, copying, or otherwise using the SOFTWARE PRODUCT, you agree to be bound by the terms of this EULA. If you do not agree to the terms of this EULA, you are not authorized to install, copy, or otherwise use the SOFTWARE PRODUCT; you may, however, return the SOFTWARE PRODUCT, along with all printed materials and other items that form a part of the Microsoft product that includes the SOFTWARE PRODUCT, to the place you obtained them for a full refund.

## SOFTWARE PRODUCT LICENSE

The SOFTWARE PRODUCT is protected by United States copyright laws and international copyright treaties, as well as other intellectual property laws and treaties. The SOFTWARE PRODUCT is licensed, not sold.

1. **GRANT OF LICENSE.** This EULA grants you the following rights:

   a. **Software Product.** You may install and use one copy of the SOFTWARE PRODUCT on a single computer. The primary user of the computer on which the SOFTWARE PRODUCT is installed may make a second copy for his or her exclusive use on a portable computer.

   b. **Storage/Network Use.** You may also store or install a copy of the SOFTWARE PRODUCT on a storage device, such as a network server, used only to install or run the SOFTWARE PRODUCT on your other computers over an internal network; however, you must acquire and dedicate a license for each separate computer on which the SOFTWARE PRODUCT is installed or run from the storage device. A license for the SOFTWARE PRODUCT may not be shared or used concurrently on different computers.

   c. **License Pak.** If you have acquired this EULA in a Microsoft License Pak, you may make the number of additional copies of the computer software portion of the SOFTWARE PRODUCT authorized on the printed copy of this EULA, and you may use each copy in the manner specified above. You are also entitled to make a corresponding number of secondary copies for portable computer use as specified above.

   d. **Sample Code.** Solely with respect to portions, if any, of the SOFTWARE PRODUCT that are identified within the SOFTWARE PRODUCT as sample code (the "SAMPLE CODE"):

      i. **Use and Modification.** Microsoft grants you the right to use and modify the source code version of the SAMPLE CODE, *provided* you comply with subsection (d)(iii) below. You may not distribute the SAMPLE CODE, or any modified version of the SAMPLE CODE, in source code form.

      ii. **Redistributable Files.** Provided you comply with subsection (d)(iii) below, Microsoft grants you a nonexclusive, royalty-free right to reproduce and distribute the object code version of the SAMPLE CODE and of any modified SAMPLE CODE, other than SAMPLE CODE, or any modified version thereof, designated as not redistributable in the Readme file that forms a part of the SOFTWARE PRODUCT (the "Non-Redistributable Sample Code"). All SAMPLE CODE other than the Non-Redistributable Sample Code is collectively referred to as the "REDISTRIBUTABLES."

      iii. **Redistribution Requirements.** If you redistribute the REDISTRIBUTABLES, you agree to: (i) distribute the REDISTRIBUTABLES in object code form only in conjunction with and as a part of your software application product; (ii) not use Microsoft's name, logo, or trademarks to market your software application product; (iii) include a valid copyright notice on your software application product; (iv) indemnify, hold harmless, and defend Microsoft from and against any claims or lawsuits, including attorney's fees, that arise or result from the use or distribution of your software application product; and (v) not permit further distribution of the REDISTRIBUTABLES by your end user. Contact Microsoft for the applicable royalties due and other licensing terms for all other uses and/or distribution of the REDISTRIBUTABLES.

2. **DESCRIPTION OF OTHER RIGHTS AND LIMITATIONS.**

   - **Limitations on Reverse Engineering, Decompilation, and Disassembly.** You may not reverse engineer, decompile, or disassemble the SOFTWARE PRODUCT, except and only to the extent that such activity is expressly permitted by applicable law notwithstanding this limitation.

   - **Separation of Components.** The SOFTWARE PRODUCT is licensed as a single product. Its component parts may not be separated for use on more than one computer.

   - **Rental.** You may not rent, lease, or lend the SOFTWARE PRODUCT.

   - **Support Services.** Microsoft may, but is not obligated to, provide you with support services related to the SOFTWARE PRODUCT ("Support Services"). Use of Support Services is governed by the Microsoft policies and programs described in the user manual, in "online" documentation, and/or in other Microsoft-provided materials. Any supplemental software code provided to you as part of the Support Services shall be considered part of the SOFTWARE PRODUCT and subject to the terms and conditions of this EULA. With respect to technical information you provide to Microsoft as part of the Support Services, Microsoft may use such information for its business purposes, including for product support and development. Microsoft will not utilize such technical information in a form that personally identifies you.

- **Software Transfer.** You may permanently transfer all of your rights under this EULA, provided you retain no copies, you transfer all of the SOFTWARE PRODUCT (including all component parts, the media and printed materials, any upgrades, this EULA, and, if applicable, the Certificate of Authenticity), **and** the recipient agrees to the terms of this EULA.

- **Termination.** Without prejudice to any other rights, Microsoft may terminate this EULA if you fail to comply with the terms and conditions of this EULA. In such event, you must destroy all copies of the SOFTWARE PRODUCT and all of its component parts.

3. **COPYRIGHT.** All title and copyrights in and to the SOFTWARE PRODUCT (including but not limited to any images, photographs, animations, video, audio, music, text, SAMPLE CODE, REDISTRIBUTABLES, and "applets" incorporated into the SOFTWARE PRODUCT) and any copies of the SOFTWARE PRODUCT are owned by Microsoft or its suppliers. The SOFTWARE PRODUCT is protected by copyright laws and international treaty provisions. Therefore, you must treat the SOFTWARE PRODUCT like any other copyrighted material **except** that you may install the SOFTWARE PRODUCT on a single computer provided you keep the original solely for backup or archival purposes. You may not copy the printed materials accompanying the SOFTWARE PRODUCT.

4. **U.S. GOVERNMENT RESTRICTED RIGHTS.** The SOFTWARE PRODUCT and documentation are provided with RESTRICTED RIGHTS. Use, duplication, or disclosure by the Government is subject to restrictions as set forth in subparagraph (c)(1)(ii) of the Rights in Technical Data and Computer Software clause at DFARS 252.227-7013 or subparagraphs (c)(1) and (2) of the Commercial Computer Software—Restricted Rights at 48 CFR 52.227-19, as applicable. Manufacturer is Microsoft Corporation/One Microsoft Way/Redmond, WA 98052-6399.

5. **EXPORT RESTRICTIONS.** You agree that you will not export or re-export the SOFTWARE PRODUCT, any part thereof, or any process or service that is the direct product of the SOFTWARE PRODUCT (the foregoing collectively referred to as the "Restricted Components"), to any country, person, entity, or end user subject to U.S. export restrictions. You specifically agree not to export or re-export any of the Restricted Components (i) to any country to which the U.S. has embargoed or restricted the export of goods or services, which currently include, but are not necessarily limited to, Cuba, Iran, Iraq, Libya, North Korea, Sudan, and Syria, or to any national of any such country, wherever located, who intends to transmit or transport the Restricted Components back to such country; (ii) to any end user who you know or have reason to know will utilize the Restricted Components in the design, development, or production of nuclear, chemical, or biological weapons; or (iii) to any end user who has been prohibited from participating in U.S. export transactions by any federal agency of the U.S. government. You warrant and represent that neither the BXA nor any other U.S. federal agency has suspended, revoked, or denied your export privileges.

## DISCLAIMER OF WARRANTY

**NO WARRANTIES OR CONDITIONS.** MICROSOFT EXPRESSLY DISCLAIMS ANY WARRANTY OR CONDITION FOR THE SOFTWARE PRODUCT. THE SOFTWARE PRODUCT AND ANY RELATED DOCUMENTATION ARE PROVIDED "AS IS" WITHOUT WARRANTY OR CONDITION OF ANY KIND, EITHER EXPRESS OR IMPLIED, INCLUDING, WITHOUT LIMITATION, THE IMPLIED WARRANTIES OF MERCHANTABILITY, FITNESS FOR A PARTICULAR PURPOSE, OR NONINFRINGEMENT. THE ENTIRE RISK ARISING OUT OF USE OR PERFORMANCE OF THE SOFTWARE PRODUCT REMAINS WITH YOU.

**LIMITATION OF LIABILITY.** TO THE MAXIMUM EXTENT PERMITTED BY APPLICABLE LAW, IN NO EVENT SHALL MICROSOFT OR ITS SUPPLIERS BE LIABLE FOR ANY SPECIAL, INCIDENTAL, INDIRECT, OR CONSEQUENTIAL DAMAGES WHATSOEVER (INCLUDING, WITHOUT LIMITATION, DAMAGES FOR LOSS OF BUSINESS PROFITS, BUSINESS INTERRUPTION, LOSS OF BUSINESS INFORMATION, OR ANY OTHER PECUNIARY LOSS) ARISING OUT OF THE USE OF OR INABILITY TO USE THE SOFTWARE PRODUCT OR THE PROVISION OF OR FAILURE TO PROVIDE SUPPORT SERVICES, EVEN IF MICROSOFT HAS BEEN ADVISED OF THE POSSIBILITY OF SUCH DAMAGES. IN ANY CASE, MICROSOFT'S ENTIRE LIABILITY UNDER ANY PROVISION OF THIS EULA SHALL BE LIMITED TO THE GREATER OF THE AMOUNT ACTUALLY PAID BY YOU FOR THE SOFTWARE PRODUCT OR US$5.00; PROVIDED, HOWEVER, IF YOU HAVE ENTERED INTO A MICROSOFT SUPPORT SERVICES AGREEMENT, MICROSOFT'S ENTIRE LIABILITY REGARDING SUPPORT SERVICES SHALL BE GOVERNED BY THE TERMS OF THAT AGREEMENT. BECAUSE SOME STATES AND JURISDICTIONS DO NOT ALLOW THE EXCLUSION OR LIMITATION OF LIABILITY, THE ABOVE LIMITATION MAY NOT APPLY TO YOU.

## MISCELLANEOUS

This EULA is governed by the laws of the State of Washington USA, except and only to the extent that applicable law mandates governing law of a different jurisdiction.

Should you have any questions concerning this EULA, or if you desire to contact Microsoft for any reason, please contact the Microsoft subsidiary serving your country, or write: Microsoft Sales Information Center/One Microsoft Way/Redmond, WA 98052-6399.

# New Features in FrontPage 2002

SharePoint team Web sites

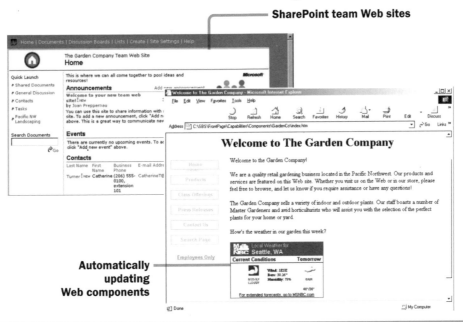

Automatically updating Web components

# Common Keyboard Shortcuts

| | |
|---|---|
| Ctrl + C | Copy text to the Office Clipboard |
| Ctrl + X | Cut text to the Office Clipboard |
| Ctrl + V | Paste text from the Office Clipboard |
| Ctrl + A | Select all the content in a document |
| Ctrl + Space | Remove formatting |
| Ctrl + End | Move the insertion point to the end of the document |
| Ctrl + Home | Move the insertion point to the beginning of the document |
| Ctrl + O | Open a document |
| Ctrl + S | Save the open document |
| Ctrl + P | Print the open file |
| Ctrl + Y | Redo the previous edit |
| Ctrl + Z | Undo the previous edit |
| Ctrl + F | Find the previous search text |
| Ctrl + H | Replace with the previous replace text |
| Ctrl + K | Insert a hyperlink |
| Ctrl + G | Insert a bookmark |
| F7 | Check spelling |
| Shift + F7 | Use the thesaurus |

### To create a Web site using a template

1. Select **Web Site Templates** in the **New from template** area of the **New Page or Web task** pane.
2. In the **Web Site Templates** dialog box, select the appropriate icon for the type of Web site you want to create.
3. Under **Options**, specify what you want to call your Web site and where you want to store it, and then click **OK**.

### To insert an existing file

1. Click where you want the text to appear or select the placeholder text.
2. On the **Insert** menu, click **File** to open the **Insert File** dialog box.
3. Browse to the folder where the text you want to insert is stored.
4. In the **Files of type** drop-down list, select the appropriate option.
5. Select the file you want from the list of available files, and then click **Open** to insert the full text of the document in your Web page.

### To insert a hyperlink to a file

1. Click where you want the hyperlink to appear, and on the **Insert** menu, click **Hyperlink**.
2. Click the **Browse for File** button, browse to the folder where the file is stored, select the file name, click **OK** to select the file, and then click **OK** again.

### To create a table

1. Click where you want the table to appear, and on the Standard toolbar, click the **Insert Table** button.
2. Point to the first cell and hold down the left mouse button. Then, without releasing the button, drag the pointer until the number of rows and columns you want is highlighted (the grid will expand as you drag the mouse to the edge), and then release the mouse button.

### To insert clip art in a page

1. Click where you want the clip art to appear.
2. On the **Insert** menu, point to **Picture**, and then click **Clip Art**.
3. Make sure that **All media types** is displayed in the **Results should be** box, and then search for the type of clip art you want by typing a keyword in the **Search text** box and clicking **Search**.

4. Right-click the graphic you want to use, and click **Insert** on the shortcut menu.

### To size a graphic

1. Double-click the picture to display the **Picture Properties** dialog box.
2. Select the **Specify size** check box, and set the **Width** to the setting you want. Make sure that the **Keep aspect ratio** check box is selected, and then click **OK**.

### To create a shared border on a page

1. With the page open, click **Shared Borders** on the **Format** menu.
2. In the **Shared Borders** dialog box, select the options you want, and then click **OK**.

### To apply a theme to a page

1. With the page displayed in Page view, click **Theme** on the **Format** menu to open the **Themes** dialog box.
2. In the **Apply Theme to:** area, click **Selected page(s)**.
3. Select the theme, select the color scheme, banners, buttons, bullets, and other graphic elements, and then click **OK**.

### To create a frames page using a template

1. On the **File** menu, point to **New** and click **Page or Web** to open the **New Page or Web** task pane.
2. In the **New from template** section, click **Page Templates** to open the **Page Templates** dialog box, and then click the **Frames Pages** tab.
3. Click the template you want, and click **OK** to close the dialog box and create the new page.

### To publish a Web site to a Web server

1. With the Web site open, click **Publish Web** on the **File** menu.
2. In the **Enter publish destination** box, type **http://<server>/<name of web>**, substituting the name of your Web server for *<server>*, and the name of your Web for *<name of web>* and then click **OK**.
3. Click **OK** when prompted to create a new Web site at the specified location, and click the **Publish** button to complete the publication of the site.